GW00497329

CLOUDLAND

QUEEN OF THE DANCEHALLS

JAMES G. LERGESSNER

Copyright © 2013 James G. Lergessner

This book is copyright. Apart from any fair dealing for the purpose of private study, research, criticism or review, as permitted under the Copyright Act, no part may be reproduced by any process without written permission. Enquiries should be addressed to the Publishers.

All rights reserved.

First published by Dr James G. Largessner

Second published by Boolarong Press

National Library of Australia Cataloguing-in-Publication entry:

Author:	Lergessner, James G., author.
Title:	Cloudland : queen of the dance halls / James G. Lergessner.
ISBN:	9781922109774 (Paperback)
Subjects:	Cloudland Ballroom (Brisbane, Qld.)
	Ballrooms--Queensland--Brisbane--History.
	Dance halls--Queensland--Brisbane--History.
Dewey Number:	725.86099431

Typeset in Arno Pro 12pt.

Cover Design: Boolarong Press

Front Cover design: depicts Margaret (*nee* Reid) and the late Colin Giese (the 'Jive King' of Cloudland).

Published by Boolarong Press, Salisbury, Brisbane, Australia.

Printed and bound by Watson Ferguson & Company, Salisbury, Brisbane, Australia.

ACKNOWLEDGEMENTS

I would like to thank the following for permission to use images contained in this work: John Oxley Library; The State Library of Queensland; Fryer Library of the University of Queensland; Queensland State Archives; Queensland Newspapers; and *The Australian*.

Thanks also go to my publicist, Kerri Ross, who submitted photos of the Thurman/Vaughan families; Lesley Tissington (*nee* Lergessner) for her editing and Cloudland 'pics'; Toby Melonie; Cliff Field; Stephen Flemington; Tim/ Maggie Adeney-West; Tana/Aaron Thiele; Ben Mellon; Tim Moroney; Chris Goopy; 'Rainbow Rob', Robyn Mortimer; Christine Burton (Hans Apel's daughter) ; Karen Foster; Marie and Bill Thurman; Frank Claude Higgenson who was Queensland ballroom dancing in the late 1930s ; Norm Wellard for a CD of a Cloudland LP, The Sounds Of Seven, Sunshine Records label; & former 4KQ radio commentator, John Knox (editing). Kerrith and Celeste Giese skilfully provided the original cover design artwork; and Janice Brown and myself created the final cover sequences.

As Cloudland was predominately a 60/40 venue for a significant period of its operation, I also wish to pay tribute to Vance Lendich, who was the venue's band leader with the 60/40 group, *The Sounds of Seven*, from 1965 to 1970. As an alternative to the charts nine or ten piece bands had traditionally used, promoter Ivan Dayman requested that Vance be paid to produce charts of current pop songs, as upgraded or rewritten material, for 60/40 events, including some new evening three-step music.

Vance and Toni Lendich have conducted the *Old Rockers Reunion* for 10 years. It features former band members from the '50s, '60s (and beyond) Brisbane music groups, as well as a few former Cloudland players. The final reunion there is scheduled for 10 a.m. on Sunday, 7th April, 2013.

PREFACE

AN EXPANDING BRISBANE METROPOLIS

This web of time—the strands of which approach one another, bifurcate, intersect, or ignore each other through the centuries—embraces every possibility.

Jorge Luis Borges

The Coat of Arms of the Amorial Ensign of Queensland 1893.

Queensland State Archives.

Besides our lost, demolished, preserved, and enduring building sites, Brisbane has come a long way since the late 1930s, the era when Luna Park (Cloudland) was constructed; and beyond 1982, the year of its total demolition. It has far outstripped its 'Hicksville' reputation, in modernising its services for all of its citizens and providing some splendid building structures about which its growing population have now become immensely proud. Space precludes my mentioning each and every socially inventive scheme, but a few topical entries in Brisbane's growth and development should not escape our immediate attention: prior to and after Brisbane being proclaimed a city in 1902.

The *Windmill* in Wickham Terrace was built of sandstone by felons back in 1828. It even housed a fine grinding treadmill. The early convicts of Brisbane had laboured wearily on this site; and two Aboriginal men were hanged there in 1841 and 1854.

The old Windmill, Wickham Tce., Brisbane.
Brisbane City Council.

Similarly, the Victoria Barracks in Brisbane's inner city suburb of Petrie Terrace was, at one time, the hub of Brisbane's law and order, including that applied to the convicts. In fact it was the city's initial post-convict gaol from 1860. From 1885 to 1974 police were trained in this facility. In 2007, redevelopment occurred. Sadly, another significant original and cultural heritage relic was to bite the dust!

The Victoria Barracks Museum.
Brisbane City Council.

The Queensland Steam and Navigation Co. constructed new wharves and warehouses adjacent to Eagle Street in 1864. According to John Laverty, *The Making of a Metropolis Brisbane 1823-1925:* "All of these wharves were situated between the Customs House and the Botanic Gardens".

The *News Queensland* archive image (*above*) (Picture research: Gwen McLachlan) depicts the wharf area in 1948; together with a moored US submarine, *Capitaine;* the Customs House; and the Story Bridge in the *background.*

During 1876, the 'Ekka' was finally opened for business.
Courier-Mail Ekka Supplement.

By 1876, the Brisbane Exhibition or 'Ekka' had commenced, only 17 years after Queensland had become a separate colony from New South Wales (within 1859), and when the first Intercolonial Exhibition was staged.

The old Queensland Museum, 2012.
Sunday Mail.

The Queens Park sports field, with the Queensland club in the background, October 1894. Picture research: Gwen McLachlan.
Sunday Mail.

In 1891 the Royal Queensland National Agricultural and Industrial Association (RNA) erected the Exhibition and Concert Hall, on the corner of Bowen Bridge Road and Gregory Terrace. Some financial problems meant the State had to subsequently take it over. It was renamed the Queensland Museum, and carried out that role until 1986. It is now an artistic centre.

The *City Botanic Gardens* in Brisbane was created in 1916, by adding to the original botanic reserve section two other parks, the Domain on Gardens Point; and Queens Park in Alice Street.

The *Brisbane Courier* and *The Daily Mail* had merged in 1933 to form *The Courier-Mail*. The latter set up its own website in 1999.

The Brisbane Markets, near the City Hall, 1930s.
Sunday Mail.

The Victoria Bridge from Queen Street, in Brisbane, 1890.
Queensland State Archives.

On May 24th, 1936, traffic lights were installed in Queen Street, Brisbane. Then, on April 8th, 1940, the city witnessed the completion of the City Hall in Brisbane's CBD—the 'Million Pound Town Hall'. Then the Story Bridge was opened in 1940, the same year that Irving Berlin penned the largest-selling Christmas song ever, *White Christmas,* with sales of more than 50 million.

In the same year, the *Riverside Ballroom* in New Farm was erected in the style of an igloo. It was initially a Naval Officers Club from that time until the 1960s. Cloudland Ballroom was also a local landmark from 1939-1940 until its controversial demolition in 1982, but more about that story later.

Brisbane's main trunk line telephone exchange also opened in 1945. It worked effectively and was eventually upgraded, like other types of communications.

Brisbane's trunk line operators, 1940s.
Courier-Mail.

Overleaf is an image of Queensland's and Australia's first known computer. Just like the telephone exchange, it was fully functional; and now we can almost laugh at such a hulking piece of technology.

The hospital which became known as the Princess Alexandra was constructed between 1951 and 1956, on the site of the *South Brisbane Auxiliary Hospital* of Woolloongabba. The new facility was designed to relieve all the congestion at the north side *Brisbane General Hospital*, presently the *Royal Brisbane Women's Hospital.*

The State and the nation's first computer, 1948.

Westfield Chermside, 1950s.

Initial construction of 'P.A.' Hospital, 1955.
Sunday Mail.

PARKING METERS SPREADING LIKE A PLAGUE

WHEN parking meters were installed we were told they were to get rid of the selfish all-day parker, allowing more people to do their shopping and carry out their business.

This sounded reasonable, but before long these money-eating monsters had spread like a plague of grasshoppers over the whole of the city area, and now they are invading the suburbs and near-city areas.

We have reached the stage where freedom-loving Australians have to pay two shillings (20c) to park for a few hours outside their own homes.

F. W. Panton, Taringa Parade, Indooroopilly. *Courier-Mail.*

By 22nd September, 1954, Brisbane's population had reached 500,000, indicating many more services such as large-scale shopping areas were required for the expanding number of people within the city metropolis. Consequently, in 1957, the very first *Drive-In Shopping Centre* appeared on the Brisbane skyline. At the time, the State's 'biggest' cars apparently lined up at Westfield Chermside, in the north of Brisbane.

Channel Nine then began broadcasts of the first television signals around Brisbane within November of 1959, three years after television had come to Australia. In 1961, the advent of a brand new parking meter system caused some anxiety, as this letter to 'The Editor' of Brisbane's main newspaper explains:

The *Courier-Mail*'s reference to this innovation.

During 1963, the aforementioned *Courier-Mail* moved to its present site in inner-city Bowen Hills as both this suburb and nearby Mayne had become a haven for the surrounding industry sector.

After the phasing out and end of trams in Brisbane in 1969, the

Riverside Expressway, linking the metro area with the south-eastern road journey to the Gold Coast (by means of the new Captain Cook Bridge), left the river bank to the north of Brisbane with a new complex of concrete pillars and their intersecting freeways. The main highway opened on 7th March, 1973, offering a combined State Government-Brisbane City Council urban corridor scheme, which then resulted in south-east Queensland's becoming a car-dependent region.

either suburban or interstate—stopped on the south-side of Brisbane. The Victoria Bridge was previously the only link between the South Brisbane and (north-side) Roma Street terminuses. Now all of Brisbane's rail networks could be linked.

The November, 1978, railway link across the Brisbane River.

Sunday Mail.

A *Courier-Mail* issue of 1962, suggesting buses were replacing trams. (21st December, 1962.)

Besides buses replacing the trams, the rail link crossing over the Brisbane River in 1978 subsequently made life less stressful for south and north-side city commuters. Up until that period trains arriving from the south—

Belle Vue Hotel, K.M. Berry, 1972.

The *Courier-Mail* edition, explaining the demolition of the *Belle Vue Hotel*, April, 1979.

As a precursor to the demolition of the Cloudland Ballroom in November of 1982, the iconic *Belle Vue Hotel* was similarly destroyed in April of 1979.

Since Brisbane graciously hosted the Commonwealth Games in September-October of 1982, and, since Councils expanded in the 2010s, early Brisbane has grown in *area* to be one of the largest cities in the world. It has also blossomed into a city offering numerous travel services for citizens, fine entertainment; and the proliferation of tidy parklands.

Cloudland's shocking and instant demolition in November, 1982, is quite lovingly remembered in these 'odes to a disappearing world',

some 'black-ringed' cards from the *Optimism* project at GOMA (The Gallery of Modern Art), Brisbane.

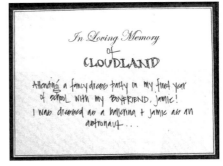

Matthew Condon likened Cloudland's demise to the 'death of a parent', particularly in view of its 'city-wide courtship significance'. (*Motorcycle Café.*)

In 1988, Brisbane hosted the remarkably successful *World Expo 88*.

Sir Lew Edwards in his role of Head of Brisbane's World Expo 88.

This South Bank event on the Brisbane River marked a watershed for the State of Queensland's capital city, both in terms of its citizen's pride; and how Brisbane was perceived by its many overseas and interstate visitors:

> Brisbane spread out below with the proud, winding river like a snake with its glistening water scales...And the sky above. The crystal depths of an Australian sky, translucence of blue and silver, like a dust of light dissolving away.
>
> [Jack Lindsay, *The Blood Vote* (1985).]

The fair's theme was 'Leisure in the Age of Technology'. 'Expo Oz' was the appropriately named platypus mascot for the exposition. The event had attracted more than 15,760,000 visitors, who purchased tickets to the tune of A$175 million.

Following EXPO 88's opening up the city to its hordes of visitors, the *City Cat* ferry services on the Brisbane River began in 1996. In 2000, Brisbane's old Powerhouse arts facility opened in New Farm upon the site of Brisbane's first Municipal Power Station.

In 2008, to match the increased usage of public transportation, a record extra 424 bus services, 120 new buses, 385 bus drivers; and three *City Cats* were added to the Council's fleet.

On the 11th January, 2011, the Brisbane River peaked at 4.6 metres, about a metre below the level set by the 1974 floods. Twenty-one people were confirmed dead; and 11,900 homes were completely flooded. It is only now in 2013 that much of the city of Brisbane and other affected areas of Queensland are getting back to some normalcy in peoples' lives, though we've been hit with more floods this year, to make other's lives in the State an ongoing misery.

The old tramway powerhouse, *c.* 1930s.
Brisbane City Council.

CONTENTS

℘ROLOGUE

This is the story of the origins and operation of the renowned Cloudland Ballroom, which sat perched atop its tiny Montpelier Heights location, in inner-city Brisbane's Bowen Hills—from 1939-40, awaiting the early hours of November 7th, 1982, when it was demolished.

This grand 'lady' began its social existence as a 2.5 hectare amusement district, 'Luna Park', before its various activities gradually took pride of place on the hill and it was basically renamed the 'Cloudland Ballroom'.

During the war years, Cloudland lay mostly idle, except for American military dances and functions. However, the Brisbane City Hall's Red Cross was an important socialising arena for any U.S. and Australian enlisted personnel. The 'menu was very austere and simple' and 'meat and two veg, meat

pies, fish and chips' received no complaints.

DURING WWII,
BRISBANE CITY HALL'S
RED CROSS CAFE FED

TWO HUNGRY ARMIES.

OUR NEW WORLD-CLASS
FUNCTION KITCHEN CAN
FEED 1,200 DISCERNING
GOURMANDS.

BRISBANE CITY HALL
EVEN BETTER THAN YOU REMEMBER

After the war, ex-service military personnel and their sweethearts once partook of elective 'R & R' at the venue, escaping from their earlier memories of the worst fighting during World War II. This impressive 'lady' also played a significant role in the social lives of at least three generations of Brisbane citizens. It was important, too, not merely as a cultural landmark, but also as a place where Brisbane residents headed for their entertainment.

Who could forget the building's exteriors—how Cloudland's myriad twinkling lights beckoned from the heights of Bowen Hills? Or its much-loved romantic, parabolic roof arch? This unique feature over Cloudland's entrance was incredibly high at nearly 18 metres, became visible for miles and was totally lit up at night. What of Cloudland's egg-shaped illuminated dome? Or its alpine (funicular) railway, designed to transport patrons up its steep hillside?

Inside, Cloudland boasted an elaborate Art-deco interior. Can you remember its springy, 'floating' timber floor?; or its domed sky-light fittings?; or its large revolving mirror ball?; its tiered seating?; its stunning stage interior?; its sweeping curtains; the lavish lighting; or its plaster lady who held onto the red fairy lights?; and Cloudland's private alcoves, upholstered seating, dressing rooms, and its perfect ventilation, the very finest of its kind?

1
BRISBANE: ONCE 'THE DEMOLITION CAPITAL OF QUEENSLAND'

PRESERVING PUBLIC BUILDING SITES

Though much is taken, much abided; and though

We are not now that strength which in the old days

Moved earth and heaven; that which we are, we are;

One equal temper of heroic hearts,

Made weak by time and fate, but strong in will

To strive, to seek, to find, and not to yield.

Alfred Lord Tennyson, *Ulysses*.

Man has always been endowed with old-fashioned reason—and common sense—with the power to create, so he may add more to what he's been granted in life. But, up until now, he hasn't just been a curator of the land and its heritage-listed buildings, but also a 'destroyer'. Forests keep on disappearing, rivers dry up, wildlife has become extinct, the climate's chaotic, the land grows poorer and uglier with each passing day; and cultural heritage edifices are demolished so they quickly vanish. Regarding the latter, it seems like our society's problem about placing a value on our many aged citizens extends to the low worth that is given to our historic structures— not very much!

My late father used to mildly rebuke "those folk who fail to learn the lessons of history". He thought that such people are doomed, at the very least, to repeat this course of action. He also said, when something was missing from our cultural landscape—especially if it was a highly-prized historic building—that it was now "a strange set-up". Observing the time we grew up in the city—relics of our own 'era' in Brisbane—it has become rather noticeable that this period of our past lives—gradually or suddenly 'disappears'. So it is like watching a movie about your own

Brisbane in its earlier years.   *Courier-Mail.*

Brisbane as it is today.   *Brisbane City Council.*

past. It's a crazy sensation, as if a part of your previous existence has vanished within the ether. Before now, you would think that others besides me would have become accustomed to these feelings. After all, growing up and living in Brisbane enabled us to not only be used to this phenomenon, we had many unaccountable opportunities to, in fact, witness aspects of parts of the city's demise. It's easy to wonder why our proud city of Brisbane does not wish to 'reconstruct' our near past, but seems fixated on either obliterating it or completely ignoring it.

Sometimes the loss of a cultural heritage icon may surface amid howls of protest, silent condemnation and street demonstrations. Then at other times, there is hardly even a kerfuffle, as there is deceit, subterfuge and stealth involved in

an historic building's passing. With wrecking balls, sledgehammers, and bulldozers, the wreckers' advance at a night's death knell—after midnight to the early hours of the morning.

In his *Sunday Mail* column, renowned poet Rupert McCall in his piece 'Our Regal First Lady' (with reference to the *Princess Theatre* at South Brisbane) echoed much the same grim sentiments:

This city has sacrificed more than enough of its cultural and architectural heritage. We have too easily become a token gesture to a long line of facades and so this voice must be heard now. Better to understand, acknowledge and appreciate what we've got while it's still there, serving its historical purpose, rather than howl when the developers are given an opportunity to circle.

Bruce Molloy, a Professor of Film and Television at Bond University, has also come up with much the same sordid sentiments and conclusions:

"I think what's happened to historic old buildings in Brisbane is diabolically bad. There's been little effort to maintain architecture for most of [them] in Brisbane, which I think is a great pity. We will never have a cultural or civilised society until we start respecting our [heritage] better than we have done".

BRISBANE'S 'DEMOLISHED CULTURAL HERITAGE SITES

Say goodbye my own true lover

As we sing a lover's song

How it breaks my heart to leave you

Now the carnival is gone

High above the dawn is waiting

And my tears are falling rain

For the carnival is over

We may never meet again…

Though the carnival is over

I will love you till I die.

The Carnival is Over, The Seekers

At the Gallery of Modern Art in Brisbane, a project about Brisbane's lost heritage offers us all a chance of redemption:

Tucked away in a corner overlooking the river at the *Gallery of Modern Art* is a very reflective spot amid the busy *Optimism* exhibition. A sign invites you to fill in your memories of Brisbane's vanished buildings on black-fringed cards, each titled *In Loving Memory*.

It's set beside a large gravestone structure, upon the back of which are names of five iconic Brisbane buildings—*Festival Hall, Cloudland, Skate Arena, Belle Vue Hotel,* and the *Victory Hotel.*

On the front the words have been altered to create different meanings.

Cloudland has changed into Land Value, *Skate Arena* to Arsen Atake and *Belle Vue Hotel* is now Hotel Levelled.

"I miss walking around them like when I was a child", reads the handwriting upon one of the *In Loving Memory* cards.

"Memories stay but the physical doesn't".

As Miranda Wallace writes in her essay in the *Optimism* catalogue: "For the generations of Brisbane's inhabitants, the ability to return to places that were symbolically significant for the experiences they hosted—a first teenage dance, a first kiss, a marriage proposal—is denied by the fact that so many landmark buildings that catered to the city's nightlife during the 20th century have been destroyed".

The untimely destruction of Brisbane's prized building sites was chiefly by accident, as fire sometimes broke out in its largely wooden, colonial structures.

The *Cremorne Theatre* at South Brisbane, in its early years, interestingly heralded: "No rats or fleas". Once managed by the impresario, John McCallum, it was destroyed by fire in February, 1954, so it escaped the actual fate of demolition. *The Queensland Art Gallery* now stands on this site. (*Courier-Mail.*)

While we keep lamenting Cloudland's loss, the question remains: what lessons have we learned from this? Maybe none!

The original *Shingle Inn* Restaurant.

Parts of the original *Shingle Inn* are in storage across Brisbane's city.

The original *Shingle Inn* shop fit-out is expected to be installed [to the refurbished] City Hall when it reopens after its $215 million restoration between December and February next year (2013). (*Courier-Mail.*)

The Milton Tennis Centre's ticket office has also been restored at the Brookfield Tennis Centre.

The initial *Shingle Inn* in Albert Street has gone, together with those scrumptious sandwich fillings. One memory of this café at Brisbane's *Gallery of Modern Art* produced this following ode: "In loving memory of the Shingle Inn, Edward St. Dark brown wood, cakes spinning slowly under glass and wondering how waitresses' head pieces stayed on". Like the *Shingle Inn*, some of our suburban swimming pools have also gone, like the one at Toowong.

The Brookfield Tennis Centre's 'ticket office'.
Courier-Mail.

Some aspects of Milton Tennis Centre's heritage have already been stashed away; and, in one case, reused:

> Parts of the tennis centre, including canvas banners, nets and even bingo sets are in storage at Tennyson as Tennis Queensland works out the best way to put them on display at their new home.

> The biggest item saved was the ticket office that sat at the entrance off Milton Rd., rescued by Brookfield Tennis Centre owners, Sue and Greg Braun, a former Wimbledon and French Open player. Mrs Braun said she had also tried for six months to save the derelict and vandalised ticket booth but the final salvage came down to a matter of hours.

> "It just broke my heart—it's part of our heritage", Mrs Braun commented on the unloved little building. Driving past on one morning eight years ago, she spotted the demolition on site and had begged them to let her save the building.

> It took [her] more than a year to find old-style tradesmen to faithfully restore the booth, even down to the toilet roll holders inside that used to hold the reels of tickets.

Unfortunately, sites and structures of high public significance which clearly defined our past, and the city's identity, too, are slipping from our grip, fully compromised. One such is the 121-year-old *Yungaba* building at Kangaroo Point. It is the only purpose-built centre for immigrants in the State. A private developer, *Australand*, purchased it in 2005; and holds the structure's fate in its company's hands.

Her Majesty's Theatre was another of the fallen icons featured in the *Gallery of Modern Art's Optimism* exhibition in Brisbane:

> "In Loving Memory of *Her Majesty's Theatre*. Somehow the dark auditorium had a [very] special magic missing in many modern venues. The curtain opened and the proscenium arch allowed special effects to unfold. Opera, ballet, musical comedy or Shakespeare—wonderful".

The *Paris Cinema* was another building featured in the Gallery's odes to dead venues:

> "I used to go to the *Paris Cinema* in Albert Street to see *Pink Panther* movies as a child. I used to sit in the balcony upstairs, it was a little art deco gem—sadly subsumed into the *Myer Centre*".

Upon the evening of September 28th, 1962, any slight hope Brisbanites had of saving the city's iconic trams went up when 65 of them were billowing with smoke and fire—an inferno fed by oil, grease and tyre rubber. With the inimitable smell of the old tram engines fresh in most citizens' nostrils, the date of April 13th, 1969, was the day of Brisbane's ultimate tram ride.

Tram wrecks after the fire.

Given Premier Joh Bjelke-Petersen's total disregard for many of Brisbane's historic early buildings, the city of Brisbane became infamous as the 'demolition capital of Australia'. It was also renowned for its midnight attacks on historic structures; and police dealing with all the protestors—while the Deens (officially referred to as Sultan Mohammed; Abdul Rahinan; Habib Allah; Mohammed Abdul Gaffar; and Haneef Mohammed; or nicknamed respectively, George, Ray, Happy, Louie and Funny), the State government's preferred demolition workers—carried out their wicked early morning demolition raids and assorted activities.

A Gallery of Modern Art (Brisbane) memory of trams from its Optimism exhibition.
Courier-Mail.

Demolition in Brisbane proceeded almost without interruption, including the *ANZ Bank* (on the corner of Queen and Wharf Street), the *Queensland Trustees Building* in 1981; *Her Majesty's Theatre* in 1984; and the *Hoffnungs* building. In this respect, by the 1980s the State of Queensland had indeed truly become in every sense of the word the *demolition capital* of the world.

Opposed by criticism and continual attacks from the National Trust, town planners and community action groups, the Bjelke-Petersen government released in 1985 a glossy pamphlet *Preserving Our Queensland Heritage*. Of the 17 sites mentioned in this booklet, all but *Government House, Newstead House, Yungaba* (the immigration centre), *South Brisbane Town Hall* and the *Museum* were based in the CBD area of Brisbane. All the structures featured were constructed out of brick or stone; and only a few—the *Mansions; Harris Terrace;* the *Commissariat Store;* and the *Old Government Printery*—had been endangered.

People stood around dejected in the early hours of the morning in 1979, the night the *Belle Vue Hotel* was demolished into dust and rubble. A landmark site of Brisbane's social life of an earlier day and era now lay abjectly in ruins.

It is interesting to know that parts of the *Belle Vue Hotel* now have a life of their own:

Not far away (from the establishment's previous site) the *Belle Vue Hotel*'s famous old iron balustrades have been included in a Queenslander-style cottage in one of Brisbane's suburbs.

The house was built in 1892, six years after the second *Belle Vue Hotel* was finished in 1886.

The hotel was demolished in April, 1979, while crowds of protesters had clashed with police before dawn.

Owner Eugene Barry said the railings run along the front of the house, topped with a timber rail.

"They were one of the reasons why we bought the place", Mr Barry said.

The brilliant *Belle Vue Hotel*'s balustrades are now on a cottage in Rosalie.
Courier-Mail.

An interstate ballroom dancing championship at the *Festival Hall*, Brisbane, 1962.
Sunday Mail.

Before Cloudland's demolition in November, 1982, the other listed cultural heritage buildings demolished by the developers in that same year included the Martin Wilson building, Brisbane's oldest commercial building, (March); the

300-year-old riverfront buildings in Eagle Street in April; the Bank of Australasia building on the corner of Queen and Wharf Streets (July); and the three Browns Cottages in St Paul's Terrace in August.

Likewise, the feeling within the city of Brisbane when Festival Hall was demolished and turned into a 41-floor apartment complex called *Festival Towers* was of utter despair. Do not forget that this building at the corner of Albert and Charlotte Streets was the location where *The Beatles* had performed four of their shows in June, 1964.

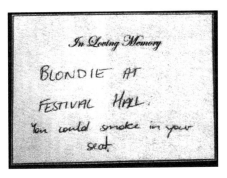

A lament for the Festival Hall's concerts.
Gallery of Modern Art, Brisbane.

The *Festival Hall*, 22nd August, 2003.
Gallery of Modern Art, Brisbane.

When *Festival Hall* was ripped down, I became nostalgic about every wrestling and boxing match I'd ever witnessed there— not to forget so many great live performances by acts like Peter Allen and *Doctor Hook*. I can still clearly picture Dennis Lacorierre from the latter band belting out his moving version of *The Wild Colonial Boy*.

After closing in 2003, a billboard sign entreated: "Seats for sale, cheaper than a concert ticket, phone 3221-5030". Notably, the newsagency upon that corner also closed the same day.

CLOUDLAND BALLROOM, 1939-1982

...in lovely loneliness

Half folded like an April bud

on winter haunted trees

THE HORN

Hark is that a horn I hear

in Cloudland...

Walter De la Mare, 1873-1956

Remember, if you so dare, Cloudland, 1939 to 1982? Even though it was demolished nearly thirty years ago, Brisbane's 'builder' generation (those born 1925-1945) and 'baby boomers' (all those born between 1946 and 1964) are still reminiscing about Cloudland. They will never ever forget it, as it was the iconic entertainment venue at Bowen Hills, which had served the Brisbane community as well as the entertainment industry for more than 40 years. But, if you've perchance forgotten, it crashed to a demolition bulldozer in November of 1982.

The 'baby boomers' and those 'builders' before them also have rather fond memories of Cloudland for a variety of reasons; in essence, it appears as if every 'Brisbanite' beyond the 50 year age bracket possesses a little bit of Cloudland in their DNA or 'nostalgia' file. Many folk reflect on the myriad joys and social pleasantries of that glorious era, but recoil when having to remind themselves of the manner of its shocking and grubby passing:

...the iconic building, with its highly distinctive dome, was the catalyst for innumerable romances and marriages after it was built in 1940. It closed during World War II, forcing diehard jitterbug fans to look elsewhere for amusement, but re-opened with gusto after the conflict was over. Within a decade the jitterbug [dance] had been ditched for the "scandalous" dance moves played out to rock 'n' roll music by bodgies and widgies and teenyboppers. Parts of the immense dance floor were roped off so all the flailing arms and legs of the young rockers did not injure older patrons. But by the 1970s the crowds had started to dwindle as more sophisticated nightclubs had emerged and so the Deens were called in to execute a lightning demolition raid. (*Courier-Mail*.)

Bowen Hills, Brisbane, the site of Luna Park (Cloudland) from 1939/40; photograph taken from the *Royal Brisbane Hospital*, 1891.
Qld Pics.

Pertinent to Cloudland's 'loss', Thomas Ryan has made this comment:

What a shame to lose such a wonderful and inspirational design. There are many other modernist buildings that are at risk of being lost today and buildings like them need to be protected, as heritage does not just mean 19th century architecture and social history.

And again, from Tony James:

Cloudland was the beacon crown of Brisbane and it glowed at night like a lighthouse from the past. I find Brisbane such an ugly city now, just a limp copycat of countless others.

We now have nothing anymore we can say is originally ours, all our picture palaces are gone, majestic buildings being plundered, without a thought of (so called) heritage listing. I think the destruction of Cloudland and most of Brisbane was criminal; and the sad thing is I'm sure I'm not alone in that thought.

Furthermore, from very this keen observer of our heritage and fumbling cultural past came the following:

I would have liked to have seen Cloudland and I was 10 years old when it was demolished, but it should have been heritage listed. Another building that should have been heritage listed is the movie theatre *The Regent* within the Queen Street Mall in Brisbane and not only just the entrance. It should be the whole building. That's what I don't like about Brisbane and they are too interested in knocking down old buildings for offices or home apartments. When I go to Hobart one thing I like is they keep their old buildings and they restore them and some of them are offices. Brisbane City Council and the Queensland State Government have a lot of explaining to do to allow all this to happen. If this happened in Europe there would be a lot of explaining to do and here in Australia it should be the same. Brisbane has enough hi-rise buildings. *Festival Hall* in Brisbane CBD is another example for hi-rise apartments.

According to the *Courier-Mail*, the 'Cloudland clock and some signs were recovered by onlookers prior to the Bowen Hills ballroom being demolished, and are understood to be in homes in Brisbane'. But some of Cloudland's heritage is still in storage, stashed away for who knows what purpose? Perhaps the last word of the debate over Cloudland's disappearance should go to Jan Power, Brisbane's food critic and farmers' market 'guru'. She compared the demolition of Cloudland to "people throwing out their good jewellery". (*Courier-Mail.*)

OUR ENDEARING CULTURAL HERITAGE SITES

"Moving the 'Mephisto' [German] tank to the Queensland Museum, Bowen Hills, Brisbane, 1919".

Qld Pics.

What, pray, of our cultural heritage sites remain largely untouched or only slightly altered? Think the *City Hall*, the *Story Bridge*, *Government House*, the old *Queensland Museum*, plus *The Mansions* building in George Street, the *Riverside Ballroom* at New Farm, the *Trocadero* at Stones Corner and Valley Swimming Baths.

The *Booroodabin Bowls Club* upon the Breakfast Creek Road, Newstead, is obviously a survivor of similar establishments in Brisbane:

The *Booroodabin Bowls Club*, established within 1888, is Queensland's oldest bowls club and part of Brisbane's formative history. 'Booroodabin' is an Aboriginal word which means 'place of many oaks'. Lord Lamington (The Queensland Governor from 1896 to 1901) was the founding patron while Sir Thomas MacIlwraith was the very first president of the club. He was also the Premier of Queensland at the time.

Newstead House on Breakfast Creek Road, Newstead, is another building that seems in pristine condition:

The 'ancient' and 'modern' look of the *Booroodabin Bowls Club*.

Newstead House, then and now.

The older and the revitalised Gassworks.

The old and the new *Miegunyah* House.

Brisbane's oldest domestic dwelling has evolved from a simple Georgian cottage in 1846 into the quintessential homestead of today. In its purest form, the *Newstead Cottage* of 1846 was an architectural style drawn from the bungalow of the Indian sub-continent. Today *Newstead House* is furnished in the exuberant appliances of the late Victorian period and with a fine colour scheme to match.

The Gassworks on Breakfast Creek Road, Newstead, is another example of a structure which has outlasted its own era:

The extraordinary journey of *Gassworks* started 145 years ago, when the *Teneriffe Gas Works* first developed. The iconic No. 2 Gasometer was built in 1873, initially down at Petrie Bight before being moved to its current location. Before the end of the 19th century it was supplying gas to Brisbane streets from Hamilton around to Toowong. The *Gassworks* will be reignited into one of Brisbane's most vibrant mixed used communities now with the iconic Gasometer as the centre point of activity.

Miegunyah House within Jordan Terrace, Bowen Hills, is another to have escaped the developer's plans 'without a bullet':

Victorian, elegant, and built when the local tradition was at its most opulent, it is now one of Brisbane's most accessible heritage homes. Step through the cedar door to enter a world of lofty ceilings, marble fireplaces, gleaming silver and the drudgery of washing day. Enjoy Devonshire teas overlooking the tree-shaded garden.

The Tivoli, located within Fortitude Valley, is still one of Brisbane's most elegant and unique venues. It possesses a spacious main auditorium, which is overlooked by an immaculate dress circle; and centrally features a stage and gold proscenium. Adding to its old world atmosphere are brass railings and subdued lighting.

The Tivoli: one of Brisbane's present-day favourite entertainment and function venues.

The old *Diamantina Hospital* has now emerged as the *Diamantina Health Care Museum Association* down at Woolloongabba. It generally acquires, conserves, researches, and exhibits materials of some significance in health and nursing care, including development and support services.

The old Diamantina Hospital on the grounds of the Princess Alexandra Hospital, Woolloongabba, Brisbane. The author's mother, Edna, wrote letters there for its patients in the 1950s.

three years to construct from 1876. The fine colonial architect, Francis Drummond Greville Stanley, expertly guided the project. The *Queensland Museum* was even housed there for a 20 year period. The *State Library* and an art gallery also took up residence on the site. In 1958, an unusual 'extension' appeared to reduce, rather than add to, its fine 'stand-alone grandeur'. It would be cultural 'vandalism' pure and simple to tamper with it once again.

The *Public Library of Queensland*, 1931.
John Oxley Library.

This unusual extension was to become known as the 'William St. Library', 1958.
Courier-Mail.

A possible heritage-building 'brawl' also loomed over a strange scheme to construct a hotel above Brisbane's old *State Library* (The *Public Library of Queensland*) building in William Street, North Quay. The clandestine proposition had formed part of Tabcorp Holdings' $260 million upgrade nearby to its own facility. The quaint old complex, copied from a 16th century Italian architectural design, took up to

Thankfully, the very Italianate-styled *Princess Theatre* in South Brisbane constructed in 1888, is still standing. It is a venue which has hosted plays and other stage productions; silent films; shown movie reels; promoted choirs; held talent shows for US military personnel in World War II; music concerts, such as *The Whitlams*; and rock 'n' roll circus troupes.

The Princess Theatre, in South Brisbane. A 'Bentley' sketch.

Sunday Mail.

The *Breakfast Creek Hotel*, built in 1889, to showcase the French renaissance style of architecture, is still going strong despite changes of ownership, renovations and flooding over the years.

The *Breakfast Creek Hotel, ca.* 1890s.

The *Regent* in its prime was only one of the numerous grand picture 'palaces' in the city of Brisbane. Sadly, the *Odeon, St. James, Metro*, the *Forum*, the *Paris*, the *Tivoli*, *The Winter Garden* and *Her Majesty's* theatres are merely the ghosts of our past. Given its elaborate grandeur, the people of Brisbane were eager to catch a glimpse of this newly-completed *Regent Theatre* on November 8th, 1929, as

if its opening was a great cause for city celebrations. As Sally Browne recounted in the *Courier-Mail*:

Opening night at the grand picture palace, which had been built for the costly sum of £300,000, was a much anticipated event. Crowds stretched around the corner into Albert Street.

A magnificent show awaited them—a live orchestra, dancers, a Wurlitzer organ played by US organist, Stanley Wallace, as well as newsreels of the Melbourne Cup, followed by two short films and the exciting feature, *Fox Movietone Follies of 1929*.

The papers had touted the arrival of the gothic empire-style *Brisbane Regent*, the grand cinema and vaudeville stage to rival any of its style in Hollywood.

Funded by the Mayne Estate (of *The Mayne Inheritance* fame) and operated by *Hoyts*, it was the last of a chain of Regents built around the country, and the most superb of them. Today, only the *Melbourne Regent* remains intact. (*Sunday Mail*.)

The cinema inside of the old Regent Theatre in the Queen Street Mall.

Courier-Mail.

Ron West, who has played the organ and run the projection for over 50 years at various venues, in the late 1970s brought 13 truckloads of carpet, curtains and seating to the *Majestic Theatre* at Pomona in the Sunshine Coast hinterland.

The Regent Magazine, Vol. 1, No. 3, 1929.
Fryer Library Theatre Program Files.

By 2010, the previous heritage-listed foyer and quaint marble staircase of the old *Regent Theatre* had been incorporated into the $800 million development of this site. A 300-seat cinema and then two 60-seat multi-purpose auditoriums were also drafted into the plans.

As the *Sunday Mail* of July 26th, 2009, reported:

> The showcase cinema, bar and vestibule on the ground floor, which were lovingly recreated from the old remains of the destroyed original 2600-seat *Regent Theatre* in 1978-80, are not heritage listed and not part of the [rebuilding] plans.

Heritage watchers now fear parts of the *Regent Theatre* may go missing with the complex's redevelopment in the Queen Street Mall. 'While developers say the Regent's foyer and decorations are being protected, critics fear its heritage value is being smashed piece by piece'. (*Courier-Mail.*)

The foyer of the Regent Theatre.
Courier-Mail. Picture: by Campbell Scott.

The *City Hall*, which opened on April 8th, 1930, is still lovingly with us all, although an estimated $200 million was needed to fix subsidence problems; concrete cancer; as well as crumbling walls or ceilings. It's perhaps ironic now—if you were an eye witness to its unveiling—to recount what the Lord Mayor, William Jolly, told the assembled crowd: 'This majestic building will stand for all time, not only as a symbol of the present generation, but as a monument to the work of the early pioneers'.

Cranes putting all the finishing touches on Brisbane's City Hall, 1929.
Sunday Mail.

The *Story Bridge* which spans over the Brisbane River, was opened on July 6th, 1940, by Sir Leslie Wilson, and is still in existence. It is the largest steel bridge built using Australian materials, with 95 per cent of the steel coming from Australia. Its Queensland-born designer, J. C. Bradfield, took up the engineering reins; and Evans Deakin and Hornibrook Constructions built the entire structural edifice.

The *Story Bridge* is looking just like a meccano structure, circa 1939.
Sunday Mail.

Interestingly perhaps, when the entire bridge is painted with its special metal-protecting paint, another team of workers starts the process all over again from the beginning, so the conservation scheme is ongoing.

2
THE PASSING OF OUR QUEEN OF 'CINDERELLA' CITY

Don't think you are going to conceal thoughts by concealing evidence that they never existed.

Dwight D. Eisenhower,
(1890-1969), *US President*

JOHANNES BJELKE-PETERSEN

Power consists in one's capacity to link his will with the purpose of others, to lead by reason and a gift of co-operation.

Woodrow Wilson, (1856-1924),
US President

It may seem odd to some or many of you to begin a tale about Brisbane's 'grand old dame', Cloudland Ballroom, by commencing with its demolition, demise or complete disappearance from the city's skyline then work backwards. But, to me, this event appears to be a logical point to commence a story having elephantine twists and majestic turns, together with a good quantity of hoary stings in its substantial tail.

The late Sir Joh Bjelke-Petersen.
Picture by David Caird.

Sir Joh Bjelke-Petersen and Russel Hinze at the height of their political power.

Courier-Mail.

English writer, actor and television personality, Stephen Fry, tells a story about the British Prime Minister, Tony Blair. He was once asked to help him with a speech; and his response was in the form of a narrative about Philip of Macedon. Apparently, Philip had hired a man whose job it was to hit him on his head with a bladder on a stick— the idea being that, in so doing, he might keep the king's ego well in check. The punch line was that Blair had no need of a man like that; he had his grim deputy, John Prescott. So it was with Russel Hinze, Sir Joh Bjelke-Petersen's deputy! Some even said they were both "tarred with the very same brush" in their ultra-conservative, even right-wing approach to Queensland's governance.

Queensland's longest-serving Premier, Sir Joh Bjelke-Petersen,

was in power from August 8th, 1968, to December 1st, 1987, when he was then deposed by Mike Ahearn. By 1982, the year of Cloudland's 'passing', Queensland had been ruled for nearly twenty years by Joh. Although he oversaw a major period of vigorous economic development, Sir Joh was unashamedly anti-heritage; and pro-development. His own way of thinking was that the country was to be exploited in a sort of 'pioneer' approach to the land. Joh's period of government was marked by an extremely hard line approach to public protest, all street marches, unions; and industrial action of any persuasion—including the *Cloudland Ballroom* and the *Belle Vue Hotel*:

Peanut farmer Joh Bjelke-Petersen became premier and leader of the (then) Country Party on this day [August 8th, 1968] after the sudden death of premier Jack Pizzey on July 31st. He went on to rule with an iron fist for just shy of 20 years before a tangled web of police and government corruption saw his beloved party turn on him.

Police make an arrest during a Brisbane demonstration.

Courier-Mail.

and that Brisbane was still a big country town and a cultural desert.

Here's how one commentator had described the political and social atmosphere within Queensland during Joh's time:

> I felt something was sorely amiss in Queensland; a feeling that stuck with me somehow…Queens-land was an outright police state. Their Premier, Joh Bjelke-Petersen, in full cry after more than a decade in power, largely set the tone of the place. By his edict, public assembly had been ruthlessly suppressed, the dissenters were bashed and jailed, big-time corruption flourished and the cops did as they pleased. I can still remember Joh's ludicrous measures to "refuse service to the homosexuals or other perverts" in bottle shops or pubs.

The very 'Instrument' of the Bjelke-Petersen control: Queensland Police force. This is worn as the officially approved badge; and had served as a symbol of Joh's crushing of any sort of opposition.

Courier-Mail.

Joh's rule appeared to confirm political scientist, S. M. Lipsett's claim, that every country has a 'Deep South'. The Premier's own adage was that he was uncomfortable "running along a barbed wire fence with a foot on either side". He said this kind of practice didn't work for him, allowing him to celebrate what he perceived as Queensland's particular 'differences'; and treating outsiders with outright contempt.

With a stark reference to the "deep north" problem which was rumoured to exist in Queensland, one newspaper report of the period put it thus:

> [There is] a perception in other parts of Australia that residents lacked democratic rights and civil liberties;

Protests like this one could not happen in the 'Deep South' of Queensland.

The Australian.

At least tacitly, Queenslanders were advised to forget the repression, corruption and social upheaval people suffered in eradicating all Joh's injustices. In essence, Bjelke-Petersen, like Groucho Marx, appeared to be implying to Brisbane residents: "Those are my principles. If you don't like them, I have others".

As one commentator remarked:

They [i.e. street marches] were not 'unlawful' in inverted commas, they were unlawful, and often deliberately so. The law, as enacted and enforced by the Queensland government under Joh Bjelke-Petersen had curtailed democratic rights that had been fought for over a period of several years by unionists, the workers, and political organisations. My unlawful actions were a conscious act of defiance in order to win back those democratic rights.

How Joh's policies converted to the Brisbane's cultural and music scene are interesting, to say the least.

It's not easy to explain to the uninitiated the effect that the Joh Bjelke-Petersen government's political and social agenda had on the population all those years ago. Police intimidation and oppression all took their toll, particularly upon all of the indigenous communities, students, union workers, rock and roll bands and anyone else on the wrong side of the political fence.

The then government's righteous and wholesome media façade contrasted sharply with the reality of life on the street. Blatant police brutality was commonplace for anyone involved in unlawful protest marches, as was the acute anxiety and paranoia induced by the frenzied clatter of police camera shutters that had documented everyone and everything. Imagine coming home to see television footage of Minister Russ Hinze in at the notorious *Bubbles Bathhouse* in Woolloongabba, declaring that no brothels existed in the State. The place was warped, pure and simple.

The media have never focused on the exodus of bands and individual artists, filmmakers, photographers, writers, poets and the DJ's from Brisbane during that era. There must have been thousands who headed down south. It was not about wanting to leave; it was about having no choice but to leave. This Queensland regime had unwittingly become an exporter of popular culture of which the rest of the Australian capital cities, primarily Sydney and Melbourne, were the main beneficiaries.

I had left Brisbane with $400 and a car load of drums. I arrived in Sydney during Monday afternoon peak hour and crawled across the harbour bridge to the muffled roar of *The Saint's Prehistoric Sounds* on my car stereo. I felt triumphant.

That very first night at the *Sandringham Hotel* in Newtown I watched Louis Tillet's *Paris Green* do the business with a smoking Louis Burdett on drums.

Celebrating my new-found freedom I wandered outside and lit up a joint, only to have a NSW police F100 wagon pull up outside of the pub at the same time and toot its horn. Flooded with residual paranoia I immediately flicked the J away into the gutter and then continued to sheepishly sip my schooner. A barman had appeared and launched himself onto the running board of the Ford and expertly slid a slab of beer into the passenger side window in one smooth movement. All I saw was an arm and thumbs up as the police re-entered the King St. crawl. Jubilantly I skipped over to the gutter and retrieved the smoke. Finally I was in big city!

Robert Lastdrazer had a similar story to relate:

During a recent night out with a couple of mates in Melbourne, conversation centred on the deaths of Lobby Loyde and Billy Thorpe, their Queensland origins and the impending reformation of the original *Saints* line-up at Brisbane's coming of age festival called "Pig City" later this year. My friends took the opportunity to remind me that I had left Queensland in the mid-1980s vowing never to return. They asked how it felt having been some 2000 kilometres from home for over 20 years. "Just lovely" was my reply.

In the early seventies my parents took me to a tourist attraction called *Bullen's Lion Safari* situated about half way between Brisbane and the Gold Coast. There on a humid 30 plus degree-day I watched a large polar bear swaying from side to side in a cage so cramped the animal was unable to turn around. "That's not right is it Pop?" I queried. "No, no it's not" the old man thoughtfully replied, shaking his head, Ironically that enclosure was to mirror my adolescent relationship now with this 'Sunshine State', the feeling of being born and trapped in a humid, cultureless cage.

Given such opposition to Joh and his National Party politics, when the former was awarded an honorary degree at the University of Queensland upon November 15th, 1984, academic staff at the institution were appalled at the idea:

There were—predictably—howls of outrage from opponents of Premier, Sir Joh Bjelke-Petersen, after the University of Queensland announced that it would award the premier an honorary Doctor of Laws. Politics aside, there was some substance to the complaints considering Sir Joh often proudly declared that he had been educated in the "school of hard knocks". He also never bothered to hide his contempt for academics. The UQ Academic Staff Association executive was appalled, saying the prestige of honorary doctorates awarded to 11 other people that year had been "reduced" by the inclusion of Sir Joh, "whose inimical attitudes towards the ethos of the university are very renowned". True to his past form, the premier was unrepentant when told his doctorate had angered university staff. "The poor creatures—it doesn't take much to upset them", he said. Thousands of protesters staged an ugly protest at the university awards ceremony in May, 1985, in which governor Sir James Ramsay was spat on. Sir Joh did not attend.

Joh's luck ran out when his own party dumped him at the end (1st December) of 1987, with Mike Ahearn becoming the new Premier.

Courier-Mail.

Brisbane's *Sunday Sun*'s triumphant headline in 1989.

In 1989, Wayne Goss and Labor finally seized power from the old National Party. (Under Peter Beattie from 1996, and latterly, Anna Bligh, they ruled the State until March

24th, 2012, when the Liberal Party under Campbell Newman won office in a landslide victory).

Premier 'Can Do' Campbell Newman's victory wave, 24th March, 2012.

Sunday Mail.

In 2005, the 'chooks were all finally fed' when Sir Joh Bjelke-Petersen had died with his family by his side. He was 94.

Sir Joh was buried in the grounds of Bethany, his family home in Kingaroy, Queensland. The plot is ringed by gums he planted there as a younger man.

1982

Learn from the mistakes of others. You can never live long enough to make them all yourself.

Groucho Marx

The year of 1982 held a certain interest for all Queenslanders, Australians and those examining international events. There was a baby boomer aerobic craze in that year, with Jane Fonda providing all her workout videos. Sardonically maybe, *Eye of the Tiger* and *Fame* were hits of the year. In the US, in the first operation of its kind, doctors at the University of Utah Medical Centre implanted a permanent artificial heart. Barny Clark, a retired dental practitioner, lived 112 days with the device.

On the home front, Sir Ninian Stephen was appointed Australia's Governor-General. Then an American male became the first person in this country to be diagnosed as having the AIDS virus.

You'd also think that no one would want to return to the '80s, the 'greed is good' decade that ended with entrepreneurs like Gordon Gekko in the US and Alan Bond of Australia in jail. In Victoria, on May 19th, 1982, hundreds of people were named in a tax evasion report tabled in the Victorian Parliament. Companies were sold to sham directors, costing the Federal Government approximately $200 million in lost revenue.

Brisbane as a city in late 1982 was going about its routine, daily business. Upon August 2nd, 1982, *The Sun*, a new morning daily newspaper, had appeared. Towards the end of this same year, the Commonwealth Games were held within Brisbane. On September 30th, 1982, Prince Philip opened the event. It closed on October 10th. To mark these celebrations Cloudland held a 'Commonwealth Games Bush Ball' that same evening.

John Colville coordinated the Queensland Folk Federation's *Bush Orchestra*, with a line-up of 35 musicians, playing for this very successful event, one of the last functions ever held at Cloudland.

This friendly chain marked one of the social highlights of the Commonwealth Games.

Brisbane had advanced a long way and come of age since its hosting of the Commonwealth Games. It was currently a *'Cinderella' city*, emerging from its frumpy clothes to presently seek salvation as a sleek new civic swan. What a pity perhaps one shocking act by a National Party Government in November of this self-same year sent us back to live yet again amongst the ugly sisters and the Bjelke-Petersen dark ages.

Matilda, the mascot, surprised the entire world with a wink and a pouch full of little joeys at the Commonwealth Games opening.
Courier-Mail.

The passing of a Brisbane iconic building should be a lesson for each of us. Its destruction is after all, a metaphor for life itself. You cop some awful decisions during your existence; you make some bad calls; you get some odd situations thrown at you; and you are sometimes 'hit for six' by what life sometimes dredges up. That's what happened to our Cloudland. If you—like the actors in the filmic version of David Nicholls' popular novel, *One Day* – could just return to one day upon which Cloudland was buzzing, that would be a dream. As for the dancehall's ignominious death, Thomas Hardy says it completely

when he refers to Tess of the D'Urberville's passing as "a day which lay sly; and unseen among all the other days of the year, giving no sign or sound when she annually passed over it; but not the less surely there". Cloudland's sad loss is fairly much like Tess's.

Sometimes a public "monument's" death makes us mourn the passing of our own lives. It's called "nostalgia". We grew up with Cloudland; it is part of us. When it died, a little bit of us passed, too. It's now debatable if many younger Queenslanders know little of Cloudland or Joh Bjelke-Petersen's severe governance of the State. If so, they may be largely ignorant of the possibility that history might just repeat itself.

From the joyous victory parades which marked the end of World War II to the often violent protest marches, political upheavals and demonstrations of the 1970s and the 1980s of Joh's 'reign' in Queensland, the State's citizens have employed the city of Brisbane's streets to speak out (regarding Cloudland's 'passing') and to celebrate and to commemorate this notable event that touched Queensland. Let's hope there is no need to do so again, with respect to any of our cultural heritage buildings.

As Leon Gellert, in *Before Action*, said about another context: *We always had to do our work at night/I wondered why we had to be so sly/ I wondered why we couldn't have our fight/ Under the open sky.*

THE DEMOLITION OF CLOUDLAND

Cloudland Ballroom sadly and involuntarily closed its doors in November of 1982. There was no choice in the matter; many others had made decisions about the former dancehall's future for her. Unfortunately, it was, at this point, time to go.

It is said that a person's anxiety is usually caused by the fear of the unknown, while also surmising that what might be going to happen is so inevitable; and entirely out of his or her control. Clearly, Tracy Dunnet's (nee McDougall's) boss in Brisbane either had a premonition that Cloudland was about to 'go' or had some insider information:

> In 1982 I worked for a company called *Stewart & Co.* (Private Investigations). The afternoon before Cloudland was demolished my then boss Henry Stewart-Koster asked me to go with him to check something out. This was quite unusual but I was always up for an adventure. He didn't ever tell me where we were going and was quite secretive. We drove up the rear lane to the top of Cloudland Hill and around to the front entrance. It was quite eerie—there was no-one there. It didn't occur to me that it was about to be demolished and if I had any idea of it I would have called the media. Unfortunately, we didn't get out of the car to have a walk around—all I remember is the sign that said *TAXIS TO THE REAR*. He then dropped me off at the train station—some cryptic comment about it all making sense by Monday. The next morning I woke up to read of the demolition in the *Courier-Mail* and he was right—our little trip on the previous afternoon did make sense.

Cloudland demolished. Aug 11, 1982.

The architectural delight of Cloudland, demolished on *7th* November, 1982. *N.B. This small reproduction of the very front page somehow carries the incorrect date!*
Courier-Mail.

George Savva of the band, *Gingerbread*, also claims how he was performing at a gig at Cloudland the night before it was torn down (November 6th, 1982). His band at the time was the *Diamonds*. As the stage was poorly lit that particular night, and the band was literally playing in the dark, George—who was, as usual, with his saxophone—had asked the lighting guy to please put some light on the stage. Before the final song of his bracket for the evening, the lighting man had beckoned George forward and showed him that most of the electrical wires at Cloudland had been disconnected. George was in no doubt of the exact reason why when he awoke the next morning to find that his beloved Cloudland was "no more".

Like some thieves in the night, the Deen Brothers demolished Cloudland in the early hours of the morning of November 7th, 1982. *N.B. The old Panorama Room to the top right of the picture is still standing!*
Courier-Mail.

Who were these nefarious Deens who were so involved in destroying such a prized heritage site? The Deens had been running a company for more than 30 years in Brisbane; and were involved in several major projects including major demolitions and earthworks. Their activities were connected with "no salvage demolition clean-ups", specialising in brick and concrete. To them, no job was too large or small. "We don't just doze around, we rip into it" was their motto. Moreover, "*all we leave behind are the memories*". In sum, the Deens were a 'no-questions-asked-or-answers-given' style of outfit, favoured by the State government and the Brisbane City Council's 'urban fathers' for such controversial undertakings.

The Deen Brothers had been connected with the demolition of several more magnificent constructions other than Cloudland. In point of fact, these brothers had achieved fame during the Joh Bjelke-Petersen era for a whole string of secret demolition activities on some of Brisbane's grandest public buildings of the 19th and 20th centuries. All of their midnight 'demos' were very common place in the 1980s and defined just how the Queensland government valued their heritage:

> The Deen Brothers have a long history of demolitions at night, bringing down the *Belle Vue Hotel* in George Street in 1979, the Cloudland Ballroom at Bowen Hills in 1982 (and later the Brisbane Tavern in 2002 all in the dark). Other prominent demolitions have included the *Gabba* grandstands as well as the *Holy Name Cathedral* foundation and crypt in Fortitude Valley. The company had also cleared land at Maleny where the controversial *Woolworths* store was built. But Mr Deen said that it was unfair that any job they performed was presumed to be 'dodgy' or controversial in some way. "It's a little bit that way. But we know we're doing everything by the book", he said.

The Deen Bros. and their work crew.

Cloudland in 1982.

In fact, the Deen Brothers' own wrecking balls, excavators and a Caterpillar D8 bulldozer had this cultural icon tumbling; and flattened it almost completely in approximately two hours.

A heart-rending plaster lady, once an adornment of a huge Cloudland ballroom column, peeps out from the rubble which had remained.
Courier-Mail, 8th. November 1982.

There was a touch of high drama and adventure about Sir Joh's handiwork in the Deens' 'illegal' actions. The 'secret' demolition took place—under cover of darkness—in the still of the night, without any word or dire warning. Moreover, the Police acted as armed guards. In this respect, there was no excusing the manner in which this 'marvellous facility met its doom' by the early hours of a November daybreak in 1982.

The after midnight demolition to 3a.m. had only served to lull the heritage debate. By sunrise, all that was left of this remarkably significant, art-deco palace of dreams-type complex was its reduction to rubble and dust in mainly a matter of an hour or so— along with generations of memories.

The much-loved romantic arch and clam-shell entrance was now just a pile of twisted metal; and the fondly remembered egg-shaped dome was totally smashed to smithereens—certainly beyond most folks' identification. The so-called springy, floating floor, which had showed all the marks of countless feet, was to be earmarked for recycling—as swimming pool decks and for children's playgrounds in suburbia. This extraordinarily breath-taking and striking establishment—replete with its breathtaking lighting , stunning domes, skylight fittings, tiered seating about the dance floor, as well as rich decorative elaborations—was now unrecognisable.

Yet, in the dust and big piles of rubble, tinsel and other decorations still shone out through the remains of broken plaster columns. Loose electrical wiring crackled continuously as it shorted near to the Panorama Room. Green upholstered chairs ladies once sat on were now buried under piles of timber, steel, fibro and iron sheeting.

"It's GOING, going, gone...the Panorama Room at Cloudland [used extensively from the 1960s] is demolished in 1982".
Courier-Mail. Picture: by Keith Morris.

Overall, the developers removed 6,200 tonnes of broken asbestos cement sheeting and pipes. It was dug up, moved in covered vehicles; and buried under two metres of soil at a Brisbane City Council dump site. The material was made up of factory rejects, used as fill when a car park was being constructed while US military forces used Cloudland's building site during World War II. In the finish, the 2.5 hectare site was now just an exposed patch of hilltop—apart from two odd-looking navigation poles. Faded

Cloudland signs upon the entrance posts were the only indication of the once stately ballroom structure.

In the 'wash-up', the Deen Brothers were fined a 'derisory small sum' of $125 for not possessing a relevant permit (the maximum penalty was only $200). The old site's new owner-developer was also fined just a total of $180.67, including court costs.

A mass of rubble. *The Panorama Room* is still standing here to the right of the image.

Ironically, perhaps, in clear hindsight, the demolition of the old dancehall had taken place despite there being no permit in place; and in spite of its National Trust listing. One observer of the devastation saw the demolition of Cloudland as "an act of bastardry [which] tore a lot of people's hearts out, including mine. For me it represented the continued erosion of not only civil liberties, but also artistic vitality. It was the last straw". Obviously, continued protests were fruitless; and what many people saw as an ugly housing development was later built on the same spot.

However, somewhere at a demolition company site in Archerfield— behind the Archerfield Airport—at Willawong Trans-Pacific Recycling Plant—there are aspects of what remained of the icon: glass panelling; beautiful lighting ; iron fretwork and the like. Unfortunately, all these 'remains' are buried there. They're not really valuable to anyone, but are the proud remnants of our once fine 'Cinderella' in the city. The Bottoffini family also owned two 'plaster ladies'.

It is has also been suggested that there could be a remnant of Cloudland's fencing in existence in thick overgrown bushland, protected by a sheer cliff face out along Cowlishaw Street, Bowen Hills, just before you reach the new apartment complex built on the former site.

'STUNNED MULLET' REACTIONS

"If tears could build a stairway,

and memories a lane,

I'd walk right up to Heaven

and bring you home again".

Peter Meij

Mammon led them on

Mammon, the least erected spirit that fell

from heaven, for even in heaven his looks and thoughts were

always downward bent

admiring more the riches of heaven's pavement, trodden

gold, than aught divine or holy else enjoyed in vision beatific.

By him first, Men also and by his

suggestion taught, ransacked the centre, and with impious

hands rifled the bowels of their mother earth for treasures

better hid. Soon had his crew opened into the hill a spacious

wound and digged out ribs of gold. Let none admire that

riches grow in hell; that soil may

best deserve the precious bane .

[John Milton, *Paradise Lost, Book 1*]

How truly wonderful it would be now to turn back the hands of time! Cloudland was a stunning edifice, and definitely represented an historic and special era around Brisbane in fashion, dance and both good-natured and old-fashioned fun. Though Cloudland was constructed in Brisbane from 1939-40, it was the major venue for many concerts; and popular dance segments, styles and programs in the city, particularly from April, 1947, until 1982.

The main hall of the Cloudland Ballroom, just prior to its demolition, 1982.
Photo courtesy of Richard Stringer.

Some of the remains of Cloudland Ballroom following the Deen Bros.' demolition job.
Courier-Mail.

fate of this great lady, once a major entertainment spectacle, perched on a rise above the city skyline, in inner-city Brisbane's Bowen Hills.

The Scream by Edvard Munch summarised how many Brisbane people felt about Cloudland's demolition.

Just think—that maybe if the Deen Brothers had not placed their notoriously destructive hands upon the establishment, what a remarkable building complex it would be to pay homage to today! Of course, there are few building structures which have become as famous as the Cloudland Ballroom for simply being knocked down. In fact, it is possibly more renowned for the act of its being destroyed some 31 years ago; as for being constructed in the first instance. Nevertheless, such was the strange

There is something about sounds heard as we are sleeping or are waking up that evoke memories; and they are generally associated with the pleasant feeling of commencing a new day. But something was lost in those quite early morning tumults; that now exist only in memory for some neighbourhood folk living around Bowen Hills that particular night. Many woke up about 12.05 a.m. to hear the bulldozers and heavily swung wrecking balls.

Some say, like Shakespeare, that 'there is nothing either good or bad, but thinking makes it so'. Such was the case with Brisbane's thoughtful citizenry that day. Let's return for a while to that time and particular place to gauge people's reactions.

When the rest of the city populace awoke to the shock of one of its iconic landmarks now suddenly missing, the deceit that was felt sparked a huge if quite futile outcry from various community groups. Despite its National Trust listing since 1977, and countless vehement, public calls and a firm resolve for the building to be preserved, this hilltop Bowen Hills site was wanted for the development of units. So when plans were put forward for its redevelopment, it was only natural that the public had wanted it preserved; and a general hue and cry went up for the developers to scotch their ideas. Ergo: Cloudland Ballroom was destined to become just another of Brisbane's old beloved buildings— like the pre-1979 magnificent *Belle Vue Hotel*—which was so ruthlessly destroyed without any consideration afforded to it as a precious cultural landmark.

The remains of the once stately old *Belle Vue Hotel*—such a similar story.

Courier-Mail.

Naturally, the developers had claimed that the old ballroom was way beyond repairing, and hence, ultimately saving. They were strongly supported by Queensland's so-called development-at-any-cost Premier, Joh Bjelke-Petersen whose whole *modus operandi* appeared to be, once again quoting Groucho Marx: "Politics is the art of looking for trouble, & finding it, diagnosing it incorrectly and applying the wrong remedies".

By later on this same Sunday morning, of November 7th, the scene on Cintra or Montpelier Hill was one of utter destruction:

It is 10:30 in the morning and the roads around Cintra Hill are jammed with cars. I am one of the hundreds of people who have come to salvage one last memory of Cloudland from the rubble. Looking through the mesh fence that surrounds the site, it becomes clear that nothing was to be saved. It seems like an act of violence rather than a demolition has taken place. Decorations and tinsel glitter from the piles of timber, fibro and iron. The green upholstered chairs are now all smashed and buried among the rubble. And there, looking out from it all is the plaster lady holding the red fairy light. It is a cheap and tacky adornment but its value, like the value of Cloudland itself, cannot be measured in monetary terms.

So significant was the role Cloudland played in the social lives of three generations of Brisbane residents, that the building was listed by the National Trust. In Queensland, such a listing does little to assure a building's preservation. Cloudland will be but one of [well] over sixty culturally important buildings in central Brisbane that will be demolished by 1990. Like my fellow mourners here on Cintra Hill, I wonder how it was allowed to happen.

They came in at 4 a.m. with heavy earthmoving machinery but

without a demolition permit. This, however, did not deter the Deen Brothers who specialise in these types of clandestine demolitions. In 1979, they earned their notoriety when they tore down the *Belle Vue Hotel* in George Street at midnight. For the Cloudland job they employed six police to guard against protestors. This was an unnecessary measure as it [only] took a mere sixty minutes to reduce the great arch and ballroom to rubble.

In the next few days outraged residents started demanding answers. The members of the National Heritage Commission, on their tour of Brisbane, will stand at this fence but not enter the site. One commissioner will remark, "that's Queensland for you". Peter Kurts, the owner of Cloudland, will argue that an improvement of its safety standards would have been [way] too costly. The Brisbane City Council will issue the Deen Brothers with a meagre fine for [their] illegal demolition. And Joh Bjelke-Petersen and his National Party, the only ones who could have saved Cloudland, will continue to drag their feet when it comes to heritage legislation.

Later, driving down the Breakfast Creek Road, I glance up towards Cintra Hill and hope that, as promised within their Yellow Pages ad, the Deen Brothers have at least left behind the memories.

(Memories of Cloudland.)

The day after Cloudland's demolition, November 8th, 1982, Margaret Throsby and David Morgan reported the chain of events on ABC radio; and John Knox on 4BK. Clearly, the National Trust's Queensland Chapter had, as far back as 1977, listed the structure as a cultural heritage site. It now also came to light that they'd

mounted a renewed campaign a week before Cloudland's demise to give it a reprieve, saving it from being destroyed. Yet, as the State held no legislation in regard to any heritage, the organisation was utterly powerless to stop anyone or possibly the Government proceeding.

The Australian Heritage Commission's Mr Gus Gehrmann and its Chairman, Mr Ken Wiltshire, in-specting the Cloudland demolition site.
The Australian, November, 1982.

Following the developer's 'quick kill' of the Cloudland structure, not unsurprisingly, the citizenry of Brisbane town were quite 'devastated', in particular all the ex-service personnel and their beloved 'sweethearts'—on remembering they had once partaken of elective 'R & R' from the 'worst fighting' during World War II and knew of Cloudland's existence after 1947.

All the many onlookers could do in the morning was to stare and gasp. The streets surrounding the demolished structure were relatively congested; and now lined with 'distraught' people who could not seem to fathom that an icon could so quickly and astonishingly disappear.

Amidst Cloudland's stark ruins was Jim Fuller, the National Trust's Queensland Manager.
Courier-Mail, 9th November, 1982.

Cloudland Ballroom before the demolition.
Weekend Australian, 11th November, 1989.

Folk who had known the 'grand old dame' from magazine features, the television coverage or just being in someway connected with visiting Cloudland claimed that the wanton disregard of its destruction had affected them all quite deeply. They were most probably telling the truth. It may sound grotesque, but the grief seemed sincere. It's a given surely that all of a person's pent-up emotion of real personal bereavement gushes out on public occasions such as these.

As the Canadian communications theorist, Marshall McLuhan (1911-1980), reminds us that: 'Only the vanquished remember history'. An editorial from the *Courier-Mail* also warned Queenslanders that there "is something wrong with a society that goes on destroying its history in the middle of the night".

Such was the reaction to Cloudland's demise that there was widespread anger and grieving. Obviously, all of us had to suppress real pain, like that caused by a loss, such as within a family. Numbness was the result. However, our feelings had to attain an outlet in some small way, and they could have surfaced dramatically when an important civic structure such as Cloudland was suddenly missing.

When it went it meant the loss of romance and adventure in the city and the apartment block that replaced it added nothing [at all] to Brisbane. (Peter Skinner, Associate Professor of Architecture, University of Queensland.)

And again:

A short time ago I had been blogging about Brisbane's Cloudland, to compare the state-approved vandalism in Chicago with state-approved vandalism in Brisbane. I wrote that "possibly every city in the world has senselessly destroyed some it its architectural and historical treasures."...

I was discussing the vandalism involved in destroying the *Michael Reese Hospital* in Chicago this month. The article was called 'Gropius' Chicago Legacy Lost' because it wasn't just about the beauty of the architecture; rather its part in architectural history was critically important.

In the response to American readers who were incensed by American vandalism, I wrote about the destruction of Cloudland in Brisbane.

According to 'Sorcerer'...

it's [also] so sad that architectural landmarks are senselessly demolished in the name of progress.

Every landmark is a part of a tradition, culture and sentiment.

People and the authorities should see that they are preserved and protected!

A *side-on view* of the dancehall's interior area, audience seating and big stage, Cloudland Ballroom, 1970s.

Some ten days following Cloudland's demolition, other views to the 'contra' had prevailed— one such by R. P. Yaxley, about the freedom to destroy a heritage building, if it was deemed wise and necessary to do so:

I REMEMBER Cloudland in its heyday and was sorry to see it go, but only for sentimental reasons. I do believe that those in our society who wanted the dreadful old *Belle Vue Hotel* and the deteriorating and less-used Cloudland preserved for posterity should have been prepared to buy these properties from their owners at [their] current values, or simply see them disposed of at the owners' discretion. If Australia wishes to maintain its heritage in buildings, as classified by the National Trust etc., then the Australian community must be responsible for the funds to purchase them, repair them and maintain them. I have no financial interest whatsoever in any such buildings, but if I lived in a 100-year-old family house and wished to replace it with a modern house with all current conveniences, I would not appreciate being told by anyone that it could not be done. (*Courier-Mail*.)

Following a stormy public reception and questions in parliament to Joh and the National Party Government, the local Heritage and Building Advisory Committee wanted to press legal proceedings on the subject of the 'unlawful' demolition. Moreover, Australian Heritage Commission members from Tasmania and Victoria said there was no way that Cloudland Ballroom would have been torn down in their home states, even if the fibro (asbestos), plaster and wooden building was in a serious state of deterioration. In their view, it should have been kept as a heritage site. However, one truism about Cloudland's dismantling will stay eternally with us—once an architectural gem like this dancehall has been destroyed and gone. Like other nostalgic icons, it cannot ever be replaced.

A wreath on the fence surrounding the demolition site sums up most people's
attitude to Cloudland's passing.

3
ꟼMPRESARIO
T. H. ESLICK

Tell me, what is it you plan to do with
your one wild and precious life?

Poet **Mary Oliver**

ꟼISPELLING MYTHS

[I]t is characteristic of human life
that we do make claims about
who we are and the shape of our
lives. This quintessentially human
activity of putting oneself forward
as a certain kind of person can, in
certain circumstances, set us up
for the fall: this can occur when the
presence simultaneously expresses
and falls short of its own aspiration.
Irony is the activity of bringing this
falling short to light in a way that is
meant to grab [just] us.

Jonathan Leal, *A Case for Irony*

We all love a good tale and an
opportunity to dispel a good myth.
However, busting one so wide
open could indeed now be tinged
within a little sadness, sleight of
hand; and ever trickery. This is
the beginning of a story about
the origins and operation of the
legendary Cloudland ballroom,
which once perched atop its tiny
hill in Bowen Hills from 1939/40
until the early hours of November

7th, 1982. It is an extravagantly spun,
gothic-style adventure in the best
dramatic tradition; and commences
a long way from the world of Luna
Park (Cloudland) in Bowen Hills.
In effect, this tale takes you back to
the 1900s when one Thomas ('T.
H.') Eslick was traversing through
the world, setting up his Luna Park-
type enterprises. Whether Thomas
was instrumental in designing and
setting up the world's first theme
park at Coney Island around
1903 is highly debatable when the
names Louis Corbeille, Frederick
Thompson and Skip Gundy have
been more or less associated
with the park's development and
ownership.

Luna Park, as in Luna Park (at
Cloudland) from 1939/40, was a
name—

...shared by dozens of currently
operating and defunct amusement
parks that have commenced on

almost every continent excepting Antarctica since 1903. The first to use the name was the second major amusement park at Coney Island, designed by Charles I. D. Looff, who had subsequently designed Seattle,Washington's, Luna Park, which had opened in 1907. The spaceship in the Pan-American exposition ride "A Trip to the Moon" gave its name to these parks…and to dozens that followed over the next century.

In 1905, Frederick Ingersoll was already making a reputation for his pioneering work in roller coaster construction and design (he also designed scenic railroad rides) when he opened Luna Parks in Pittsburgh and Cleveland, the first two amusement parks to be covered with electric lighting (the former was adorned with 67,000 light bulbs; the Cleveland park had 50,000). Ultimately, he [then] opened 44 Luna Parks around the world, the first chain of amusement parks.

Despite the death of Ingersoll in 1927 and the closing of most of his Luna Parks, the name's popularity continued with newer parks with the name opening with regularity. As a result, 'Lunapark" now translates into "amusement park" in Dutch, German, Italian, Bulgarian, Croatian, Polish, Greek, Turkish, Hebrew and Macedonian.

Luna Park is [hence] the name of numerous amusement parks, from the Coney Island original, to the over 40 Luna Parks designed and constructed by Frederick Ingersoll, to amusement parks which received their names after Ingersoll's death in 1927. For a short time, Ingersoll renamed his parks **Ingersoll's Luna Park** to distinguish them from the Luna Parks to which he had no connection.

"The Main Tower of the initial Luna Park at Coney Island, ca. 1905. Many subsequent amusement parks would have their own 'towers'."

US Navy.

A picture of the whole of New York's 'Original Coney Island'.

THE LUNA PARK SAGA

> One can understand life looking backwards, but one must live it in the future.
>
> **Kierkegaard**

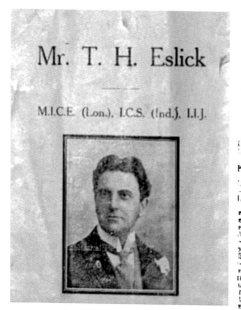

Mr. T. H. Eslick

M.I.C.E. (Lon.), I.C.S. (Ind.), I.I.J.

T. H. Eslick, the Luna Park entrepreneur.

The strange and largely incredible activities of Thomas Henry Eslick, related to his failed venture in 1939-40, Brisbane's Luna Park, are worthy of a unique position in Cloudland's history. In fact, Cloudland Ballroom was the only aspect of his ideas to actually survive into the 1980s even though he boasted to others that he was a 'consulting engineer' for Coney Island.

Thomas Eslick appears in Brisbane until around 1944, when his Luna Park scheme stumbled into failure and bankruptcy. It should be explained that he had been engrossed in a big losing battle—the park's construction (1939-40) coincided with the onset of World War II.

Interest in all Thomas' business ventures peaked with the pronouncement, in the local newspaper, of his upcoming bankruptcy hearing within Brisbane's legal system.

for the said Auguste Albertine Wilhelmine Engel, Laidley Town Agents: MORRIS FLETCHER, & CROSS, Solicitors, Brisbane
IN THE COURT OF BANKRUPTCY. District of Southern Queensland No 17. of 1942 Re H. GORDON GRAHAME, of Verney Road, East Graceville, Builder
Date and Place of Public Examination: 10.30 a.m., on 4th August, 1942, at Bankruptcy Court, Fourth Floor, Commonwealth Offices, Brisbane.
No. 18, of 1942 Re TOLMACH HERRIORR ESLICK (known as Thomas Henry Eslick), lately of 24 Cleveland Road, Morningside, Company Director, but now of Amusement Pier, Manly, New South Wales, Amusement Architect
Date of Petition: 22nd June, 1942
Date of Sequestration Order: 30th July, 1942.
No. 19, of 1942, Re J. W. MOFFAT, formerly of Massey Street, Hamilton, now of 117 Woondooma Street, Bundaberg, Foreman Plumber.
Date of Petition: 26th June, 1942.
Date of Sequestration Order: 30th July, 1942
Note: All debts due to these estates should be paid to me.
J. E. THEODENZA,
Official Receiver,
Commonwealth Offices, Brisbane, 24th July, 1942
NOTICE TO CREDITORS.
Re THOMAS COSTELLO, Deceased.
Notice is hereby given that all persons having any CLAIMS or DEMANDS against the Estate of Thomas Costello

A court of bankruptcy mention of "Tolmach Herriorr Eslick, known as Thomas Henry Eslick".

Courier-Mail.

Oddly perhaps, even with the newspaper's unforgivable spelling, no one with that particular moniker *above* appeared in the baptism,

THE LONDON GAZET⁊

THE BANKRUPTCY ACT, 1914.

RECEIVING ORDERS

No. 1,486. ALLEN, Charles Talbot, 20, Canterbury-road, Brixton, Surrey, formerly of Eden House, Cobham, Kent. COMMERCIAL CLERK.
Court—HIGH COURT OF JUSTICE.
Date of Filing Petition—April 21, 1926.
No. of Matter—491 of 1926.
Date of Receiving Order—April 21, 1926.
No. of Receiving Order—285.
Whether Debtor's or Creditor's Petition—Debtor's.

No. 1,487. BANFIELD, George Josiah, 15, Melcombe-court, Marylebone, London, N.W. 1.
Court—HIGH COURT OF JUSTICE.
Date of Filing Petition—Jan. 4, 1926.
No. of Matter—9 of 1926.
Date of Receiving Order—April 20, 1926.
No. of Receiving Order—284.
Whether Debtor's or Creditor's Petition—Creditor's.
Act of Bankruptcy proved in Creditor's Petition—Section 1-1 (G.), Bankruptcy Act, 1914.

No. 1,488. CIBULA, Davis, 94, Greenfield-gardens, Cricklewood-lane, London, N.W. 2, and 17, Frith-street, Soho, London, W. 1, TAILOR, and lately residing at and carrying on business at 89, Berwick-street, Oxford-street, London.
Court—HIGH COURT OF JUSTICE.
Date of Filing Petition—April 20, 1926.
No. of Matter—484 of 1926.
Date of Receiving Order—April 20, 1926.
No. of Receiving Order—278.
Whether Debtor's or Creditor's Petition—Debtor's.

No. 1,489. CLAYTON, G. F. (Male), of 83, Windsor - road, Leyton, London, E. 10. TIMBER MERCHANT.
Court—HIGH COURT OF JUSTICE.
Date of Filing Petition—March 25, 1926.
No. of Matter—395 of 1926.
Date of Receiving Order—April 20, 1926.
No. of Receiving Order—277.
Whether Debtor's or Creditor's Petition—Creditor's.
Act of Bankruptcy proved in Creditor's Petition—Section 1-1 (G.), Bankruptcy Act, 1914.

No. 1,490. DAVIES, William Gardiner, resided and carried on business at 127, Rathbone-street, Canning Town. BACON MERCHANT.
Court—HIGH COURT OF JUSTICE.
Date of Filing Petition—April 19, 1926.
No. of Matter—478 of 1926.
Date of Receiving Order—April 19, 1926.
No. of Receiving Order—275.
Whether Debtor's or Creditor's Petition—Debtor's.

No. 1,491. ESLICK, Tollemache Heriot, 48, Rupert-street, London.
Court—HIGH COURT OF JUSTICE.
Date of Filing Petition—March 18, 1926.
No. of Matter—345 of 1926.
Date of Receiving Order—April 20, 1926.
No. of Receiving Order—279.
Whether Debtor's or Creditor's Petition—Creditor's.
Act of Bankruptcy proved in Creditor's Petition—Section 1-1 (G.), Bankruptcy Act, 1914.

The British court entry for Eslick.
London Gazette, 1926.

birth, death and marriage records of Australia or overseas. T. H. had once advanced in a newspaper interview that his birth place was India. In another interview, he proclaimed he was London born. We can point to a listing of 'Tollemache Heriot Eslick' in Australia's electoral rolls; and another, where, using this exact name, he entered the United States. But there was, however, an item in a London newspaper. It is advisable here to examine the final entry: Tollemache Heriot Eslick, Rupert Street, London, aged 48 years.

The Royal Courts of Justice, Strand Central London.

The 1926 court case in England established the veracity of Eslick's plea that was made in his Brisbane court appearance—of his falling upon hard times and money losses in California and Europe.

Eslick's background is worthwhile speculating on here. His father Stephen J., and mother, Mary, and a young family including Thomas Henry, had supposedly lived at Foxteth Park at St Aberdare House, Lancashire, in 1882. But it was more likely that Thomas was born on August 28th 1887; although some have argued that he was born on May 23rd, 1877, at Aberdare, Wales.

Story Of Reverses In Bankruptcy Court

BRISBANE, November 27.— T. H. Eslick, amusement architect, formerly managing director of Luna Park, Brisbane, stated in the Bankruptcy Court yesterday he had lost £22,000 in Brussels 22 years ago, which he had invested in fire insurance companies. The money went in one night. He also lost a £43,000 fixed deposit in a Californian bank crash when over 100 private banks were closed. His assets were stated at nil and liabilities £1382. He told the Official Receiver he wanted his discharge as soon as possible as he wanted to get busy and pay every creditor in full. The examination was adjourned sine die.

The details of T. Eslick's Brisbane Court hearing.

Courier-Mail.

Thomas' father, Stephen Eslick, was a map Dissector Master employing six men and two women. He was undoubtedly a man of education, distinction and reasonably well-off. So learning and education were the correct mechanisms as well as breeding grounds for a youngster like Thomas Henry to advance in life.

It is easily concluded that Thomas Eslick was indeed a man of countless facets and various aptitudes. Besides constructing Luna Park as well as the Cloudland dance palace, his amazing brain-child, his boasts about his unique abilities stretched to engineering, architecture, building and managing projects. As he tied such powers to the years prior to his supposed arrival in Australia, 1911, this oversight makes all his claims and counter-claims so wildly unbelievable. His latter boast, organising, suggested he possessed the skills as a self-publicist in the realm of the public domain and work relations. In such aptitudes as these, though, he had often displayed a canny facility.

A later image of T. H. Eslick.

What seems clear, however, is that T. H. graduated from the Victoria University in Liverpool in 1898, even though some of his studies appeared to be by way of correspondence.

PORTOBELLO MARINE PARK, EDINBURGH

The Scottish National Exhibition of the year, 1908.

Scottish Newspapers.

The 'scent' of Eslick's trail connects him back to May 2nd, 1911, where he was a successful applicant for employment at the Portobello Zoological and Marine Park, Edinburgh, Scotland. Back in 1908, the people in Edinburgh were experiencing extreme 'loss' symptoms in the wake of the gala National Exhibition of Scotland, somewhat like the antecedent of modern EXPOs, like that in Brisbane of 1988. For a six month period, three and a half million people welcomed mass bands, took thrills and spills on scintillating roller coaster rides, and gaped at the side show exhibitions.

Edinburgh Marine and Zoological Gardens.

The "funding" fathers of Edinburgh wondered, now that the exhibit program had finished, whether a permanent amusement venue would now be suitable. A new fun park, based upon public subscription, plus a committee to guide the park's creation, were instigated. The idea was that Edinburgh's park would be a beacon for greater Scotland; and the remainder of the United Kingdom.

The site of the Scottish National Exhibition, 1908.

A site across town on Portobello's shoreline was chosen, ignoring the existing site of

Edinburgh's National Exhibition. However, several of the exhibition's buildings and amusements were retained, and moved across the city. This laudatory project, referred to as the Edinburgh Marine and Zoological Gardens, using infrastructure from the prior exhibition, welcomed people to its opening on May 31st, 1909. A valued employee of Blackpool's Amusement Park in the south of England, William Holland, was appointed as the General Manager. The venue was up and running.

Given the park's success, it was required of William Holland that he needed to employ some further organising staff. Needless to say, T. H. was anointed as the Advertising and Amusement manager by the park's directors.

Eslick's stay in his appointment suggested a style of flippancy, of exotic French phrases, witty lines in advertisements, treating all the readers as his comrades; and offering suggestions to write back, being part of a fun package he had set out for each of them. Such an approach was now to mark the T. H. Eslick advertising strategy for the future to come.

Subsequently, just a few months later than May, 1911, when the newly inaugurated King George V visited Edinburgh, he omitted to visit Portobello's park. Eslick then found out through newspapers of the period that the monarch was to travel to the sub-continent, to India for his attendance at the magnificent *Delhi Durbar*. He was now to be crowned 'Emperor of India'.

Two pictures of the Edinburgh Marine and Zoological Gardens.

Scottish Newspapers.

INDIAN DURBAR

Success is going from one failure to the next with no loss of [any] enthusiasm.

Winston Churchill

Eslick's progress from hence would mark a 'high tide' in his future life. Just after King George V's sojourn in Edinburgh, on August 23rd, 1911,

Thomas saw the announcement that he had been granted the position of managing the king's incredibly honoured *Indian Durbar* in December, 1922. Previously dealing with all of Portobello park's blurbs of publicity, it was an amazing break for a youngish man of just 33 to have this situation of such a prestigious responsibility fall into his lap.

THE GREAT CORONATION *DURBAR* OF DECEMBER 12TH, 1911

A great event at the height of the British Raj

Occurred during the Visit

Of their Imperial Majesties

the King Emperor and Queen Empress

to INDIA

Naturally, the Scottish Directors at the Gardens and the workers there embraced the news as welcoming. Eslick was allowed to cancel out his Edinburgh contract, making for London the very same day; and sailing for Bombay the next week. This would only allow Thomas' three whole months to manage a highly expensive and fairly complicated Royal event. Whether Eslick's participation was real, or otherwise, Thomas made the *Durbar* the feature of all his publicity distributions to the press. Over the years, these would be too many to recount.

"Going to the Saman Burj for the Darshan".

King George V.

terms of communications within this early period of the twentieth century, people were known to falsify their work histories to hoodwink prospective employers. Yet, it was rumoured that the 9,000 Hindus who were employed by Thomas referred to him fondly as 'Barra Sahib Adme Jokahm Bennati-Hia'—the big wig 'who gets things done'.

According to *Courier-Mail* journalist, Kathleen Noonan, a chap like T. H. may be typical of some folk having a double life. But he's untypical in resisting our ability to render him a simple hypocrite:

The great Indian Durbar. Here the Royal pro-cession is passing by the municipal buildings.

The Indian Times.

Construction of Luna Park's Scenic Railway, Melbourne, 1912.

It seems highly debatable now in what capacity Eslick ever was connected with the Durbar, least of all organising which aspects of it; but his 'fame' appears to have preceded him, particularly in the publicity material for Luna Park's Melbourne opening. As countries and continents were far apart in

We all have a cover story, an alibi in life, to appear cool, in control. Most days we believe it and you believe it too. We carry it off. Some people do a fabulous impersonation of an events manager or an architect or a good wife. Mine is, I am a journalist. And every week I sit down and attempt to produce the evidence that that is true. I want to prove it with unreasonable doubt. I want the alibi to be airtight. You never do truly make it, which means you're always reaching for that next piece of work.

In T. H., any painstaking efforts to disentangle the individual from his own myths have led to the emergence of a very different Eslick: a less than ideal specimen, but one whose flaws are magnetically and munificently human. We have uncovered a fellow whose immense capacity for veracity did not extend to those closest to him; a dreamer with a shrewd eye for the bottom line; a sentimental schemer; and an industrious charlatan. For all his espoused fame and general gregariousness, T. H. emerges from his exploits as a forlorn, solitary figure.

Eslick's new publicity brochure for the opening of Melbourne's Luna Park.
Argus News.

LUNA PARK, MELBOURNE

Metropolis Steel Roller Coaster, Luna Park, Melbourne.

Thomas Eslick's appearance within Australia during January of 1912 symbolises the commencement of a mythology about his exploits—one which catapults him into the heady atmosphere of those famous and finding success. It is indeed strange that, only a matter of several months following the once-fabled *Durbar* in India, Thomas emerges within St Kilda in Melbourne's suburbs. An American gentleman, Jason Dixon Williams, is constructing an Amusement venue, Luna Park, part of his own company venture.

At this especial juncture Eslick's credibility appears to break down. In its publicity material about the Luna Park enterprise, Thomas is acknowledged as the Melbourne fun park's main designer and constructor. A later brochure trumpets...

The chief designer/builder was T. H. Eslick, who had worked in the amusement park industry for over fourteen years in many countries. The Scenic Railway is reportedly a replica of a roller-coaster he built for the Great *Durbar* Exhibition of Old Bombay for the visit of King George V in 1911. His stay in India is thought to be the inspiration for the Mughul/Moorish entrance façade; and the flanking towers built at Luna Park.

And again:

[A sign] outside Luna Park [in Melbourne] says: 'The first Luna Park was built at Coney Island New York in 1903. Luna Park was designed and built in 1912 by T. H. Eslick and 20 builders from Coney Island for North American entrepreneurs J. D. Williams and the Phillips brothers.

Luna Park, Melbourne's Souvenir pamphlet.
Argus News.

It should indeed be stated at the outset that Luna Park's Scenic Railway in Melbourne was originally designed by La Marcus Adna Thompson of New York. He also instigated the world's first 'roller-coaster' at Coney Island in 1884. As Thomas did not turn up until January of 1912 in Australia, he hardly had enough time to construct or design a somewhat complicated roller-coaster. When challenged about this instance years later, Eslick claimed he had served an apprenticeship under Thompson for quite some time. What had appeared to have been forgotten were the excellent crew members J. D. Williams borrowed from America—three expert Phillips brothers; plus the skilled Louis Corbeille, Luna Park's initial manager, as well as Coney Island's in 1903.

Although the brochure clearly depicts Eslick as the head of the publicity section in Melbourne, the wording of a souvenir leaflet compiled by he himself stated that he was the park's 'Consulting Engineer and Publicity Officer'.

The park venue, Melbourne.

The massive scenic railway was the magnificent feature of Luna Park, Melbourne, when it had initially opened. Herman Leon and Harold Phillips conducted operations there for so many years, building the *Palais Theatre* opposite the venue. J. D. Williams returned to Hollywood in 1913 and established a major film studio. By this juncture, Eslick's work could be seen all across the western world; in fact, Thomas had been designing amusement parks for 14 years.

The subsequent several years witnessed Thomas travelling between Adelaide and Sydney. He was now engaged in the establishment of an amusement venue rather like the Portobello enterprise in Edinburgh. His 'White City' creation was such a rip-roaring success in Sydney; as we'll later discover, he wanted to repeat this experience in Adelaide.

"WHITE CITY" FOR ADE-LAIDE.

A STRANGE AND BEAUTIFUL ATTRACTION.

TO COST FROM £15,000 TO £20,000.

The "White City," Sydney, and the similar resort in Melbourne, are well-known to South Australians, if not from personal inspection, at all events by name. This pleasure rendezvous, the realisation of the most quaint, the most beautiful, and the most strange of all forms of amusement, has introduced to Australia the latest ideas in open-air entertainment in America and Europe, and now Adelaide probably is to have a "white city." Mr. T. H. Eslick entertained a small party, including representatives of the press, at luncheon at the South Australian Hotel on Wednesday, and explained the proposition which has been laid before the Adelaide City Council in connection with an application which he has made for a lease of a small portion of the Adelaide park lands as the site of a "white city." Mr. Eslick, who was born in India, and brought up in Lancashire, is a civil engineer by profession, and served

A news article about Eslick's campaign for Adelaide.
Adelaide Newspapers.

Eslick called a press conference to advertise his latest proposal. However, there was a snag. Before the 'White City' fun park was to be created as a viable option he had to assist the city's City Council to move their hold over

a sizeable section of an Adelaide park. Additionally, he was obliged to extract some £20,000 from local investment. In such times, these figures boggled most people's minds. Unsurprisingly, the fine folk of Adelaide and their Council found it difficult to relinquish their park or their savings. Remember, also, that Thomas was managing a similar 'White City' establishment at Sydney's Double Bay; and it was likely both derived from much the same Eslick model.

White City in Sydney, c. 1914.
Sydney Morning Herald.

The Grand Scenic Railway in White City, Sydney.

At an Adelaide press conference to promote his 'White City' scheme, Eslick had declared he was born in India, but raised in Lancashire; that he was a professional civil engineer; and that he had served out an apprenticeship under L. A. Thompson at Coney Island, the "inventor of the switch-back railway". That may well have had a sense of truth to it; Thompson did design and construct the scenic railway in St Kilda, even though T. H. later claimed the scenic railway there was virtually an 'identical copy' of the one Eslick prepared now for the 'Great *Durbar* Exhibition of Old Bombay'. There may have been a modicum of truth in Thomas' claims as he could possibly have taken his apprenticeship under Thompson's tutelage. Yet Thomas doesn't stop there. He went on to inform reporters that it was he who would construct the initial 'scenic railway' in Europe upon Blackpool Beach; and 'pleasure parks' in Moscow, St Petersburg, Berlin, Cairo, Nancy, Madrid, Paris, Cologne and Vienna. He had further added that he was the superintendent of the Delhi *Durbar* exhibit. Though it was held in Bombay, he insisted he became its 'director general'.

Thomas had also told the press conference that he was the possessor of diplomas from the 'Institute of Engineers'; he was an honorary fellow of 'Academic Francaise'; he was a civil engineer based in New York, and was appointed a life member of the Indian Civil Service. He left out his graduation from the 'International Correspondence Academy', and side-stepped his studying in architecture and advertising. Clearly, such diploma studies eventuated in the period prior to his employment as advertising and amusements manager in Edinburgh; or, in the intervening time from between Edinburgh and his Melbourne appearance in 1912.

Mr Harry Rickards.
La Trobe State Library of Victoria.

Not satisfied with 'achievements', Thomas was not finished yet. Imbued with political passion, Eslick sought to contest the New South Wales elections, for the seat of Paddington. Predictably, he then lost in the ballot. In the 1910s or so, T. H. turned his attention to the 'Royal Palais des Danse Adelaide', and a 'new pleasure resort' called White City on North Terrace in Adelaide. At White City, the objects of the company were as follows:

This company is formed to acquire from Mr T. H. Eslick the

option of lease for seven years of a magnificent site of about four acres on the Payneham Road, Hackney... [It] will be conducted on high class lines and all its entertainments are expected to appeal to a very wide public; good taste will be the keynote and no rowdyism or larrikinism will be tolerated. As there appears to be some misunderstanding in regard to the exact location of Palm Place, the chosen site for White City, the promoters desire to state that it is situated upon North Terrace, Kent town, a few yards past the penny section on Hackney Road and nearer the city than Payneham Road.

Unsurprisingly, T. H 's Adelaide 'White City' scheme failed to eventuate. But, in his new role as G. M. of 'White City' in Sydney, Thomas was relishing a new challenge. About December of 1913, White City, Sydney, showcased 'open-air' pleasure grounds occupying some 10 acres managed by T. H. Eslick. It featured 'a scenic railway, caves, stalls, a ballroom, a Japanese village and had a strongly Oriental accent', but closed in May of 1916, with T. H.'s transfer to the *Palladium*'s activities.

Thomas then wrote glowing advertisements for the '*Palladium Dance Hall*', each one with his 'Radiantly Yours' signature. But, at the same time, he was becoming tied up with Mr Harry Rickards' latest venture, the 'Tivoli Roof Garden Theatre' in Brisbane.

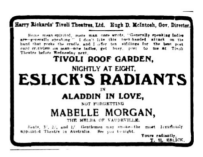

Eslick's sugary advertisement in H. Rickards' White City at Sydney.
Sydney Morning Herald.

An advertisement for the regal Tivoli Theatre in Brisbane.
Sydney Morning Herald.

On December 19th, 1914, the *Brisbane Courier* trumpeted that the

Tivoli "should be a valuable addition to our places of amusement".

"The Tivoli is the latest thing within theatres. For once there has been an effort to build a theatre to suit the climate, and first impressions suggest that it has been successful. The Tivoli is really two theatres—an enclosed theatre, so admirably ventilated, and a roof theatre, which will be a delight in the hot summer nights. Mr. H. D. McIntosh has spared no expense or trouble, and he has secured something novel as well as satisfactory. There is a suggestion of Orientalism in the Market-square front, but the architectural effect generally is very striking". (*Brisbane Courier, May 15th, 1915.*)

The architect, Henry E. White, designed the Tivoli main auditorium to house 1800 people in three levels while the Tivoli Roof Garden Theatre was then built as an open-air venue holding 1200. (*Companion to Theatre in Australia* 604 and *Brisbane Courier*, May 4th, 1915). "The Tivoli's main auditorium is specially cooled by a large air plant, which pumps in 40,000 cubic feet of ice-cold air through the theatre every minute" (*Brisbane Courier*, October, 1916). Plush ruby carpets were then installed (*Brisbane Courier*, May 3rd, 1915).

The Tivoli Roof Garden had boasted open sides which were designed to let evening breezes cool the audience while specially designed steel shutters could protect the audience from [any] rain. According to *Australian Variety* the Tivoli Theatre was one of only six theatres in the world to have a roof garden at that time (*Australian Variety, December 29th, 1915*) and it was promoted as "the Coolest Theatre within Australasia" and the management claimed that it provided "full protection for inclement weather" (*Brisbane Courier*, February 10th, 1916).

The Tivoli Theatre.

A Tivoli Theatre performance.

Thomas' connections with the Tivoli in Brisbane were from about May 25th, 1915. In 1916, Eslick became involved with the Sydney Grammar School project in Yurong Street, City. The building, 'which had provided a gymnasium, language laboratory, subject classrooms and a lecture theatre, was erected [during 1916] on the Yurong Street frontage. This had replaced the old Palladium building'.

T. H.'s associations with the Tivoli in Brisbane were still being creatively maintained all this while. On September, 18th, 1917, the Tivoli's newest attraction—according to T. H.—was *Aladdin in Love*. In its Thursday, September 27th, 1917, issue the *Courier-Mail* had suggested there were "two more opportunities remaining for witnessing the bright entertainment by Eslick and the *Radiants* at the Roof Garden, Tivoli".

In 1919, T. H. 'entertained the Prince of Wales in Australia, taking him to one of his ballrooms. He had met him before as a boy.

LA MONICA BALLROOM

In the business world, the rear view mirror is always clearer that the windshield.

Warren Buffett,
US financier/businessman.

Eslick's next venture for the ensuing few years was to involve himself more with the aforesaid revue group which we have previously gleaned he had whimsically christened *Eslick's Radiants*', later on becoming a 'Special Commissioner' for Paramount Theatres, to advertise and put on the latest 'Hollywood talkies'.

Santa Monica Pier, California.

Maybe Thomas was a recipient of work 'for one of the boys', as his old employer, Jason Dixon Williams, at Melbourne's Luna Park, was the sole power behind the throne at the Warner Brothers Film Company in Los Angeles. Meanwhile, Eslick travelled continually between Adelaide and Rockhampton going up as far as Innisfail in North Queensland; but with numerous stop offs in Sydney and Melbourne where the 'White City' projects continued to run. Here T. H. linked up with the Paramount theatres in Townsville and Rockhampton.

A publicity poster for the Paramount Theatres.

The US film Archives.

Within the year of 1920, T. H. turned his hand to producing the music to *Hullo! Girlie* with W. H. (Billy) Romaine who was to feature prominently in all Cloudland's dance programmes of the 1940s. This fine sheet music was featured by Val Royal.

Warner Bros., 1920.

The logo for Warner Bros. Entertainment Inc.

By January, 1921, after a plethora of publicity machine advertisements in Australia, T. H. had seemed to 'disappear' from the world's stage, but he reappeared in Adelaide from February to May, 1921 (*The Mail*, 26th February, 1921) for a 'Brilliant Opening Night' (*The Mail*, April 2nd, 1921); 'Giving out prizes' and 'Many Happy Returns' for the *Palais Royale* (*The Mail*, 20th May, 1921). After again being in the Australian spotlight he reappeared under the auspices of the Hope Theatre in Dallas, Texas (1922); the winter Gardens in Detroit, Michigan; the Coliseum Ballroom in St Petersburg, Florida; and the Bohemia Park Culver City in California. Somehow, he'd managed to get his foot in the door in the latter American state. So he surfaced three years later in Santa Monica, a fun city by California's seaside.

As luck would have it, a business consortium had purchased an amusement 'pier' over at the 'beach playground' of Santa Monica. Thomas, as an architect, was conscripted to design a ballroom at the end of the jetty. It did not escape attention on the publicity material for the project that Thomas had developed similar 'attractions' all around the world, including 'the (sic) *Delhi Durbar*'. Eslick commenced work, selecting a Spanish idea for the building's exterior design; and a 'French Renaissance' design for its interiors. A huge ballroom (at 2227x180 feet or so in size), it was supposedly big enough to house more than 5,000 'patrons' at any function, the largest on the west coast.

Santa Monica, California.
The Santa Monica Newspapers.

La Monica Ballroom, California.
The Santa Monica Newspapers.

By 1924, the *La Monica Ballroom* had opened its doors with all of the pomp and circumstance the Californians could then muster. The Hollywood famous, including several screen stars, as well as some other wealthy Americans, had then appeared in an array of quite glistening limousines. A twenty-piece orchestra provided much of the dance music.

A journalistic report of the era noted:

The architect's simple yet perfect system used for checking wraps, many spacious entrances to the dance floor, numerous ticket booths, a beautiful promenade: and a mezzanine balcony furnished with upholstery chairs and divans gave everyone a pleasant experience. Refreshments were available at the *La Monica Fountain and Café* located on the east side of the mezzanine level.

The ballroom's 15,000 square foot hard maple floor had beautiful inlaid patterns to break [up] the monotony of its immense surface. Thirty-six thousand strips of maple in ten foot lengths were used to achieve all its effects. Beneath it was a 'spring floor' made by layering the dance floor on an especially constructed subfloor.

Thirty-six bell-shaped & transparent chandeliers were [all] suspended from the ballroom ceiling by gold ropes. The wall decorations, painted by Russian artists, had depicted a submarine garden. The effect gave to patrons the illusion of dancing on coral. The final cost of the building had exceeded $150,000.

T. H. had pulled off a stunning victory in America! He had added several new, impressive lines to his remarkable resume—starting off from lowly advertising and publicity, to dance hall organiser, engineer, manager-entrepreneur, and then latterly as an architect. Surely the International Correspondence Academy should further advance his causes as a 'star' in their firmament.

T. H. brought the world of entertainment and of vaudeville charmingly to life in California. There was anxiety with every audition and act that was booked; the camaraderie; the lengthy hours; the constant quest for improvement; the travel—often across to icy destinations. Moreover, there was the *La Monica Ballroom* itself, with its brilliant 'sprung' floor! Now there was an idea he might use in the future. (The 'sprung floor' idea even made its way into Cloudland's ethos; as we learn later, the only reason its floor bounced was because of sagging!)

By 1925, T. H. had graduated to helping organise the Worlds Fair at Wembley in London, England. According to its March 31st, 1925, 'blurb' about Balboa Park in San Diego: 'T. C. Eslick [was the] engineer in charge of construction of devices of Luna Park, Mission Beach'. He has 'outlined plans for the $125,000 fun palace yesterday'; the 'decorate theme will be futuristic'.

THE 'FLORIDA' EXPERIENCE

> Whether I shall turn out to be the hero of my own life, or whether that station must be held by anybody else, all these pages must show.
>
> **Charles Dickens**

Eslick's circumstances in California soon drastically altered. Within February of 1926 a huge tempest almost destroyed the Sana Monica pier. It followed that the pier had sacrificed too many of the 'pilings' underneath the ballroom; so that this edifice was being supported by fewer that two-thirds of the pilings required to hold its large mass. Some £38,000 worth of repairs would be necessary to bring the structure back to its original safe design.

Interestingly, another beneficial experience beside the *La Monica Ballroom* miraculously surfaced now for Thomas. It was clearly a case for Eslick of quitters never winning and winners never quitting. Prior to the Californian episode, Eslick had befriended a prosperous Florida land developer, David Paul Davis. There Thomas had found himself in a highly remunerative employ, designing the constructions for a promising new development, upon an island in the historical precinct of St Augustine.

D. P. Davis, aged 40.

The *Castillo de San Marcos*, within St Augustine, Florida.

The Davis Island Coliseum.
Florida Newspapers.

A Cunard poster depicts the entire fleet of ocean liners.
Florida Newspapers.

'exploits' had criss-crossed the Pacific and Atlantic coasts, Davis then commissioned Thomas Eslick to now construct what was later termed as the biggest 'enclosed coliseum' in the south-eastern part of the United States. The edifice was completed in 1925; and went on to hold dances, auto shows and concerts.

The Winter Gardens, Blackpool.

But as the project's developer, Davis was soon in trouble. He was having difficulty raising the money to close off the deal—one that included swimming pools, tennis courts, five star hotels, luxury domiciles and two golf clubs. Nevertheless, as news of Thomas'

About this same time T. H. may well have offered long-term assurances to Davis; and even his continuing involvement in the St Augustine building scheme. In truth, he could even have advanced his own capital. Yet, in the following year of 1926, Davis, after negotiating a huge life insurance payout policy, in an act open to dispute, action and controversy, had suddenly disappeared from inside his Cunard Liner cabin, *en route* to France. So he was never sighted again. These events occurred about the same period that T. H. was in the United Kingdom, seeking to appeal his bankruptcy brief in London's High Court of Justice. While there, Thomas appears to have dabbled in Blackpool's Winter Gardens advertising to help make ends meet, viz:

> The Empress Ballroom is a 3000 capacity entertainment venue, in Blackpool, Lancashire, England. It is located within the Winter Gardens, the ballroom is a Grade 11 Listed Building. It is operated by Crown Leisure Ltd, on behalf of the Blackpool Council, who purchased the property from Leisure Parcs Ltd. as part of a £40 million hand-over.

The Winter Gardens site, Blackpool.

After acquiring an American spouse, Thomas returned to Santa Monica in 1928 to manage the renovated and reopened *La Monica Ballroom*. On April 29th of 1929, however, the *Oregon Journal* mentions 'the possible deportation of a T. H. Eslick to Wales'.

The following year T. H. had connections with the British National Pictures Studios in Elstree, London. Presently, he had accumulated 32 years in these types of experiences. On May 25th, 1930, Thomas recounted his visit to India in the *Oregonian*.

On Friday, June 13th, 1930, daily perusers of the Oregonian newspaper were welcomed by another of T. H.'s smooth pitches as they sipped their morning coffees. 'If I Were You for Just One Day', had read the advertisement, 'And that day was on tomorrow—Boy! Girl! Believe me! I wouldn't hesitate. I'd know just where to go. Eh!—Where?—Why? To Lotus Isle'. Not unexpectedly with Thomas Eslick, the printed 'come-on', signed '*Yours Radiantly, T. H. Eslick*' was just a few weeks premature.

The ad for Lotus Isle.

In actual fact, the 'Million Dollar Pleasure Paradise' the fine print professed and promised wouldn't be available until June 28th. Only the bath house, supervised by the 'nationally known swimming instructor and lifesaving expert, Captain Emil Vodjansky, would greet Portlanders that particular weekend'.

T. H.'s plans were up to their usual 'grandiose' standards:

Lotus Isle, an amusement park located on what is now known as Tomahawk Island in the Columbia River between Portland and Vancouver, Washington, was an ambitious project. T.H. Eslick, in addition to his knack for promotion, had a reputation (perhaps self-perpetuated) for thinking big. In Delhi, the newspaper had reported later that month, this "stolid Britisher with a trace of a Yorkshire burr" had been dubbed *Burra Sahib Adme Jokahm Bennati-Hia* ("the Big Chief who Gets Things Done") by the "nine thousand Hindus" who worked under him to construct a great royal *durbar*.

For the Lotus Isle, Eslick had commissioned the Puget Sound Bridge and the Dredging company's dredge *Olympia* to run three shifts a day with a crew of 50 men, bringing up 750,000 cubic yards of sand to build a "dyke" around the entire island, higher than the highest water ever known on the river and wide enough for a road on the top. In March, 1930, the project then added two hundred workers to the hundred already building the park, aiding Portland Mayor George Baker's "relief drive" to combat unemployment.

A $150,000 "scenic railway" wound between two artificial mountain peaks decorated with a few scenes from the life of the Chief Multnomah. Seven and a half miles of drain pipe could pump five thousand gallons a minute from the island site. The front entrance, eight hundred feet long and featuring twelve golden minarets, was modelled on the Taj Mahal.

A central double lake crossed by bridges boasted an illuminated waterfall, with "water flowing over plate glass upon which lights of changing hues played constantly". The wide veranda of the grand ballroom extended out over the lake. Captain Vodjansky had ordered 5,000 swimming suits for patrons of the bathing pavilion. With tracks extended from the Faloma station on the Vancouver street car line to Lotus Isle and the fare fixed at ten cents, the park was just about ready for its full debut.

The *Oregonian* suggested there was at Lotus Isle about "every type of amusement anyone could ever wish for": bathing; dancing; the wild ride over Mount Hood; to "hitting the 'nigger doll baby' in the eye". Undoubtedly, the good people of Portland, Oregon, flocked to these fair-style entertainments, even though they had appeared racist and child-abusive in their themes.

By December 1st, 1931, T. H.'s connection with the Lotus scheme was to end in tears when *The Oregonian* had made reference to Eslick's salary lawsuit with Lotus Isle.

On May 19th, 1932, T. H. had married Florence Thiele in Walla Walla, Washington. The subsequent year he was involved in 'A Century of Progress' in Chicago, USA. From 1934, Thomas had provided assistance for the T.T.D.A. (Tourist Trade Development Association in Vancouver). 'Mayor Leeming sought out Eslick's advice', calling T.H. Eslick an 'amusement engineer'. From the following year, in 1935, T. H. was connected with 'The Show Boat' in Victoria, British Columbia, Canada.

When Sydney's Luna Park was officially opened in 1935, it was also—like the Lotus—said to be T. H. Eslick's masterpiece—featuring a 'brace of Moorish towers' as well as 'an almost demonic "Mr Moon", whose open mouth was the venue's main gate. An electrical sign completed the overall effect, one practically 'unprecedented in Australia'. Suffice it to say there is no 'Mr Moon' connected with Coney Island or other Luna Parks which arose in the United States.

As we would all know, T. H. Eslick, the self-heralded 'Pied Piper of Portland', was just starting on his path to big scale projects. Clearly, T. H.'s dabbling with fate and Luna Park-like experiences had enabled him to present a glittering resume to the world. This wealth of accumulated knowledge would soon take him to Australia, specifically Brisbane, to design that capital city's splendid Cloudland Ballroom.

4

LUNA PARK (CLOUDLAND), BOWEN HILLS, BRISBANE, 1940s

Luna Park (Brisbane) Limited

The Most Modern Amusement Park In Australia

Directors:
C. STEWART, Brisbane.
W. K. McLUCKIE, Brisbane.
T. M. AHERN, Brisbane.
T. H. ESLICK, Brisbane.
J. DIXON, Melbourne.

Mr. T. H. Eslick is well known as an International Amusement Park Designer, Engineer and Executive. He designed and constructed Luna Park, Melbourne, White City, Sydney, and 43 other Amusement Parks in all parts of the World.

His services as Managing Director of the Company have been secured for a term of five years, with option of renewal.

CONSTRUCTION HAS COMMENCED—PARK OPENS JULY 1939

Luna Park, Melbourne, has paid over 20 per cent in dividends since 1913, 20 per cent

An advertisement for Luna Park, Brisbane. Note the very ambitious finish date here of July, 1939—as its building had only commenced in April, 1939.

T. H. ESLICK AND THE BIRTH OF LUNA PARK (CLOUDLAND), BRISBANE, 1939-40

From the early 1800s, particularly at the time of the Moreton Bay Penal Colony at Brisbane Town, the Bowen Hills site where Cloudland was to stand from 1939-40 to 1982 was merely bare bushland with a tree- studded hilltop above the emerging settlement.

By the 1920s, Montpelier Hill featured *Cowlishaw House,* a grand old home constructed by James Cowlishaw. It was an immense property with structured and tiered gardens overlooking the Brisbane River—and could be found between the city centre and the plush northern suburbs of Hamilton and Ascot. Who would have thought it would be the site for Luna Park (Cloudland) in 1939?

James Cowlishaw (1834-1929).

The Cowlishaw Residence.

A last stage of the demolition of the old Cowlishaw residence. It was razed to make way for Brisbane's Luna Park, Cloudland, on Montpelier Heights. The old chimney stack in the act of toppling was erected in 1849. Cowlishaw was a well-known landmark for nearly 100 years.

The Telegraph, April 11th, 1939.

In the late 1920s, Bowen Hills was not the leafy suburb it is today—pretty, well serviced and not far from Brisbane's CBD. So many trees had been cleared for house blocks in this decade; roads, streets and paths were unsealed; pedestrian foot traffic and carriages carved out well-worn tracks on suburban heights; the houses were mostly new ones; and gardens were in an initial state, so were yet to flourish.

Arriving back in Australia, together with his wife and her offspring from a previous marriage, T. H. Es-lick would now need to sense his way by establishing new projects and creating brand new schemes. By 1937 he appeared in Sydney advertising as a 'door to door salesman' to plug educational materials, perhaps encyclopaedias. By 1939, the *Courier-Mail* of

Wednesday, November 23rd, announced: *Brisbane Luna Park Plans Go Ahead*: "Mr T. H. Eslick, designer and builder of Luna Park, St Kilda, is in Melbourne completing arrangements for the construction of a Luna Park within Brisbane". All the while, T. H. had been flaunted as a very capable 'American'.

Thomas's quite intimate knowledge of Sydney's 'White City' and Melbourne's Luna Park enabled him to issue an official prospectus for the Brisbane venue within the early days of 1939. New Farm and Breakfast Creek were considered as sites for the Brisbane structure, with *Cowlishaw House,* established at Montpelier Heights in Bowen Hills, receiving the nod of approval.

After a stint in the southern States combing similar Luna Park venues, in that same year, T. H. was back in Brisbane, presenting to a group of directors the notion of a Luna Park for Queensland's capital. Each time he spoke to others, the same wily approach was again promenaded: the (**sic**) *Delhi Durbar*; Luna Park in Melbourne; and the like. Left out now was door salesman; bankruptcy in London; vaudeville promotion; advertising movies in the north of the State; or Thomas's correspondence course education.

> The statutory meeting of Luna Park (Brisbane) Ltd. which was held yesterday was attended by about 40 shareholders.
>
> The managing director, Mr T. H. Eslick, outlined the company's progress and [the] forward programme.

> Shareholders expressed confidence in the company's prospects.
>
> Reference was [then] made to the death of Mr C. Stewart, chairman of directors. It was stated that his place on the board would not be filled at present. (*Courier-Mail*, April 25th, 1939.)

The commanding site was originally intended to possess a fully-fledged fun-style park, such as Luna Park in Melbourne, which T. H. Eslick boasted he 'built' in 1912. It was to be the largest free-standing building of its particular kind in Queensland's capital city; and, on its hill top site above Brisbane, Cloudland's "distinctive parabolic laminated roof arch, nearly 18 yards high, was [to be] highly visible". T.H.'s idea was to make the venue's entrance as impressive as Sydney's Luna Park with its huge laughing face. As for the 2,000-2,500 capacity ballroom itself, T. H. focused special attention on the renowned dance floor (*a la* the *La Monica Ballroom* in California). It was reputed to be the best of its kind in Australia; and T. H. wanted the entire venue to be "the best ballroom in the Southern Hemisphere". Little did he know that it was later to become a most famous entertainment centre for many balls and festivals.

After convincing the Directors, led by its Chairman, Mr W. K. McLuckie, of the merits of his plans—ironically, the year the motion picture *Gone With the Wind* premiered in Atlanta in the USA—T. H. was allowed to proceed with the project. Southern investors predominately purchased five shilling shares after their public issuing. In the process, Thomas sold 20,000 £1 shares to help construct the £65,000 Luna Park building complex. Adolphus Parry-Fielder was established as the project's architect. It was he who would copy the alpine design for the funicular railway from one he'd seen at a European exposition. Mockingly too, perhaps, *Over the Rainbow* was fittingly on the hit parade at this time—maybe a portent of T. H.'s grandiose ideas for his lofty 'Cloudland'.

On March 19th, 1939, the first sod for Luna Park, Brisbane (Cloudland), was turned by the Deputy Governor of Queensland. Daughters of the original owners of *Cowlishaw House*, the Misses Cowlishaw, and Thomas's wife, Florence, were in attendance. In real Eslick fashion, not just 100 but 1,000 pigeons were set free to celebrate the event. The actual building of the enterprise would begin after April of 1939.

Luna Park would take eighteen months, not the extraordinarily strange prediction which T. H. had notified the local press of only five months. Given 1939 marked the year that World War II broke out, the Luna Park project suffered from a shortage of manpower and supplies; hence the lengthy period of its construction.

After tenders were considered, Evans Deakin had won the right to supply 64 tons of construction metal for Thomas's project, including skeletal frames for the structure's roof.

The 'Tower of Dreams Ballroom', Vista Café, in Luna Park, Brisbane. Its official opening was supposedly on an impossible date in July of 1939.

Tana /Aaron Thiele; Kyle Fysh.

'Cloudland', Luna Park Ballroom, in Brisbane, was constructed on the peak of Montpelier Hill at Bowen Hills from 1939 to the year of 1940. In the latter year, *Whispering Grass* became a worldwide hit on the music charts. In keeping with the nation's being on a 'war footing', Nugget introduced a new boot polish, 'Military Tan'. On home soil, in July of that same year of 1940, there was a ceremony in honour of opening the new Story Bridge, Australia's second longest span bridge.

Initially, following its construction, an open-air type alpine tramcar arrangement (a funicular railway) pulled itself up and down the sheer hillside, at the rear of Cloudland's entrance. It used two car carriages, each having around a capacity of 30 passengers. They would transport eager patrons a distance of 330 feet from Breakfast Creek to Cloudland Ballroom.

Photographic Resume of the Luna Park, Brisbane
Construction Progress
Specially Prepared for our Out-Of-Town Shareholders

A photographic resume of Luna Park, Brisbane. Featuring the construction progress especially prepared for 'out-of-town' share-holders.

Aaron/Tana Thiele.

...the complex did have one unique attraction. Its alpine railway was designed to transport patrons up the steep hillside to all the attractions above from the trams upon the streets below. The railway did not survive as long as Cloudland [did], having been damaged in a mini-tornado. (*It was only Rock 'n' Roll*, Geoff Walden.)

As for the project itself, Eslick's Luna Park scheme, in actuality, involved the 2.5 ha site on one of the highest points in Brisbane, as a playground of open air amusements, picnic grounds, shady walks, motor avenues, the aforementioned alpine railway and the ballroom. All told,

£24,000 worth of new attractions were promised for the 'show' side of Luna Park's activities, including Australia's first Electric Racecourse. This had involved twenty full sized, life-like wooden horses which were electrically propelled along a 600 foot track, with riders to control the speed of horses; plus a big dipper ride. (Sadly, most of these Luna park-like features were never built.)

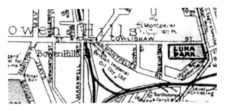

Luna Park at Bowen Hills, Brisbane. The venue appears here to be in the wrong place. It should be immediately to the right of the Bowen Hills words, adjacent to where 'Montpelier' is in the diagram.

Cloudland was to become typical of the stream-form ballroom architecture of the 1930s, exemplified by its central archway, columns, interior lights and balustrades. Regarding all these latter features, the internal décor of the ballroom had pillars made from telegraph poles, chicken wire and plaster; and was also notable for giving architects headaches later on in its existence.

In June of 1940, a fire broke out in Luna Park's construction zone; and then a night-watchman was assaulted; then he shot at his assailant, who escaped. The *Brisbane Courier* newspaper reports of the time said the building under construction was worth £15,000;

and was insured for £12,000. Police claimed the fire had been deliberately lit; but T. H. Eslick had believed that little damage had been caused. Perhaps predictably, the culprit who ignited the fire was not found.

At the Luna Park ballroom's official opening, on August 2nd, 1940, the Managing Director, T. H. Eslick and the Chairman of Directors, W. K. McLuckie, both gave brief speeches. Vice-Mayor, Alderman A. H. Tait, praised Mr Eslick's "genius", particularly in relation to the ballroom's 'so-called' famous "sprung" floor. He hoped that the promoters, directorate and stockholders could now be rewarded for their "pluck in investing £65,000, so that Brisbane can enjoy the best ballroom in the Southern Hemisphere". Mr McLuckie added that "the ballroom was designed to give pleasure to all the residents of Queensland, particularly those in Brisbane, and he hoped that [they] would make full use of it". (*Courier-Mail*, August 3rd, 1940.)

On this balmy August evening of 1940, Luna Park's enormous arched dome towers at Bowen Hills heights were visible to those present at the official opening, as well as Brisbanites who observed the night sky. Miss Minty Barry was the evening's hostess.

With its myriad of twinkling lights beckoning from off the heights of Bowen Hills, Cloudland, Luna Park's ballroom attracted hundreds to the official opening by the Vice-Mayor (Ald. A. H. Tait) last night. The dance programme began shortly

after 8.30...and soon 100 couples were dancing to the music of *Billy Romaine's Orchestra*, and hundreds more had watched from all the alcoves and galleries. (*It was only Rock'n'Roll*, Geoff Walden.)

A hand-painted watercolour presented to T. H. Eslick, upon nearing the 'completion' of Luna Park, Brisbane. It was actually his employees' letter of July 24th, 1940, thanking him for his guiding leadership with Luna Park, Brisbane.

After its official opening, further essential completion work on the Luna Park section of the Eslick plan was set back by a fierce cyclone exhibiting strong winds in November of 1940, six months after the fire there. This storm destroyed part of the scaffolding and framework of the scenic, switch-back railway. Moreover, the structure intended for the big dipper roller-coaster collapsed, becoming unusable; and some of the park itself was completely destroyed (such as the 'Dome of Death' and 'slide down the hill'.) £2,000 of non-insured damage ensued; and it seemed a legitimate case.

The site was now exhibiting union problems with its workers, as well as sideshow owners looking for a stable completion date. The notion that the Luna Park aspect of Eslick's project, besides the ballroom, would keep the ballroom attraction relatively viable—or vice versa—was at the forefront of the directors' thoughts prior to its evolution. However, Luna Park, as a large-style ancillary and themed entertainment spectacle for its acclaimed ballroom—which had been proclaimed as a viable, exciting project "managed by international businessman, T. H. Eslick"—was currently in quite serious decline. Initially planned to be finalised at around the same time as the ballroom, the funfair, amusement section of Luna Park was never to fully come to fruition.

Meanwhile, the war had escalated and the overseas news was bad. T. H. Eslick then tried to drum up support for less entrepreneurial activities at the venue: such as vaudeville acts, public dance lessons, zany advertisements, and his predictable tag line, 'Radiantly Yours'. With the Luna Park rides and show part of the business still to occur—and the finished Big Dipper not in use—Eslick's scheme for the venue was in terminal disarray. Although the new amusement section of Luna Park had opened

at the very same time as the ballroom—August of 1940—it only lasted six months, until the park aspect finally closed up in January of 1941.

By April of 1941, even though T. H.'s overall concept for Luna Park was good, as well as credible, shares bought for 5/- realised a paltry 6d. Further into the bowels of World War II's consequences, work on the amusement park had stopped on its closure; the big dipper was dismantled, never to be rideable; and the scenic railway was likewise closed.

Luna Park was now up for sale. In this uneasy of economic climates, no bids were forthcoming. Eslick was now making plans to declare himself bankrupt and the park's investors were on the end of a large loss.

After the end of 1940, Luna Park as a separate attraction to Cloudland Ballroom had floundered under Thomas's leadership, with the result ending up in dismal failure. So official bankruptcy and ruin were once again making their presence felt with T. H.'s sensitivities. Till the end of the war, Eslick would be involved in a messy court case involving his bankruptcy and the 'sequestering' of property. His odd dual identity (Tollmache Herriot Eslick) and previous London bankruptcy of the 1920s had come back to haunt him.

It was a crying shame, wasn't it, that T. H. and his fellow employees could not see a catastrophe looming at the venue; and that those worldwide events over which T. H. had absolutely no control—such as the onset of a second world war— would jettison any firm chance that Luna Park in Brisbane required for success.

T. H. Eslick was a perennially clever individual. Entertainment was the prominent aspect of his theatrical passion. Perhaps he should even be anointed as 'the forerunner' and 'the creator' of the many themed parks of today. Then, maybe, he should not be so. You'll recall that the 'Portobello Marine Park' was well up and running before his involvement as Publicity Manager; yet that marine park of 1909 did embody the characteristics and design of the modern versions of that original idea. As regards Cloudland, T. H. **was** instrumental in building it. However, fate and world events constrained Thomas's own requirements to then follow this scheme through to a considered, logical conclusion.

Facing a possible catastrophe, T. H. made one ultimate dive into his continuing fantasy world to try to steady the sinking ship.

Apparently, Thomas disappeared from Brisbane soon afterwards. For only what some outsiders saw as a brief time period, Luna Park (Cloudland) appeared to be more or less forlornly abandoned. But 'other management strategies were now in place' and it carried out some of its activities unabated until 1941. (In time, the abandoned amusement park aspect of Eslick's operations became a car park.)

Island Utopia Lures Luna Park Designer

MR. T. H. Eslick, designer of Luna Park, is searching for people to join him in establishing a little commonwealth of perfect peace on a Utopian island in the Pacific.

First news of his quest was when an advertisement appeared in The Sydney Morning Herald, describing "a permanent home in a Pacific island where life is lived easily—security, health, and contentment under blue skies and soft breezes in a community-owned, non-profit commonwealth of intelligent people, who are tired of working to pay taxes, of living to please neighbours, of surrendering personal liberty to keep faith with a regimented, over-governed, soul-tiring civilisation."

Inquiries revealed that the advertiser was Mr. Eslick. In an interview in Sydney, he said: "I have spent my life visiting crowded cities in four continents. If civilisation is what we know to-day, then I'm better off without it. I spent years working in America, and when I came back to Sydney in 1938 I found it had become a metropolis, and King's Cross a microcosm of the world's dissipations. I don't object to these things, but I have had enough of them.

"I want to make my dream a reality, because I believe there are thousands of people like myself who are longing to float into a safe harbour of peace, content, and simplicity. If that is not so, then I shall still start an island community—just myself and my family."

Mr. Eslick, who is an Englishman, has been the designer and constructing engineer of amusement parks in many parts of the world. His Australian work includes Luna Park, Melbourne, and White City, Sydney, as well as Luna Park, Brisbane.

This newspaper interview re-counts Thomas's deep-seated 'despondency'. Reproduced in the *Sydney Morning Herald*, January, 1941.

There were 164 replies to T. H. Eslick's call in Sydney on January 23rd, 1941, to establish this Pacific Island paradise. In one week to 10 days, T. H. was to organise a meeting of those interested. There were no more of these same sessions, though, before the end of the war. Men in business, Thomas hoped, would take up his new idea, although his plea attracted a small population of 'cranks' and 'faddists'. (*Central Queensland Herald*, January 30th, 1941.)

For a time, perhaps to think over his uncertain future, T. H. moved to Vancouver, Canada; and then in 1947 back to Blue River, Oregon, in the United States. *The Eugene Register* (Oregon) produced a May 4th, 1948, obituary for a T. H. Eslick. It states 'that he was born in Wales and that he lived for a time in Australia'. The Oregon Death Index lists Thomas's first name as 'Tallemach', so it seems to fit his description and past history. 'Surviving are his widow; three step-children, Mrs Frances Farmer, from Blue River; [a] Mrs Maxine Sutherland, Vancouver, British Columbia; and Charles Thiele, Portland; and four grandchildren'. (Oddly, perhaps, another T. H. or Thomas Eslick had died within September, 1965, aged 78 years. His last known residence was in Alabama in the Southern United States.)

LUNA PARK'S BALLROOM

As we are now aware, Cloudland Ballroom with its partial theme park complex operated as a fine dance palace and Luna Park entertainment venue from August of 1940. It would be hard to imagine, at this stage of its origin, that the ballroom venue atop its hilly and leafy location in Bowen Hills was now later to become the city's foremost entertainment venue for well over forty years. In sum, it would later be significant both as a major landmark; and as a place where "generations of Brisbane residents" headed for their entertainment. The distinctive arch over its entrance, which was incredibly high, was to be visible for miles, and totally illuminated at night. Inside, it boasted an elegant 'Art Deco' interior. Around the period, its constructors suggested that with "its private alcoves, upholstered seating, dressing rooms, and perfect ventilation…the ballroom will be the finest of its kind in [the nation]"—

…Cloudland was so closely identified with all the [later] Americans…It was designed to be a show piece as Brisbane's finest answer to Sydney's Luna Park. £130,000 was invested to construct the best ballroom in the Southern Hemisphere to provide for the leisure activities of the residents of Queensland, particularly for those of Brisbane city. *The Courier-Mail* (02/08/40) reported.

In 1940, Noel Coward, the English dramatist and composer, entertained our Australian troops at the Grovely military camp in Brisbane; visited Cloudland; and performed at a Red Cross Concert within *His Majesty's Theatre*. Coward would discover that this particular year's program of music at Cloudland went something like this for September, the month after its opening:

CARNIVAL NIGHT

AT CLOUDLAND

That part of Luna Park dedicated to dancing feet which is symbolised in Cloudland Ballroom holds considerable charm for Brisbane revellers of the night. The style of dance entertainment provided is original. A contributing reason is Bill Romaine and his band whose nuances in playing provide elegant music. Fortunate are the dancers that have this combination playing the accompaniment.

Carnival will hold sway to the ballroom to-night which means that Romaine will let his drummer go into frenetic music of the kind you will not find this side of voodoo land. In addition Helen and Charles will entertain in exhibition dances and Molly Hislop will raise her sweet voice in song. What more do you want? Two carnivals?

Amusement devices are in full swing in the park area and offer opportunity for light relaxation. (*Courier-Mail*, September 5th, 1940.)

And again:

CLOUDLAND BALLROOM

The *Courier-Mail* Saturday, 16 November, 1940. ...**CLOUDLAND BALLROOM** Modern dancing is a feature of the programme at **Cloudland Ballroom** every Saturday night, when the latest music is played by Billy Romaine and his orchestra. Diversity is provided by Billy Romaine and [his] show, to which members of the band and a 'croon-ette' contribute. In the park...

CLOUDLAND BALLROOM

The *Courier-Mail* Saturday, 23 November, 1940.

...**CLOUDLAND BALLROOM** Mr Billy Romaine's orchestra provides the music for dancing at **Cloudland Ballroom**, Luna Park, where the programmes are varied nightly. Modern dancing is listed for to-night. Novelty items presented by the band will provide bright interludes. A wide range of amusement...

CLOUDLAND BALLROOM

The *Courier-Mail* Thursday, 28 November, 1940.

...**CLOUDLAND BALLROOM** a programme of modern dance numbers will be featured at the Cloudland ballroom, in Luna Park, to-night. Bill Romaine's orchestra will supply the latest music, and members of the band will give comedy numbers at intervals. Attractive amusement devices in the park proper offer...

Bill Thurman *(left, top)* and three mates at Cloudland.

Around this same time, the *Billo Smith Band*, formerly of the *Trocadero*, with R. Phillips, Manager, took part in the ballroom's entertainment and organised all of its prime scheduling. During all these heady days of 1940, Cloudland hosted many dances that particular year. The highly reactive, wooden floor, which had appeared to be 'sprung' but wasn't, was made fine use of by thousands of sashaying couples. Of course, no great night out would be complete without that usual photo momento with the 'Luna Park-Cloudland' monicker up at the top. In fact, these same folk with friends and family often had their evening 'captured' against the backdrop of a crescent moon, stars, willow patterns and an evening sky.

Kath Cristie recalled the days when—

"We used to have two queues which were so long they went from the ticket office right down to the front gate"...

"I worked in the ticket office with another girl then and we were so busy we used to throw all the money on the floor in the ticket box and pick it all up later".

WORLD WAR II

The subject of a US Defence Series postcard, 'Ansons in Cloudland'.

Orson Welles in the studio, enacting his radio play.

Running parallel to all these events at Cloudland from 1939 to 1940 and beyond that period was the imminence, and later stark reality of a world at war conflict. Orson Welles' Halloween Night radio plug of the sci-fi classic, *War of the Worlds*, created widespread anxiety, then panic, in the United States. There were scenes of "hundreds fleeing to hills; and folks shooting up a New Jersey water tower, fearing it was a Martian death tripod"

Alarming events happening world-wide were now beginning to give rise to these same intense concerns and troubled minds as Welles' dramatic radio broadcast had caused. In actual fact, there was to be an "eerie silence" about events, as complete as when the last Martian in Welles' *"War of the Worlds"* carked it.

The air raid shelters in Elizabeth Street, Brisbane, 1942.

The front page of the *Courier-Mail* carrying the news of war.

War was declared on Germany on September 5th, 1939. But the events in Europe, though a tad troubling, did not now seem to lull our relaxed 'Aussie' mentality. As Brendan O'Malley declared in a *Courier-Mail* column:

> The Christmas holiday season of 1938/39 was the last carefree summer break Queenslanders would see for the next six years.
>
> Despite the alarming news from Europe, where hundreds of thousands of refugees were fleeing Germany and the surrounding countries, and from Asia where Japan had invaded China, the holiday makers Down Under were so determined to make the most of a scorching summer.

Brisbane pub photo, US goodwill visit out to Australia, nine months before Pearl Harbour. *Courier-Mail.*

Literally within months of all those glorious Australian summer vacations, the largest crowd gathering in Brisbane's history had turned out to welcome the American fleet on Tuesday, March 25th, 1941. This parade, snak-ing from Fortitude Valley to the City Hall by means of Queen Street, formed part of a 'goodwill' visit and tour by the American Naval Squadron. Within nine months from that date, following on Pearl Harbour, the United States had boldly entered World War II.

'Goodwill' visitors' parade, in Brisbane.
Courier-Mail.

The symbol of US military might.

On December 22nd, 1941, the first of the US troops seen within Australia disembarked at Brisbane, which was soon to develop into a major strategic base for US forces in the war against Japan. They were all cheerfully welcomed as representing a Pacific defence for the Australian nation:

It was the start of what soon became a flood of GIs, whose presence forever changed the city and the coastal centres such as Townsville and Cairns. The 4,600 troops were [all] on board a convoy of seven ships escorted by the

cruiser *Pensacola*, which had been on its way from Hawaii back to Manilla to reinforce the Philippines. It had been ordered back out to Hawaii before US President Franklin D. Roosevelt redirected it to Brisbane. The convoy was carrying a brigade from the US Field Artillery Corps, but there were also many Army Air Force ground crews on board. As well as troops, the ships were additionally carrying 70 (disassembled) fighter planes. The "phoney" war had ended in Queensland by then. The rationing and cutbacks were starting to bite, including police road patrols designed to stop any of the people taking their cars for Christmas driving holidays. And air raid shelters were taking shape in Brisbane after Premier William Forgan Smith ordered the Council to build 200 public shelters.

A welcome for the US Navy in Brisbane, December, 1941.
The Weekend Australian.

Alas! Poor Brisbane folk were to experience life during the anxious, dark days of World War II "when public air raid shelters lined the streets, children wore identity discs;

and thousands of American and Australian troops inhabited camps around Brisbane". (*Courier-Mail.*)

American military police outside of the Central Hotel in Brisbane, 1942.

The Brisbane Courier.

To the editor

WARDENS are doing their best to supply every household with sand for sandbagging, yet some people are so cantankerous that they will not walk across the road to get their bucket of sand because it is in a different Council division. What is to be done for such people?

"Bulimba Warden", December 24, 1941

THE success of the Japanese surprise attacks in the Pacific was doubtless due to detailed information supplied by their own spies. Japanese in Australia should be watched and even the Chinese nationals should be checked, for physically the two peoples resemble each other.

E. H. Hunter, Southport, December 23, 1941

IN this national emergency, I suggest that many of us work part-time in the war factories as a contribution to the war effort. I am prepared to work for 12 hours a week in a war factory and others, I

am sure, would do the same if given the opportunity.

R. E. Hunter, Wooloowin, December 21, 1941

The US Army, Navy and war departments subsequently had prepared and issued *Instructions for American Servicemen in Australia*. It included:

...a guide to slang, ranging from drongo (rookie) via sarvo (this afternoon) and Oscar or Oscar Ashe (any hard cash) to poke borak (to insult), matilda (tramp's bundle) and barrack for [to root for], which probably added to the confusion in some situations].

An instruction manual for US troops in Australia, 1942.

The Australian.

Other illustrative material was also utilised to help induct the 'Yanks' to our Australian life by means of *A Pioneer Land: The People Down Under.*

An explanation of the true character of the Australian Soldiers from A Pioneer Land: the People Down Under.

Courier-Mail.

The Aussie money was something else. They [all] talk about quids and bobs. Nobody could figure it out". (*Courier-Mail*.)

The 'iconic' Brisbane tram.

Courier-Mail.

As Brisbane had readied itself to become a garrison city for the Allies fighting in the 'Pacific Theatre', some American military personnel were somewhat confused about how the city appeared to them:

"We knew nothing about this place", one of the first US soldiers in Brisbane noted. "Houses on stumps with red roofs; cable cars in the middle of the roads; the Aussies called them trams. Some girls were in town; they looked pretty, dressed well, kinda classy.

"The Brisbane Stadium as it appeared during WWII." *Notice the military vehicles and a person in uniform and the Bulimba Beer truck to the left of the photo".* It was chiefly a wrestling and boxing venue.

LUNA PARK (MILITARY) CAMP, 1942-1946

A side image of the near exit out of, or entrance to, Luna Park (Cloudland) during World War II. It was maybe the Boyd Street entry way, near 'Cintra', an historic house in Bowen Hills. It is believed that the vehicles parked nearby are "outside of the photographic laboratory for the Army Pictorial Service" of the United States Army.

A front on image of the entrance to Luna Park (Cloudland), World War II.

Charles J. Stehlik.

By 1942, the good citizens of Brisbane, despite the presence of an American garrison in their capital city, had exhibited serious worries about the war in the Pacific. As Terry Sweetman recalled in the *Courier-Mail*:

The year 1942 was when the fear of Japanese invasion and the reality of barbarism brought war literally to our doorsteps.

The further from the events, the less clear they become. There is now an historians' war waged over whether the Japanese had truly intended to invade Australia.

But whatever the intentions in the war rooms of Tokyo, Australians felt the very real threat of invasion, which made the year 1942 the darkest in our history.

It was horrible enough for what people knew. It was hideous for what they didn't know.

The Japanese had invaded Malaya and would soon take Singapore.

In the calamities that followed, it is sometimes forgotten that the Australian forces suffered 1789 dead and 1306 wounded in the campaign, hardly the walkover often portrayed.

In the timeframe, there were casualty rates well comparable with the slaughter of the Great War.

The Japanese avalanche had swallowed up 22,376 Australian prisoners. The majority of them (14,972) were in Singapore, but others included 2736 in Java, 1137 in Timor, 1075 in Ambon and 1049 in New Britain.

On February 19th, 1942, some of those same Japanese forces which attacked Pearl Harbour struck Darwin.

A World War II wartime poster.

The Australian.

feel about the place as well as the presence of welcome visitors.

The bombing of Darwin.

A later poster, released between 1943 and 1945, "calling for Australians to avenge these deaths of all those who perished aboard the hospital ship, *The Centaur*.

Australian War Memorial archives.

An American Army advertisement to draft various prospective US military personnel.

With the nation seemingly under attack; and the war in the Pacific by now at full throttle and engagement, the folk in Brisbane town were happy with the American "occupation" of their capital city. With the range of US military camps established in many of Brisbane's suburbs, there was a 'safe'

As the war within the Pacific overtook peoples' worldwide emotions, by 'cultural exchange' necessity, the 6.4 acre site of Luna Park at Boyd Street in Brisbane, as well as the large ballroom at Bowen Hills, was 'commandeered' by the military during the World War II period, to be used as an American camp, office and headquarters. Requisitioned for its prized facilities by the American Army under the Australian Government's National Security Emergency Regulations of the Day, it was often now affectionately referred to as "Camp Luna Park" by the Americans and Australians serving in the military. During the mid- war years, Cloudland also served the US military as its office headquarters; an officer training base; and as MacArthur's typing pool. Highly sensitive work was carried out by the US Army when it took over the ballroom. Desks, stretchers and office equipment filled the venue. Huge search lights were also placed on the main structure's roof.

One service officer remembers this era vividly:

Technical Sergeant Don Moreland of the 837th Signals Service Detachment slept on cots set up on the floor of Cloudland Ballroom which he knew as Luna Park. Don remembers that there was a cable car there which carried visitors up the steep hill to the dance hall. It was not in operation when he was there. Don said that the ballroom floor was mounted on top of springs and tendered to sway when people walked across it.

Don Mooreland also helped to establish and to then operate all the IBM tabulators for General Douglas MacArthur's top secret signals intelligence unit which was known as Central Bureau. The IBM tabulators were located in a large garage behind a big two storey house at 21 Henry Street at Ascot, Brisbane.

An engineering work camp detail of some American soldiers within Queensland, in World War II.

The Australian.

An image of Luna Park, Cloudland, in World War II.

Charles Stehlik.

Another vantage point of Cloudland and Luna Park, World War II.

Charles Stehlik.

A World War II photo of Luna Park, Cloudland. Cptn. Owczkowsky's Dispensary in on the left.

Jason Harty.

Director (Military) October 1943 Telephone

Restricted

HEADQUARTERS - USAFFE

HEADQUARTERS COMMANDANT:

C.O. Headquarters Company: Capt. Hopkins, H.S.

Executive Officer: Lt. Bryant, E.A.

Orderly Room Dispensary: Capt. Owczykowsky, B.J.

Inside of Cloudland (Luna Park), World War II. Possibly a US Signal Corps photograph.

Jason Harty.

US Naval Base facilities in the Brisbane area.

This interior of the Cloudland Ballroom, Luna Park, taken on 8th February, 1943, was used by the US Army for quartering troops. *Note* the numerous 'cots' with mosquito net hangers and the in-door volley ball court. (US Army photo.)

The following, related to the image, is an extract from the official Military Telephone Directory of October, 1943, setting out the incumbents at the American Army Headquarters at the Luna Park Camp.

Within Brisbane, an office was also set up for General Douglas MacArthur, the Commander-in-Chief of the Allied Forces in the South-West Pacific Area. MacArthur had used his AMP buildings city digs while he was plotting for his return to the Philippines, where he just made a harrowing escape: 'I shall return.'

The US Army's 832nd Signal Photographic Detachment's personnel were billeted at Newstead House. Some meals were provided within the large living quarters of Camp Luna Park and others at Crosby Park nearby Ascot Raceway. Miegunyah House, an elegant Victorian era home in Bowen Hills, also served as HQ for 'Z' Force, well known for clandestine forays into enemy territory.

this tragic accident—as the pilot did not survive—the street which now connects Hamilton Road and Murphy Road was named 'Kittyhawk Drive'. (After the US military had left Cloudland's premises, the ballroom was again closed.)

MacArthur's headquarters in Brisbane, Queensland.

Australian Prime Minister, John Curtin, with the Com-mander United States Gen. Douglas MacArthur.

In the late afternoon of Saturday, 13th November, 1943, there was an incident of sorts when a US fighter aircraft crashed in Sparkes' Paddock, now 7th Brigade Park, in Chermside. From the period it occurred, there has been controversy about the kind of plane that was destroyed. Some say that it was possibly a *P-47 Thunderbolt*. To commemorate

Members of the 832nd Signal Service Battalion – *Cintra* House, January 26th, 1945.

S/Sgt. William H. Ettenger.

2nd Lt. Joseph Pinto and Harry C. Hillochy, of 832nd Signal Service Battalion,
January 18th, 1945.   *Pvt. Roger Feuereisen.*

A *P-47 Thunderbolt.   Chermside & Districts Historical Society.*

5

THE POST-WAR YEARS AT CLOUDLAND, 1940s

THE LEGACY OF THE 1930s AND 1940s

According to Brisbanite, Peter Ryan, a gentleman was originally characterised "as a well-educated man of good family and distinction or [as] an independently wealthy man with no need to work" (*Sunday Mail*). Such were the folk who had inhabited Cloudland Ballroom in the 1940s.

Brisbane on 19th February, 1943.
Ovid Di Fiore, US Army.

My late mother and father were of the old school. They were old-fashioned and private people. The world they saw and went back to in memory is gone. So is the period in which we grew up. These years are now very much a thing of the past. 'O death in life', wrote Lord Tennyson, 'the days that are no more'. My mother and father remembered back to when they were a little girl and boy. All their beloved fathers, rest their souls, went everywhere in a hat. They would doff it to every lady passing in the street.

Lady Race-goers in Brisbane, 1940.

Men also moved onto the outside of the footpath. This was presumably to protect all their womenfolk, as there were always splashes of water, spots of mud, and the imminent dangers caused by the morning traffic:

> The *Courier-Mail* [suggested] that when a man met a woman in the street, "the hat should not be raised until the pipe or the cigarette has been removed from the mouth".

> Street conduct was a complicated business involving a [little bit of a] soft-shoe shuffle. The man should always walk on the gutter side of the footpath with one or even two [of the] women, "the elder next to him…when crossing the street, however, he should take the centre position".

I well know that things have changed noticeably since those previous years. You could say there is sometimes a lack of erstwhile courtesy in this modern world. It is often caused by the demise of those old-established good manners. Life poses a lot more worries with every passing day. I believe we should focus more on others; if only, perchance, to be treated properly ourselves. In thinking like this, as I do, we only need to look as far back as 'Old Brisbane' and those well-remembered earlier years. They had provided us with a true and modest grounding. The point was that we were our own moral guides. It was up to us to behave with manners. This was indeed the same model that we used for all those lost and bygone years up to the 1930s and 1940s, including the war and post-war years in Brisbane as well as dances at Cloudland.

As Banjo Patterson remembered times past in his *Song of the Future*:

> But times have changed, and changes rung
>
> From old to new—the olden days,
>
> The old bush life and all its ways,
>
> Are passing from us all unsung.

If only we could recover the worth, behaviour and the manners of those early decades!

THE CITY CENTRE AS A RENDEZVOUS POINT

"Awkward in patent leather shoes"
          tuxedo
brilliantine hair combed flat

he led her

like an amateur hour Astaire

over the swaying floor there. *Foxtrot*

Quickstep

Blue Skies string of Pearls

Golden Wedding

till her head spun heart sang,

was it beating

like drums from the *Billo Smith Orchestra*

when he kissed her? Could he hear?

Maureen Freer, *Cloudland*.

Though Cloudland Ballroom was thriving during the war year of 1940, with various dances and nightly functions, when the

Americans arrived in Brisbane from December 1941, the iconic venue's status changed, as I've iterated, from a popular dancehall to a strategically central army base in inner-city Brisbane. Hence, from 1942, Cloudland more or less closed down as a ballroom dance venue (except for military-style dances) owing to its occupation by various US military personnel.

Mrs Douglas MacArthur and a Chinese maid, Lt. Charles W. Downs and Lt. A. Stevens, *Cintra* HQ, Luna Park, 21st December, 1942.

The American Army attending here at a Christmas party, Luna Park, 24th December, 1942.

US Archives.

Of course, many Brisbanites already had an idea about the 'Yanks' as fun-loving, happy souls. After all, the whole world had access to such classic tales as *Little Orphan Annie*, a daily comic strip created by Harold Gray (1894-1968). Though written in the Depression of the '30s and war years of the '40s, it enabled its daily readers "to get outside of [their] woes and everyday trouble[s]. [The storylines offered you] something that showed you hope or gave you a life. [They] just [had] heart". (The *Sunday Mail.*) The implication drawn from Gray's column was that all Americans expressed these happy attitudes.

Little Orphan Annie.　　*Sunday Mail.*

Nat Kipner, who had co-produced the *Bee Gees'* first big hit, *Spicks and Specks,* was based in the city during those early years of the 1940s:

During World War II Kipner was stationed with the US Army Air Corps in Brisbane, arriving in December, 1941, shortly after the Pearl Harbour attack. He also served in New Guinea, where he was wounded and received a

Purple Heart. He later joked with members of '60s band *The Purple Hearts* that he was the only one with the real Purple Heart. Kipner met his wife, Alma Moore, in Brisbane during the war. Their son, Steve, was born in the US but they returned to Brisbane while he was still just a toddler.

Further:

Socialising with American servicemen led to marriages for about 10,000 Australian women, and nylon stockings for many more, which partly explained the occasional riots between Australian and American troops, most notoriously in the so-called *Battle of Brisbane* when, over two nights in November, 1942, Australian and US soldiers had fought each other on the city's streets. One Australian was killed.

Mostly, however, relations between Australians and Americans were good. (World War II, *The Australian*.)

By 1945, when ladies' hemlines were long, men's' attire was formal, and World War II was finished, all the songs from Frank Sinatra up to the *Andrew Sisters* were played at wartime and post-war dances.

In many respects American GIs influences were far-reaching:

AMERICAN GIs flooded our shores throughout the war years and changed the face of Queensland forever. US soldiers camped out in Brisbane and Townsville came armed with far greater weapons than we could ever have imagined. They stormed our shores and captured our young people with nylon stockings, the sound of swing and promises of freedom.

American ex-pat, Nat Kipner. He died in California, December 1st, 2009.
Courier-Mail.

Things began to really change when Queensland's young men were shipped off to the war, leaving the women to work in factories and keep businesses running. With newfound freedom and a steady wage, many women threw themselves into the social whirl of wartime Brisbane and Townsville, which together boasted the largest US army presence in Australia.

In the '40s, teenage girls were out jiving, jitterbugging and carousing with cashed-up US troops, while the sedate citizens of Queensland grew increasingly concerned. Authorities even forced any teenage girls to attend VD clinics in Brisbane.

As one Brisbane woman, a teenager at the time, remembers: "In spite of the war, the social scene was pretty hectic. The Americans were everywhere and they had more money than our men. When we got engaged you could not purchase a diamond ring in Brisbane; they'd bought them all up. We got a sapphire ring".

During these war years Brisbane also became a major destination for US swing bands who came to entertain homesick troops. This inspired young Queenslanders to emulate their modes of dress and dance, setting the stage for the emergence of our bodgies and widgies.

Quite a few venues were set up for dancing, congregating and meeting the opposite sex in Brisbane:

The Trocadero, in Melbourne Street, was Brisbane's main *'palais de dance'* till Cloudland was built in the early 40s; and its great Big Band centre. There was also the Blue Moon Skating Rink, and a dozen old fashioned verandahed pubs, the liveliest of which after the war was Manhattan Gardens. (Later, when the whole area was levelled for the Brisbane Expo, a good many of the pubs were preserved and incorporated into this site; and [they] have survived into the new one.]

Lola Taylor had 'light hearted' wartime memories. A local girl, she worked for the US Army Post Office in Brisbane; and had married a demobbed Australian naval serviceman.

My workmates and I went to dances at [Cloudland and] the *Trocadero* in South Brisbane where Billo Smith's band played the latest hits, *Deep in the Heart of Texas, Yours, Paper Doll* and many other tunes which I have forgotten. I tried what I thought was jitterbugging. Just 'shimmy-shaking' really, as I had no idea at all how it all went. But shake I did.

Lola also joined the American Red Cross as a volunteer and hospital visitor.

Dances became a feature of all Lola's volunteer work:

One of her duties was to attend the almost nightly dances at the American Red Cross Centre in the city. There she enjoyed luxuries like coffee, Coca Cola and donuts during the breaks and was required to wear a membership badge and to dance with any American serviceman who asked her.

But on Sunday nights, the highlight of the week was the City Hall dance.

"Here the huge American Army band played in the Glenn Miller style, with each part of the orchestra performing in special roles, standing and flashing their trumpets, saxophones or trombones from side to side", she remembers.

"What exhilaration when *American Patrol, One O'Clock Jump* or *Golden Wedding* erupted into the big band sound".

"My friends and I wore brilliant red lipstick at the time, so when Jackie Fisher, that lead singer who had sounded just like our idol Frank Sinatra, sang *Tangerine*, we would linger close to him and wet our lips to be just so like 'Tangerine with her lips like flame'.

"It makes me smile just to recall it".

Lola Taylor (with an admirer) upon a break between all her dances. City Hall, World War II.
The Senior News.

A soldier plays the saxo-phone at a Brisbane military hostel during 1941.

Besides Lola, many of Brisbane's local "lasses" learned hand movements to the popular '40s tunes, such as the 'Hand Jive', gleaned from the US soldiers during World War II.

Estelle Pinney also vividly recounts those World War II-style entertainments:

Flash back to the 1940s and Estelle Pinney, 85, remembers a few good nights out at the *Princes* nightclub in the city.

"It was during the war years and it was a real favourite haunt of the servicemen. It was an upmarket club and you had to have a partner to gain entry" she says.

"Men wore suits and women their best dresses. We used to shuffle around the dance floor to the lovely music of the orchestras".

"These were expensive nights out and it was usually only the American servicemen or Australian officers who could afford to go. Single men and women would more than likely go to all the dance halls for a night out. That was much more affordable".

She recalls the dulcet tones of Perry Como and Bing Crosby being played when the orchestra was on a break.

"There was never any trouble, they were wonderful times", she says.

June Adamson in her delightful classic 'Brissie" book *Don't Rock the Boat* also does not want to be left out of the World War II 'Yank-style' entertainment.

When American fleets in port saw the City evenings awash with starkly white uniforms on brash and over-confident Yanks, wartime days and the US invasion were remembered. I was jiving while one sailor stood by watching me, moving with the music, anxious to join in. He gestured to me and called out "Hey, this lady likes to dance just as much as I do" and asked me for the next bracket. This is big, I thought; he chose to partner me and he's from America where all this rock and roll stuff began. We jived together in instinctive harmony, him in his whites, throwing back his head and hollering and me in my element.

It was an Adamson rule that when I [crept] in from my evening exploits I was to cut through the chorus of snores that almost shook the furniture to let my parents know all was well. On this night, I was so excited that after I had gained something like parental attention, I talked a little longer telling how I'd jived with an American.

Dad was almost back to sleep and sunk in snoring by my boring tale when I added a little extra information. Why did Dad suddenly come to attention, sitting upright, eyes now wide open, body almost falling from the bed when I just happened to mention how well the stark white uniform contrasted with this serviceman's coal-black skin?

In 1943, the Seabrae Hotel in Redcliffe held a high-ranking officers' 'do' for the US military forces. Further around by the Redcliffe peninsula, the Redcliffe Comforts Fund also became the centre for the whole surrounding area and American GI visitors. *The Pier Theatre*, Luna Park, was established in August of 1944 (on site of the current saltwater lagoon); and the Redcliffe Roller dome was also a popular component for what was a seaside entertainment precinct out near the Redcliffe jetty. The venue was open until 1966. It is strange indeed, in hindsight, to record here that a 'Luna Park', modelled in some ways on what was originally conceived for Luna Park (Cloudland), Bowen Hills, or elsewhere, was constructed at Redcliffe only a year before the war was over. It was now the first municipally-owned attraction:

> Luna Park, an amusement park, was erected on an unused section of the foreshore just north of Sutton's Beach at Redcliffe Point in late 1944. The owners, Redcliffe Town Council, had appointed Messrs W. Scott and Philip Wirth as amusement managers. Later on, the enterprise was sold by the Redcliffe Town Council to local businessman Hal Buchanan who sold it on to the Roman Catholic Archdiocese of Brisbane, which sold it again in 1952. Amusements included a steam train, Ferris wheel, sideshows and car-rides as well as a salt-water swimming pool.

The front of the cinema, Pier Pictures—at Redcliffe, 1950—& situated amongst a group of tiny shops and the Advance Milk Bar and Café; so popular as 'haunts' for American GIs.

Luna Park, Redcliffe, 1962.

As local George Howes recalls the Luna Park establishment:

> Between the main street of Redcliffe and Sutton Beach, of course, there was an area down on the front there at the Oxley Memorial, which was Luna Park, and that was formed towards the end but not at the end of the War [1944]. I distinctly remember there were great aspirations for Luna Park, how it was going to be as big as Sydney's Luna Park and was going to be as big as Brighton in England! It's so amazing how local dignitaries can get carried away with those sorts of imaginations, but I never did...Having said all that, there were quite a lot of amusements down there...

Then Luna Park got going and there was a slippery dip going down from the Oxley Memorial. There was a chair-o-plane down the bottom; there was quite a big chair-o-plane and they even had the big Ferris wheel [and a shooting gallery] at one stage and a Merry-go-Round was over upon the side. I still remember it—this ride used to seem to be left in neutral at night. We'd go down there and you'd be able to push the Merry-go-Round around and start it up then hop on and have a ride, a free ride.

I remember one night there was an American guy trying to impress this lady with a baby and he said, "Come on you guys, let's push this merry-go-round, let's get it going" so my mate and I got round the opposite side to the American, hopped on and we got motivated by that guy—he was doing the whole legwork and we had a great time! It was all simple fun; it was very, very simple. It was an egalitarian society; nobody had very much money so you virtually made your own fun.

THE 'POST-WAR' PERIOD

Brisbane celebrations following World War II.   *Australian Senior.*

Hope is the thing with feathers that perches in the soul

And sings the tune without the words

And never stops at all.

Emily Dickinson

On August 15th, 1945, a nation's spirits were greatly lifted when Australia's Prime Minister, Mr Ben Chifley announced the end of World War II. Brisbanites took to the streets for what many in our capital city regarded as the greatest occasion of the twentieth century.

On 9th May of 1945, Australia had mildly celebrated VE Day, announced in the UK the previous day. It would be in August before any official Aussie events.

example, about 127 babies were born per 1,000 people.

War brides within Brisbane.
Thurman family photo.

A soldier with his sweetheart, 1945.
State Library of Queensland.

By 1945, and the end of war hostilities, people felt free and unburdened: peace had arrived. In this self-same year, 30 out of some 1,000 Australian newborns died; and 17 babies were born per 1,000 people. But the infant survival rates improved after 1946. By 1947, for

After the second World War, women, in true sexist mode, were urged to relinquish their daytime jobs, retreat back into the kitchen, and get themselves married; and 'conspire' to produce healthy offspring. This campaign proved eminently successful. The products of these unions were then publicly acclaimed; and the new 'baby boom' which ensued lasted several decades.

Between 1946 and 1964, nearly four million babies—called 'baby boomers'—were born in Australia. Overall, an unusually large number of men and women 'tied the knot' and started families. Everyone appeared to be having a child. Husbands and wives, reunited after the war, also extended their progeny. But the scars of World War II were everywhere.

Brisbane's bustling city centre, c. 1940s.
Courier-Mail.

Marriage after the war years. Marie Vaughan and her father on the way to her wedding ceremony.
Thurman family photo.

As people breathed huge sighs of relief at their new-found freedom, they wanted to give their children everything they'd perhaps missed out on—a better life for their offspring: home, school, a secure family and a car for outings. The greatest wealth was no longer contentment with just a little. Following the war, young people also had enough money to go out dancing; and attend 'shows' in the evening. It should be noted that they were the first generation to really do so. In fact, in 1945, women's wages were raised up to 75 per cent of male wages, so both sexes were free to enjoy nightly entertainment. It seems that each generation looks back at the previous one; and laughs about their method of communicating over big distances. Most people by now owned or had access to a telephone; and so many folk possessed cars, making "dates" with the opposite sex and visits to Cloudland unproblematic.

Bill Thurman and his bride, Marie Vaughan, signing the marriage register.
Thurman family photo.

'CLOUDLAND BALLROOM'

After the war was over, peace was again restored in the Western world, the Luna Park Camp name was then dropped from its position beside the word 'Cloudland'; and the edifice became known from then on as simply the 'Cloudland Ballroom'. Consequently, in the late 1940s, Cloudland Ballroom on Montpelier Hill became quite a popular rendezvous point for many post-war romances; and grand celebrations.

This two-and-a-half hectare Cloudland site was then purchased by two Sydney women—sisters Mya Winters and Frances Rouch for £16,000; and it reopened its doors on either the 24th or 26th of April, 1947—a date about which no one seems entirely certain, for weekly dances and social function occasions.

Following the dancehall's re-opening Roy Phillips managed the Cloudland Ballroom for the Rouch-Winters ownership, organising the venue's dances and social evening functions from 1947-1950. Billo Smith was our front of the house band from that time period until January 25th, 1957. From 1947 to 1960, annual Postal and 'Med Balls' were also a big feature of the venue's activities. A country/hillbilly artist, Cora Ruhe, also fulfilled a six month residency there, booked by her agent, Marshall Palmer. Finally, Miss Queensland and Miss Australia Quests reigned supreme.

This group of musicians was typical of those around Cloudland in the mid-to-late 1940s.
Sunday Mail.

A poster proclaiming the re-opening of Cloudland.
The Telegraph, 17th April, 1947.

Breathy versions of Fats Waller's 1936 classic *I'm Gonna Sit Right Down and Write Myself a Letter* again echoed around the walls of the relatively 'new' dancehall:

I'm gonna write words oh so sweet

They're gonna knock me off my feet

A lotta kisses on the bottom

I'll be glad I got 'em...

As one patron recalls those years in and after, 1947:

For 40 years it was the place to go in Brisbane if you wanted to woo a girl—or simply if you liked to spend all your Saturday nights showing off the latest dance steps.

Originally, the grand old dame was going to be an amusement park, but instead a huge ballroom with a landmark curved dome, reminiscent of the sails of the Opera House, went up on the site in the 1940s.

It enjoyed commanding 270-degree views, just the touch needed for a romantic night.

Such was its visual appeal that up to 500 tourists a week used to visit, mostly southerners on one-day excursions from their holiday base on the Gold Coast.

Although [mostly] closed during the war years, it bounced back in 1947 in time for the emergence of the 'radical' new dance moves imported from America, particularly the *jive*.

Throughout the 1940s, Cloudland Ballroom had hosted some 47 gatherings, together with dances and debutante balls.

As local commentator, David Gibson, confided "before Cloudland's paint started peeling and the majesty began to wear [in the early '80s], it was a place to heal and find love in post-war Brisbane". In fact, many a romance blossomed at regular dance events held at the ballroom during the post-war years.

Calvin Lowney traverses his memories to dredge up the post-war 'jitterbug' craze:

Do I remember Cloudland (*Viewpoint*, Oct., 20)? Do I ever. It was just after the war; the Yanks had gone but had left us their jitterbug dance. There was a section of the ballroom that was roped off where the "jitterbugs" could dance and not interfere with the ballroom dancers. We would listen to Billo Smith and his 25 piece orchestra and jive the night away. I used to borrow my dad's car so I could take a girl home if I got lucky. (*Courier-Mail*.)

A *side view* of Cloudland's entrance (1946).
Photo courtesy of "Odyssey".

The *front entrance* of Cloudland "in 1946, with all of its original glory". *N.B. The archway entrance was not present in World War II.*

Photo courtesy of "Odyssey".

'BILLO' SMITH AND HIS ORCHESTRA

Many famous musical artists, acts and bands appeared at Cloudland. This classy venue became a symbol of elegance, hosting numerous balls and evening dances. 'Billo' Smith was among the main musicians who performed at Cloudland. He had "worked at Cloudland from 1947 to 1957":

W. J. "Billo" Smith was born to professional musicians at Brisbane, Australia, in 1930. He studied piano from age five, but his musical career really began at 13 when he studied the clarinet with his father, a prominent Brisbane musician and band leader. At 17, Billo joined his father's 12 piece band at Cloudland Ballroom playing the sax and clarinet. Aspiring to a classical career, he won the Queensland clarinet championship at the Brisbane Eisteddfod in 1956. A scholarship to enter the New South Wales Conservatorium closely followed, where he studied clarinet, piano and was a principle (**sic**) member with that orchestra. Whilst there, he took up oboe, flute and double bass, playing for many classical recitals and sang (**sic**) in a Minotti opera. After two years full-time study he realised his forte lay in the jazz arena. In 1972 he moved to Queensland's Gold Coast where he teamed up with ex-Horrie Dargie men, Vern Moore and 'Doc' Bertram, to form a vocal and harmonica trio with the *Ted Preston Band*. Although retired

from playing, he is heavily involved in composing, arranging and publishing music in all styles.

"A couple dancing at Cloudland, ca. 1948. A photographic memento of one night out"…

John Frederick ('Bunny') Hodgins had also played the banjo with Billo Smith and his band for several years.

As 'Bunny' also remembers, "Billo Smith had come to Brisbane in 1925 from the *Sydney Cavalier*; and he had held the best jobs until 1957, first at the *Trocadero*; and, after the war at Cloudland Ballroom. As many as 2,000 dancers would pack the dance floor of the *Trocadero"*.

'Bunny' Hodgins, 24th June, 1972.

Dawn Lee was only a 'slip of a girl' when she 'chanced' by Cloudland to see her dad, John Blakeway, play trombone in Billo's band. Although he played the *Trocadero*, the *Ritz* and Cloudland, it was only at the latter that she was allowed to watch—and later dance to—his performances. Then, on reaching the age of 16, in 1948, Dawn could go along to the dances with her friends.

As she was still young during the immediate post-war years, Dawn did not miss out on Cloudland's mostly closed days during World War II.

At the ballroom, in the late 1940s, Dawn danced the various differently programmed event nights for a couple of days each week. There was always the consolation of a commemorative Cloudland photo with her own group of friends or dance partner.

When Billo and the band broke from playing for a well-needed vacation, Dawn holidayed with all the group's members, plus their families. She'd also lounge about the beach at Coolangatta, with Billo, his wife, Nessie, and their son, Billy.

As well as Billo's band, Harry and Don Lebler also played at the Bowen Hills venue as *Axiom and the Mixtures* during the late '60s and '70s.

'Billo' Smith.

Two of the local Queensland waltz tunes which may have been played at Cloudland in the late 1940s, published prior to 1930.
State Library of Queensland.

Sir Laurence and Lady Olivier.

Although Noel Coward, as I've already indicated, had visited Cloudland Ballroom in 1940, the playwright did not really have the

profile of 'Hollywood' stars, like Clark Gable and Laurence Olivier.

Sir Laurence and Lady Olivier out at a debutante ball in Brisbane, 1949.
Courier-Mail.

On September 2nd, 1948, Laurence Olivier and Vivien Leigh paid a visit to the venue at Cloudland, following a play performance of *School for Scandal* at a Debutante's Ball for the 'Royal Society of St George'.

Olivier had only recently been knighted but was not one to put on airs, which was just as well in egalitarian 1940s Queensland. He apparently even refused to talk to anyone who had addressed him as "sir" instead of plain old Larry.

The British glamour couple were in town in 1948 for the Old Vic Company's show *School for Scandal*.

His Majesty's Theatre was packed with a who's who of the city, described by the *Courier-Mail* as the "most brilliantly dressed audience since before the war".

Despite the subtropical heat the women were decked out in evening gowns, gloves and furs, many of which had no doubt been gathering dust in wardrobes for years.

Lady Olivier—talented actress Vivien Leigh—drew "oohs", "aahs" and remarks like "doesn't she look beautiful" when she arrived in a striking black gown.

There was thunderous applause when Sir Larry gave a courtly bow to the audience and told them: "We have travelled many thousands of miles to come here and it is a joy to say welcome to the people of Queensland".

Near the completion of this decade, ballroom dancing championships returned to Cloudland and other major Australian cities:

A professional dance championship of Australia and New Zealand will be held this year for the first time since 1935. State and New Zealand couples will compete in Sydney on December 1.

Queensland representatives will be chosen at a dance festival at Cloudland Ballroom, Brisbane next Saturday afternoon. (*Courier-Mail*, November 2nd, 1949.)

A policeman directs some vehicles across the Victoria Bridge, Brisbane, April, 1940.

6
'BODGIES' AND 'WIDGIES'

THE 1950s: A DEFINING DECADE

Robert Menzies.

The 1950s was a decade of rock'n'roll music, milk bars, peace following two previous world conflicts, a baby boom; and black and white television. Following the war years and well into the decade of the '50s, Australia's Prime Minister, Robert Menzies, wanted to produce a nation of strong, self-reliant people.

By September 22nd, 1955, the population of Brisbane had reached 500,000; and there were a record number of births in Australia during 1958: 222,540. In 1959, towards the last part of this decade, television had also arrived, although we watched the Melbourne Olympics on a rental set in 1956.

Despite changes to the social and cultural landscape, Australia within the 1950s was largely built on 'a cup of tea, a Bex, and a good lie down'. Brisbane, of course, was no exception. Sunday was usually a quiet, brooding kind of day. It was a day of rest, the customary meal or religious observance. As dawn broke, the roosters in the chook pens all across the suburbs performed an oratorio of joint crowing, beckoning us all to rise from our deep slumber. Few shops were open, but sport was played. Most folk would rise late as a family, perhaps visit relatives and then attend church. Sunday school included singing and also various scripture lessons. Sometimes, children visited the larger church to receive prizes, exchange gifts or to display their work.

REMEMBER WHEN?... the 1950s in Brisbane.

Although Brisbane in the 1950s could frequently be described as 'one-dimensional', it was generally a place where there could often be a limited tolerance of differences. Some observers even spoke of the 'long 1950s', a time that in a certain 'neck of the woods' in this country had been said to last until *ca.*1967. Ever since the Australian entertainer, Barry Humphries, had 'savaged' suburban Melbourne in the 1950s, some sophisticated observers have also assumed that a house with a yard and garden do not quite gel with everything that is 'hip' and 'happening' in the now. But many audience members who had

witnessed Barry's skits back then emitted a belly laugh and had all returned to their happy domiciles— in the suburbs.

Barry Humphries (Edna Everage) and Barry Crocker in *The Adventures of Barry McKenzie.*

The Australian.

Like Humphries' Melbourne, Brisbane was a city of verdant, expansive suburbs in the 1950s, the time I was growing up and attending school. In the crowded inner city suburbs, the creamy or white painted houses, with their light galvanised crimson or grey-hipped roofs—myriads of them—flourished on both sides of the winding Brisbane River, only separated by the occasional tree or so from their neighbours. Further afield, on the various reaches of the river, or in its surrounding hills, or else on its timbered slopes, nestled the houses of the outer suburbs.

ᴱENTERTAINMENT, 1950s-STYLE

Bill Thurman and Marie Vaughan, dressed to impress at the dances, 1950s.

Johnny O'Keefe in concert: the 'Wild One'.

Cloudland was the venue where Australian bands from the 1950s to the early 1980s played regularly. In truth, because it was an old-time/pop/rock/punk/musical entertainment venue, the ballroom hosted literally many thousands of dances and band concerts in the 1950s, '60s, '70s and early '80s, including a number of significant events. Several 'Aussie' stars of the rock'n'roll era entertained at Cloudland, including Normie Rowe and Johnny O'Keefe. It was also lucky enough, for instance, to host two of the six concerts played by rock'n'roll legend Buddy Holly on his only Australian tour in February, 1958.

Cyril Kerr managed Cloudland Ballroom from 1950 to 1954. Within October of 1954 Apel & Sons purchased Cloudland Ballroom for only £20,000 from Winters & Rouch. H. R. Apel then managed the venue from 1954 through to February of 1964. In this same period, Apel developed a scheme in 1962 to construct the 'Panorama Room' adjacent to Cloudland for his various entertainment functions.

From the mid-1950s—

Vince Hardiger played lead trumpet in the *Billo Smith Orchestra* three times a week. His first gig was in 1954 and he remembers Saturday nights where up to 2,000 people filled the dance floor. Vince says it was a joy to play and watch the action from his prime vantage point. He's now 85 years old and still regularly picks up his trumpet.

Chas Walker used to dance at Cloudland in the fifties, but confesses he always longed to be on stage with the orchestra. He played alto tenor and baritone sax and says the big band era was [huge] fun for the musicians of Cloudland who were all great mates. Chas also met his wife at Cloudland.

On January 25th, 1957, Billo Smith had handed over his band control to Frankie Thornton.

Messrs. 'Billo' Smith, Hans Apel and Frankie Thornton, in 1957.

Courier-Mail.

The interior of Cloudland Dance Hall, Bowen Hills, 1950.

John Oxley Library.

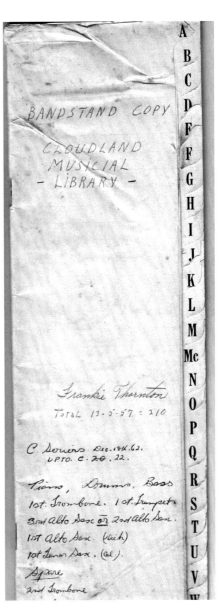

A playlist from Mr Frank Thornton's band, the late 1950s.

Ege Snook & the Apel family.

Another happy customer from those 1950s, Bev Bailey, also reminisces about these good old days:

Thank you all for those lovely memories of my "other home"—Cloudland. I was involved in my Ballroom dancing with the studio of Dick and Noela Orchard for many years and spent almost all my free nights at Cloudland in the early '50s. Many nights my cousin and I walked home when we missed the last tram to Kedron. Never had any fears—what a lovely era. One of the members of the band, the late great Eric Hall, who played alto sax and clarinet, worked with me in the insurance industry; and brought the dancers to the edge of the stage when he and Harry Lebler played the *Golden Wedding*—what a band with Billo Smith and Nessie—ah!! those certainly were the days.

Though at Cloudland for a vastly different reason, Rod Laver has latterly "cast an eye over Brisbane's increasingly cluttered skyline, mentally floated back into his teenage years, and then asked: 'Whatever happened to Cloudland'?" He had remembered going and seeing the American Calypso King, Harry Belafonte, at the iconic ballroom.

One keen observer with an eye for nostalgia remembers her family stories about Cloudland Ballroom in the 1950s:

My introduction to Brisbane's Cloudland Ballroom took place sometime during the '50s when, from the front veranda of my aunt's home on the north side, I became fascinated by that brightly coloured arch perched above the inner city suburb of Bowen Hills. The arch was attached to a majestic ballroom which beckoned romantic dancers; and those emerging rock'n'rollers to colonnaded alcoves, [its] floating dance floor and the panoramic views of the city, such as it then was.

Often, the after-dinner conversation held around my aunt's table included references to Cloudland and to the various couples who had encountered their futures there of a Saturday night within the early years of the war and just after. There were photographs of my Uncle Jack with his beautiful young bride, Alma, shown sitting on a crescent moon against a backdrop of twinkling stars.

Norma Hourigan also recalls Cloudland fondly:

Because I was fond of dancing, I'd gone out with girlfriends to Cloudland Ballroom and Len came up behind me and asked me to dance. A year later I had met him again at Cloudland! He then asked could he write to me and that's how our courtship began. We were married in St Anne's Presbyterian Church in 1955.

Len and Norma Hourigan.

Taking his management duties at Cloudland seriously, Hans Apel set about to dress up the ballroom as best he could: by repainting Cloudland both inside and out; building a new ticket box; a foyer was installed; the interior décor was enhanced; and the royal blue and gilt ceiling was repainted. Over time, major quests such as Miss Queensland and Miss Australia would be decided there, and so would the Queensland 'rock'n'roll dance championship' on June 5th, 1957. In fact, one of the largest 'big bands' seen at the venue after its welcome 'facelift' was Tony Cornwall and *The Knights* on April 2nd, 1958.

'BODGIES' AND 'WIDGIES'

'Widgies' at a car rally.

distinctive teen culture. They came to this latter part of the decade as consumers and money spenders—a new commercial target group—splashing out on things such as records, clothes, cosmetics and also travelling to the movies. One film in particular, together with its sound track, helped to create the initial stirrings of children's obsessions about rock'n'roll.

When the 1950s commenced there really wasn't any such official 'animal' as a teenager. Then, from about 1953, and as the decade drew to a close, people of that age not only had a monicker now, but they also possessed a voice and an identity, inventing their very own

Sinatra, Pat Boone and Connie Francis. Around March of 1955, I drove visitors to our Heaslop Terrace home in Annerley mad with my 'apeing' of Johnny Ray 'crying' (handkerchief and all). I had loved the way he was mobbed in all the places where he performed that month around Australia.

The new picture, *Blackboard Jungle*, starred Sidney Poitier and received its thrust from a stirring song along with a thumping beat entitled *Rock Around the Clock* performed by 'Bill Haley and the Comets'. Gob-smacked teenagers were now suddenly riveted to the excitement of this new type of music. It seemed primitive, like a kind of jungle sound. Up to this time, I had thought rock music was a version of my grandma's old rocking chair lullabies.

Johnny Ray at the Brisbane Stadium.
Courier-Mail.

Two covers (45 r.p.m.) for Bill Haley's Rock Around the Clock.

Before this Haley hit record on the music charts, the pop music 'scene' had been inhabited by artists who appealed more to adults than to teenagers—like Nat King Cole, Perry Como, Doris Day, Frank

From around this time of 1954-5, Bill Hayley's *Rock Around the Clock* was screening continually at the *Tivoli*. Rock'n'Roll had arrived in Brisbane. The 'City Fathers' had already begun to speak about some family breakdowns and poor behaviour. Police were now to be on the lookout for 'Bodgies' and 'Widgies'. Emotions also ran high when Australia's local version of Elvis Presley, Johnny O'Keefe, "blew in from Sydney".

Elvis Presley in a recording studio.

Bill Haley and the Comets letting their hair down to Rock Around the Clock, all the rage during [the 1950s].

Courier-Mail.

It appears that any *'bodgies'* were the 'Aussie' equivalent of the UK's 'teddy' boys and of American 'biker' boys. In essence the name had derived from the slang term "bodgy", which means an imitation or bogus. So, in effect, our own teenagers were viewed as bodgie versions of US teens. Yet no standard or satisfactory explanation for the odd term *'widgie'* has ever surfaced in this country.

In January of 1957, by now one of rock'n'roll original all-stars, Bill Haley, with his band the *Comets,* provided full-on, back beat rock concerts to a gasping Australian public. He had recorded *Rock Around the Clock* in 1954; and we'd all seen the movie *Blackboard Jungle* by then which featured the song. *Rock Around the Clock* quickly outstripped the very first 45 r.p.m. record released and sold in Australia the very same year—Darryl Stewart's, *A Man Called Peter.*

On January 10th, 1957, the *Courier-Mail* trumpeted:

Bill Haley and his *Comets* shook a packed [audience] into convulsive movement at the climax of their rock'n'roll concert last night.

Teenagers and some older men and women had clapped, fluttered their arms, gyrated their knees and jigged their heels. Whole rows of the audience swayed in rhythmic unison from side to side, stamping and singing in time with the band. But there were no real attempts to dance or to start a rush. An estimated 10,000 people or so attended last night's concert.

Patrons paid 9/6d. and 39/6d. admission for the Bill Haley concert, quite a sizeable amount at that time.

In milk and coffee bars, and, on record players at home, the decade's brand new seven-inch EP records had made the throbbing strains of the music last so much longer. Various types of apparel and behaviour led to some separate hordes and different cults. Brisbane, no less now, still had their 'bodgies' and their 'widgies'.

This 'phenomenon' of teens, as it was to be called later, was once defined as:

Bodgie, noun, colloq. (esp. in the 1950s), one of a group of mostly young men usually dressed in an extreme fashion, esp. tight trousers and slicked-back hair, and given to wild, delinquent behaviour. **Widgies** were their girlfriends, & of similar sartorial and social inclinations.

The 'establishment's' anger towards bodgie and widgie dress was loud and extremely vocal, especially when Elvis begged *Don't Be Cruel*, Little Richard presented *Long Tall Sally* and Carl Perkins put on his *Blue Suede Shoes*. Surfing in the wake of rock'n'roll music, bodgie and widgie exponents were quite keen to take in Chuck Berry's pretty sound advice: '*Gotta be rock'n'roll music if you wanna dance with me*'.

The 'rise' of a brand new sub-culture, 'bodgies' and 'widgies'. *Courier-Mail*. Picture research: Gwen McLachlan.

In the city, some of my older friends had graduated to the flashy, bodgie look. Several of them now wore tight black 'cigarette legs' or 'stove-pipe' trousers and loose-fitting jackets. Sometimes they had appeared in skinny black ties. A few widgies wore white blouses, flared skirts and high heels. Some said they were now 'all the rage'. As we were on the verge of the 'swinging sixties', life as we had known it had changed markedly.

This emotive letter to the editor of the *Courier-Mail* by G. A. Dredge of Wooloowin, in 1951, summed up some parents' points of view about the change to Brisbane's social fabric. (Of course, others stressed that adults were caught up in "old-fashioned moral panic" and that there was no need to feel concerned.)

I am in complete agreement with those deploring the state into which [our] modern youth seems to be drifting. I am not really perturbed by the jitterbug antics, having learnt by this time to tolerate their actions. It is the mode of dress which moves me most. From surface appearance it is almost impossible to tell most of the[se] effeminate boys from their female counterparts, both wear baggy trousers which [all] finish slightly below the knee. Some of the females who wear skirts look as if they employ a shoehorn to get into them. Faces of all are usually imbecilic and devoid of all expression, contorted only by jaws masticating gum. They all speak a language indecipherable to the average Australian and leave myself and many others completely disgusted.

And again:

A taxi driver told me that since the police started to break up the groups of bodgies and widgies who stood around well-lighted milk bars, he and other taxi drivers have seen the results. They often drive these young people to dark parks where they drink intoxicating liquor and are so helpless when driven home afterwards. Surely here is the opportunity for some church organisation to do something for these unfortunate young boys and girls, many of them belonging to broken homes. Couldn't milk bars be run especially for them so that, even if they were a bit too noisy, that could surely be controlled? They would be enjoying themselves together, in their own way, instead of being forced to take strong drink, and then be much harder to approach. Wouldn't it be worthwhile to show them that they would be welcomed at a milk bar instead of being moved on continually as undesirable, with dire results?

Another individual, this time a father, was so exhausted after a teen's birthday celebrations:

Being an indulgent father, I turned back the carpet, then gave them a pound or two for some new records. What I witnessed makes it clear that they all need psychiatric attention.

"It went on to the early hours and they seemed to finish in a daze, a dancing daze".

Another man chimed in: "If you would only read a little world history, you would understand young people.

"Dancing excitements have been with us down the years. Have you, for instance, heard of the *tarantella*?"

"It's a dance, and 500 years ago it became a mania. The young people danced it with complete abandon until they fell to the ground exhausted.

"The *tarantella* went on its merry way for 300 years".

The father asked: "You mean *rock'n'roll* could go on forever?"

"No", countered the other man.

"The young people of today are more sensible, better educated; and healthier than any young person the world has yet known".

For boys, the bodgie dress could be duck-tail hair style cuts and tailored clothes such as tight suits and long hairy jumpers; and then there were, needless to say, those strange pointed-toe winkle-picker brogues. Hairstyles for the bodgies involved lot of grease, short hair on the sides and some length on the top. With regard to girl 'widgies', they had 'rocked up' to events in their skimpy tops, sparkly dresses, poodle skirts, with wide belts and lurid make-up.

As Tony Lathouras of Sunnybank recalled in the local newspaper:

I was a pre-rock'n'roll (about ten years from 1945) bodgie who married a widgie. Male dress was double-breasted draped suits with the pleated trousers and pegged cuffs, white shirts and loud windsor-knot ties. You could not buy the suits ready-made so they [all] had to be tailored. The widgies wore mid-length dresses with cork platform ankle-strapped shoes.

Older people in this era, as I've already indicated, were certainly afraid of the effects of the rock'n'roll concerts and music upon their young. They feared an 'outbreak' of juvenile delinquency: an 'orgy' of rock'n'roll immersion; kissing, dancing and drinking; and going to wild parties. The elderly did not want the young to develop bad habits or head in the wrong social directions. Especially with the threat of the Cold War and nuclear weapons being held over Queenslanders' heads, many believed it would be foolhardy to liberally unleash an emerging rebellious youth culture on an already worried public.

However, as far as Cloudland was concerned, the 'bodgie' and 'widgie' influence through 'jiving' would affect the dance crazes there for decades until the early 1980s.

ROCK'N'ROLL GEORGE:
THE ORIGINAL 'BODGIE'

It's the eye of the tiger

It's the thrill of the fight

Risin' up to the challenge

Of our rival

And the last known survivor

Stalks his prey in the night

And he's watching us all

With the eye of the tiger.

Frank Sullivan, *Eye of the Tiger.*

George Kyprios' nickname, "Rock'n'Roll George, was linked to those heady days of the original Cloudland. Evidently, he "used to go there to dance. Some guy had made up a number plate with 'Rock'n'Roll'; and it was believed that this moniker was connected to the type of dancing existing at Cloudland. From there the name stuck". George "was a reminder of a nicer and more gentle time, when [people would] go through the city [and to Cloudland] and have a good time".

George's FX Holden parked in Queen Street, Brisbane.

No one created interest or city excitement more than this inimitable character of George, harmlessly cruising Queen Street and West End during Brisbane's late

1950s, 1960s and 1970s, 'doing the rounds' every Saturday night in his fox-tail adorned 1952 FX Holden Special. George's 'station' "was just outside the *Black Cat Casket Agency*, which used to be on the corner of Queen and Albert Streets, where *Hungry Jacks* now stands. There he stood, arms folded, admiring the passing female "scenery". He wore neatly pressed stove-pipe trousers, defiant of fashion trends, well [past the 1950s and] into 2009. George also possessed a different pair of brightly coloured stove-pipe pants for every day of the week which he had made so acceptable well into Brisbane's post-Cloudland future. Clearly, he became stuck in a time warp and he adored being there.

Rock and Roll George outside the old New York Hotel in Queen Street in the *ca.* 1980s.
David May.

George Kyprios was such an iconic figure and feature of Brisbane's social landscape he 'inspired' the 1960s song Rock'n'Roll George. "*Up and down Queen Street/ past the City Hall/ who's that in the driver's seat/ it's Rock'n'Roll George*".

George represented something timeless: regular as clockwork he cruised the city, with radio blaring and [also] wearing his trademark stove-pipe trousers. As he and the car aged George became a local legend, a classic 'character' who was a constant in a city undergoing rapid and irreversible change. To fill in the gaps in the mystery about just who this old rock'n'roller was, [many] stories emerged around George. Fact and fiction became part of the mystique (Brisbane Museum).

A local barber, Bill Diacos, says he cut George's locks for three decades at his West End establishment.

[George], who was born and raised in the suburb, would visit up to seven times a day for a chat. He was a very independent person. If he liked somebody he was generous and talkative, but if he did not like you he was angry and gruff. But he was a lovely, lovely man.

John La Motta also claims he cut George's hair in the city:

John...started working for the original Col Naylor in the city in 1948. This is when he started cutting George's hair. When he opened his own shop in 1959, George had followed him. My father cut his hair every fortnight for the following 30 years. When my father [John] had retired in 1989, I cut George's hair for the next three years until we closed our door for a redevelopment (Joseph La Motta).

Peter Young recalls Rock'n'Roll George in the early 1970s 'cruising' Adelaide Street:

I was driving the Brisbane City Council buses. I would appear in a blue *Leyland Panther* (one of "Clem's Clippers"), give George a toot and he would do his best to get out of the way. All the bus drivers knew him and would wave. It was the same in the '80s and the '90s when I was driving cabs.

There would be George—ever the gentleman and always trying not to get in the way of those trying to earn a living.

I'd known the end was so near, I'd have a moment out of a hectic inner city scramble to wish him well for what was just around the corner.

This busy thoroughfare of Queen Street, redesigned in 1982 into a pedestrian mall.

Rock and roll dancing—comparable to that at Cloudland.

It was the end of an era in post-Cloudland Brisbane with the death and funeral of Rock'n'Roll George Kyprios, the youngest of nine children. George, a splendid fixture against the city's skyline, passed away on Sunday, November 29th, 2009, ages 82. His funeral was held on Thursday, 3rd December, at the Greek Orthodox Church in South Brisbane. There had been a lot of changes to Queensland's capital city since George's heyday. As we know, the original Cloudland venue, where he had danced the sultry nights away, had long ago been bulldozed. Queen Street, where he paraded in his Holden, had been transformed into a pedestrian mall and shopping strip.

Rock and Roll George's 1952 FX Holden performing its final lap of honour in around Brisbane's CBD. Photo: Tony Moore.

As 'Mata Harif' recalls:

Until a week ago [in November, 2009], the forlorn and wafer-thin figure of George could be seen most afternoons at the entrance to the Myer Centre...Sad as he was, the wonderful rock'n'roll attitude George had, still prevailed. If only

Following tributes to George from his fellow Queenslanders, the then Lord Mayor, Cr. Campbell Newman, requested that Rock'n'Roll George's famous vehicle be saved for the people of Brisbane, if George Kyprios' family and friends consented to the idea.

I would like to get it for the Museum of Brisbane, but one of my practical problems would be that I don't know where to put it. We don't have room for it, but I think that it would be fantastic, if the family were onside. It should be saved. George is an iconic figure and he will be greatly missed... George's great nephew, Michael Anastas, said the Holden should remain linked to the family, but were (*sic*) not against the idea of the car being used in some ideal way to preserve [George's] memory...[It should remain in the family, however, to be used in such a way that would allow George's own memory to live on as a tribute. It has close connections with the family and we would like to see it remain in the family, but to be used in a way—with appropriate partners—to recognise the man who he was and for his memory to live on.

The famous car was bought for George by his mother to try to wean him away from football at the Souths Rugby League Club at West End. He played for Souths as a winger and he used to get bronchitis every time he played. His mother said: "If you stop playing football I will buy you a car and that was the *first one* off the production line".

No doubt, one of Brisbane and Cloudland's great characters and his unique legacy to the city's rock'n'roll past will be suitably honoured sometime soon as Jack and Scott Hutchinson purchased George's famous car. It is now on loan to the Queensland Museum. A 1952 FX Holden built at Eagers at Newstead was also bought by the Hutchinsons as a replica of George's original. It was probably a 1948 model which went from '48 to 1952.

A storm brews over Brisbane suburbs, 1950s.   *Courier-Mail.*

7
BUDDY HOLLY, CLOUDLAND, FEBRUARY, 1958

A 'portable' record player of the 1950s.

REFLECTIONS ABOUT CLOUDLAND FROM THE 1950S

When Elvis Presley started in the 1950s, people were saying that his music was going to destroy society.

William Bor

With rock music top of mind for most teenagers and young adults within the 1950s, Cloudland Ballroom 'hotted up' as a 'must visit' dance venue.

Then things really got wild as Chubby Checker, Elvis Presley, Johnny O'Keefe, Johnny Ray and other purveyors of rock'n'roll unleashed a revolutionary type of music and dancing on an eager new generation.

The young funsters were kept roped off in a special section of the huge dance floor—reputed to be the biggest in Australia—in case their flailing limbs caused injuries to more sedate dancers. (*Courier-Mail*.)

Some Rock and Roll moves, Brisbane-style
Courier-Mail.

Two views of Cloudland Ballroom.
Brisbane City Council.

It was Colin Giese who had become the 'Jive King of Cloudland', a popular vote by all the ladies lined up to catch just a dance or two with him. Unfortunately, even Colin's wife had a hard time getting a dance slot with him on some evenings.

At least one keen observer, "Sour Sixteen", from Stanthorpe, saw the

worth of such social gatherings as those on the hill at Bowen Hills for young people:

> Why do so many people believe they can reform bodgies by forming youth clubs, etc. These represent the very things teenagers hate—organisation and adult supervision—and anyway, who wants to do handstands and play leapfrog? I think the teenage cabaret idea is very worthy and many more of these "nightclubs" should be formed. They encourage teenagers to act like adults and give them a place to meet which is entirely their own, yet off the street. They find the absence of a whinging adult very refreshing. (*Courier-Mail.*)

Don Carlos of Brisbane recalls issues between national servicemen, 'Nashos', with the Brisbane community:

> Half a dozen men in Army uniforms stood in the midst of the crowd that had gathered at the front of the City Hall to meet the New Year. Not satisfied with making loud remarks and behaving like badly brought-up children, these Aussie soldiers manifested complete lack of respect for religion (and the freedom of worship for which they are supposed to fight) by ridiculing the hymn singing and the prayers of an elderly minister. There are many fine young men in the Australian Army, boys who not only are willing to fight and die for the uplift of Australia, but—which is just as important—live and do all their utmost to contribute towards a better Australia. The uniform does not entitle a man to abuse another or to disrespect young women. On the contrary, the man in uniform should always bear in mind that he is an example for the young generation. Furthermore, if he wishes others to respect his uniform, he must respect it himself.

Timothy Kelly, in an article 'Memories of Cloudland', recalls his experiences in 1957 as a 'Nasho', taking on the bodgies in a fist fight:

My mate Bill Blackburn can hardly recognise me in my Nasho uniform. He's looking pretty pleased with himself in his Country Club shirt and Sixty Minute slacks. I'd be looking Ivy League too if I hadn't been called up to do National Service.

We all catch the tram from Adelaide Street and then pass through the Valley. We are travelling on down Breakfast Creek Road and so Billy's giving me a hard time about having to live out at the Wacol Barracks. I don't mind as I have only got another month to serve. With a mischievous smile he then raises his leg to reveal a hip flask in his sock. Knowing Billy, there's also another one in his other sock. They will both contain gin as it mixes well with any of the legal drinks available at these Cloudland dances. We get off at the foot of Cintra Hill and board the finucula [sic] railway. It creaks and shudders as it's hauled to the top of the hill by cables.

Peter Ray has been waiting for us in at the entrance to the ballroom. He takes off through the gardens in search of a place to stash his grog. As I watch him wander around all the shrubs and fish ponds, I imagine what the area would have looked like if the original idea for an amusement park had gone ahead.

Moreover:

Cops and bouncers in dicky-shirts watch us suspiciously as we join the lines of people entering under the shell-like archway. Inside, Billo Smith is leading the band through a [great] mixture of Rock'n'Roll and swing tunes. There's no *Pride of Erin* tonight; just Glen Miller, Arty Shaw and Bill Hayley songs all night.

Girls in hoop skirts jive with Ivy leaguers and Nashos. They all go sliding around on the sprung dance-floor which has been covered with "pops" to make it slipperier. Tonight, as usual, an army of greasy-haired bodgies patrols the room looking for trouble.

The opening bars of the *Golden Wedding* bring everyone to a standstill. They applaud the trumpet solo and go wild for Harry Lebler on drums solo who, until now, has shown great restraint. Then dancing resumes for the *quickstep* and the *fox trot*. I am reminded of a night when the floor actually collapsed during a *Gypsy Tap*.

Women sit on green upholstered chairs waiting to be asked to dance. Although I'm feeling confident in my Nasho uniform I decide to first hunt down Billy for a swig of Dutch courage. I find him in one of the alcoves sitting at a table with two jugs of orange juice. Every now and then he bobs under the table with one of the jugs and he emerges smiling.

Tim continues:

Despite the usual police presence, the bodgies are still making trouble. Three of them are pushing a Nasho around in the centre of the dance floor. I've now only been in the National Service for two months, but I feel a stirring of loyalty. So I'm in. Soon every Nasho and Bodgie had joined the fight. This time the bodgies were [well] outnumbered by belt-wielding Nashos.

In the watch-house I see Peter Ray sitting alone in the corner of the cell. Apparently, the cops got a bit suspicious of his leaving the ballroom every twenty minutes. He had been charged under the Liquor Act which states it's illegal to drink and dance at the same time. We will be let out in an hour, but for us the night is over.

A typical Nasho uniform of the 1950s.

June Adamson in her work, *Don't Rock the Boat,* never experienced 'bodgies' versus Nashos' at Cloudland, but has some interesting insights about why there may have been trouble at the dancehall:

Though I have heard accounts of clashes between bodgies and the Nashos at Cloudland, I never saw any of this myself. It's likely that it did happen, as that's the nature of tightly aligned groups with inflexible beliefs, but as so many Nashos had been bodgies and were waiting for their term of enlistment to end, it may have been that the beer was talking. Is it not the worldwide truth that chauvinistic uniforms and very uncompromising loyalties meant to unite, whether the drab khaki/green uniforms or garish football club jerseys, usually end up provoking greater conflict?...

The National Service Act of 1951 had been introduced following Communist insurgency in S. E. Asia and the declaration of war in Korea, targeting boys of eighteen years of age and enlisting them in the Citizens Military Forces. This met with a mixed reception from those boys involved; some enthusiastically threw themselves into the CMF experience; others merely endured [it]; but what a shock for some of my jiving friends when they found themselves suddenly in the ranks of Nashos, uniformed accordingly for six months or so while billeted at Wacol Army Camp or Amberley for the Air Force lads.

Smart threads were discarded temporarily and now replaced with coarse khaki; duck's-arse haircuts and side-burns trembled as they lined up to be converted by the scissors of the smirking Army shearers into no-nonsense short back and sides; twinkling dance feet were well and truly grounded in clumsy boots. Two of the happiest and the most accomplished of our jiving friends, Tommie and Alfie, almost unrecognisable without their sideburns and trendy gear, had turned up at Cloudland only a couple of times and sat with us, suddenly quiet and self-conscious, unwilling to take to the dance floor in their shapeless khaki and old-man haircuts. They just wanted the National Service to be over and some boys didn't turn up again in public until after their stint of service when their own clothes were upon their backs and their hairstyles regrown.

Naturally, incidents and unusual behaviour was not the sole province of the blokes at Cloudland. As June Adamson again reveals:

Of course there were other scandals. Helen had a well-earned reputation for being very easy. We all knew her, as when she'd been a Grammar School pupil she'd always carried a large Art portfolio with her phone number prominently displayed in over-size print when she passed the boys' school.

I watched her strut unsteadily into the ballroom one Saturday evening and knew she was primed for trouble. She was hyper-active, a blonde time bomb looking for action, a little under the weather I guessed, and wearing a tiny full skirt and a very skimpy one-shoulder top. Restlessly, she'd paced the edges of that dance floor, a little eddy of excitement surrounding her. It was impossible to ignore Helen as she just radiated "something". Her outfit in itself was a little daring but when the evening got under way and she jived and jumped, the bare-shouldered top rolled down and had exposed—not the rigid conical cotton brassiere that modesty and the fifties decreed—but a bare white breast and pink nipple!! No brassiere!! The word was out.

What a bonus for the males, many who'd never seen a real breast on public display, who formed a circle and had cheered or waited as Helen hoisted the top back into position before soon shimmying it down again. Even the police officers on duty as security found it necessary to join the circle; no doubt they found it onerous but hey, some-one had to do it, didn't they? Everyone watched to see who'd "take Helen home" that evening!

ᴀN IMMIGRANT'S TALE

In my book, *From Olive Grove to Eucalyptus Tree: An immigrant family in baby boomer Australia,* a work of fiction, I detail the lives of the De Falla family of New Farm, Brisbane, during the Cloudland era. Isabella De Falla recounts here her vivid memories of the ballroom:

In the period following my 'Deb' appearance it was apparent to everyone who attended, and even to their new partners post-ball, that we'd all seek to continue our general dancing. Within Brisbane, there was, unquestionably, no rival to Cloudland.

Folk of all 'persuasions' and from the various walks of life had 'rocked up' to Cloudland. Pretty much rigged out like our debs, the girls in white gloves and organza dresses danced at the palace *on top of the hill. Then there were the bodgies,* widgies and the so-called teeny boppers, rather like myself and Avra at the time. Patrons would show off their *waltz* steps*, jive* (which was legendary in its day),

rock'n'roll, hop and so many other dance moves and crazes around the period. The young ones had to make allowances for the 'oldies', so to speak, so the dance floor was cordoned off accordingly.

The Saturday night dances at Cloudland offered the huge open ballroom, the cute landmark curved dome (similar to the sails of the Sydney Opera House) and 270° views of the city. It also offered Billo Smith and his 25-piece orchestra. If I saw someone who looked a bit like 'Little Joe' in the television show *Bonanza*, combing his hair or appearing with shiny brilliantine on his straight auburn or black locks, waved and shaped at the back, I'd sidle straight up and talk to him; perhaps even more so if he showed me that sleep-eyed James Dean disinterested look, as only lads on the brink of manhood revealed. If he also had an accent, and was a former immigrant, like I was, I would even be more interested. Among the girls' hooped skirts across the room, and the boys' suits on the other, I'd sense his presence on the dance floor.

"By this stage of my young adulthood I'd borrow Dad's car so I could drive up to Mount Coot-tha with my find if I was lucky, or if Avra had danced enough and needed a lift home. Of course, I was always on my 'mettle' if I paired with someone. I'd heard many a baby had been born as a result of a night at this place called Cloudland. But my resolve at the time was that my life was about to begin, what on earth could cause it pain?"

A typical night-time dance.

Flipping out rock'n'roll dancers, Cloudland Ballroom, performing acrobatic feats to their music during 1957.

Courier-Mail.

IT'S ONLY ROCK'N'ROLL, BUT I LIKE IT...

Earl Lloyd (Tich) Bray, a sax/flute/ band leader at Cloudland in the late 1950s, 1960s.

Brian King, pianist, vocal entertainer and composer, Cloudland, in the late 1950s, 1960s.

The era between World War II and rock'n'roll's arrival at Brisbane dance venues marked a period of rapid social change in Australia. During the 1950s, the population of Queensland's capital city increased by one-quarter; automobile numbers had doubled; wages rose by half; as well, the cost of living increased; and individual debt suffered a four-fold increase. Though the rock phenomenon did not really emerge till some ten years after the war, the influence of American pop culture was prominent at this time. The sedate, pattern dancing of waltzes and foxtrots, stable Friday and Saturday ballroom events; and, traditional, big band music, were on the exit path. Such changes, as we've noted, were fanned by Bill Haley's appearance with the *Comets* at *The Stadium* (Brisbane) in January of 1957; and rock'n'roll generally with Jerry Lee Lewis, Buddy Holley, Little Richard and Chuck Berry.

The *Brisbane Stadium*, 1940s.

For quite a set period of the 1950s, the ballroom dancers at Cloudland had their own way as the jivers were discouraged:

Carol Shepherd remembers starting to go to dances in 1952. She was only about 15 years old and ballroom dancing was still in vogue. Cloudland was the place to be but the *Riverside Ballroom* in Oxlade Drive, New Farm, still figures so prominently in her memory. Both venues had an area roped off for people who wanted to do boogie-woogie. (*It was only Rock'n'Roll*, Geoff Walden.)

And again:

One night John and Aileen [McCourt], along with some friends, noticed at Cloudland that there was more room on the table to dance than what had been allocated to the jivers in the back corner.

AM: So on one night they were playing some rock'n'roll music and John had decided we didn't have enough room.

JM: They kept sending us all down to the corner and the only thing I could see with any room on it was a big eight-foot diameter table so we jumped up on that and were dancing.

AM: And then everybody followed us and we thought the police again for sure. So, the band stopped, and there must have been a dozen couples on different tables dancing, and putting on a bloody good show if I might say so; the ballroom dancers stopped to watch. Eventually we got off and went home and we thought that if the management finds out about all this, we may not be allowed back. But we sort of made an agreement that for one night a week, the whole floor would be given to jive. (*It was only Rock'n'Roll*, Geoff Walden.)

Gradually, as the momentum for change in dance styles grew in numbers and in enthusiasm,

Cloudland's dance promoters roped off an area two yards square at one end of the hall in those early days:

...Jan [Kerwin] lived at Carina and had a group of about eight friends with whom she used to go to dances. Tuesday night was Cloudland night and while she started the night in traditional dancing, she would always end up jiving in the roped-off area. There was a danger involved in this because she always wore her high heeled shoes, stockings, rope petticoats and a wide belt. (*It was only Rock 'n'Roll*, Geoff Walden.)

In her book *Don't Rock the Boat*, June Adamson also experienced much the same 'jive' fever:

...The action behind the rope appealed to me and I had just a few lessons at *Jack Busteeds* before launching myself onto the Cloudland jive scene where I had immediately felt at home. Behind the rope was where my friends and I preferred to be, with interesting boys with a bit of go in them; with rhythm and imagination who could jive up a big storm, often improvising as they went. These were the pegged-pants boys with duck-arsed haircuts, and shoes with soft thick soles colloquially known as brothel creepers and girls with swirling skirts and legs fake-tanned from bottles, as was the fashion. If not a swirling skirt then the opposite, a tight black sheath with a slit, still modest as the hem rested at the top of the knee.

Quiet music meant slow jiving and smooching, with many couples now sneaking away to canoodle outside on the upper balconies or a trip to the innocent soft-drink kiosk for something cold...

I often jived so long and energetically that the liquid fake-tan mixed up with sweat and dust and brown runnels seeped down my legs and into my shoes giving my petticoats inches of stained hemline on the way and making Mum's laundry-day more of a problem than it was already.

A blast of the same rousing jazz standard every week acted as the signal for the "Last Dance"—I think it was a version of Goodman's *Stomping at the Savoy* or *American Patrol*. As this signature tune blasted out the rope was removed and a jiving scrum took over the whole space. The sprung floor bounced under a sweaty sea of stamping feet; a colourful mosaic of skirts and shirts and gyrating bodies as innovators let fly with their latest jive interpretation.

By the last dance the pairing off had been negotiated; couples going steady strolled off together; girls with a new partner trying to tactfully elicit whether or not he had a car as "I'd rather be dead that be seen on public transport", both of them wondering what the rest of the night would bring.

Cloudland Ballroom, July, 1959.
Queensland State Archives.

Bands such as Billo Smith's at Cloudland were able to meet the initial challenge head on, offering music for jiving, jitterbugging or rock'n'roll in the mid-1950s. But their hearts were not in it. A new form of music and distinctive atmosphere needed to be incubated in Brisbane; so several new instruments, bands, musicians, music and venues came into vogue.

Cloudland approached the rock'n'roll challenge with relish. From 1956, they had advertised about a set of rock'n'roll competitions on Wednesday evenings (in the *Brisbane Telegraph*). This ended up as a final jive competition held on Wednesday, November 28th, 1956. In fact, Cloudland continued advertising rock'n'roll on Wednesday nights up until December 19th, 1956. They then showcased a different series of competitions in a new season up to the New Year of 1957; with a competition promoted by their new band director, Mr Frankie Thornton:

Music at Cloudland for much of the 1950s was supplied by Billo Smith's band. According to a report and photo in *The Courier-Mail* (25/01/57), Billo Smith had been the conductor of the Cloudland orchestra for 10 years when he retired from the job on the previous day. The photo depicted Mr Smith handing over the baton to Frank Thornton, oddly described in the article as an American saxophonist; and he had earlier been advertised as a headline act for the Rock'n'roll Festival held at the [Brisbane] *Stadium* on November 21st, 1956. Mr Smith did not favour the new styles of music and of dancing. According to the McCourts, "old Billo Smith wasn't greatly in love with us". He did well financially from all his time at Cloudland with his wife on piano; he was the band leader and his son played sax. (*It was only Rock'n'Roll*, Geoff Walden.)

After an initial opposition to this new rock trend, non-jiving patrons were also beginning to see its merits at Cloudland. Despite the new dance form's popularity, the pay for musicians during this period appeared to be 'lousy'. Allan Campbell of the *Dominoes* was only paid £3 a 'gig' in 1959. But it didn't take very long for rock music to catch on.

As Ron Carroll, the piano man of the *Rockettes* and later, *Blue Jeans*, recalls:

"We got banned from a few halls but not for long. By that time there were a dozen rock bands playing. You couldn't stop it. Big crowds came to Cloudland to see us and other bands such as *The Hucklebucks, The Planets* and *The Dominoes*".

"I'll always remember one night when Johnny O'Keefe was on the bill with us at Cloudland and he finished the night by getting up with the *Blue Jeans*. There were about a dozen musicians on the stage; the people were going crazy".

The *Blue Jeans* playing in Brisbane.

Toward the end of the 1950s, competition from up-and-coming new bands had led the *Planets* and the *Hucklebucks* to try to develop different sounds on the local Brisbane scene in Cloudland to match their overseas idols. The innovative *Hucklebucks* had devised tweeters for their performances by using empty eggshells. Similarly,

they developed woofers for their bass guitar by using an emu egg.

An early publicity still of *The Planets*.
Photo courtesy Rob Tonge. *It was only Rock'n'Roll,* Geoff Walden.

As the rock'n'roll dance and music craze took over Brisbane, it was not out of the ordinary for other bands to broach an old-fashioned rivalry:

Allan [Reed] remembers that at the same time the *Hucklebucks* and the *Dominoes* were playing at Cloudland the plan was to give these other bands a 'bit of a shake-up'. As was their wont at each gig, a coin was tossed to see which band went on first. This particular time it turned out to be the *Hucklebucks'* opportunity to commence the evening's proceedings. They started off with *Shake Rattle and Roll* and *Hippy Hippy Shake* and then produced this *"lovely big sound, huge booming bass. We could not get over it because nobody had a bass, nobody had a bass player"*. Hans Apel (the owner of Cloudland) and his son both came out on to the floor to look and listen while the crowd froze.

"You can just imagine the sound. It was unheard of, this glorious big bass coming through and my lead guitar screaming out there and we were really whacking it out. The crowd just roared." (Allan Reed.)

Huck Berry & *The Hucklebucks*.
Photo: Johnny James. *It was only Rock'n'Roll*, Geoff Walden.

Furthermore:

For a number of its years, Cloudland hired two bands to ensure there was non-stop music for the night. Such a situation was bound to lead to some competition and Allan Reed was again involved in some "good clean sabotage." Alan Campbell relates:

At Cloudland a few times the Hucklebucks used to play, and my band the Teenbeats, right, and Allan Reed couldn't play guitar very good, he'd just play E, A, B, that sort of thing. I can just see him playing E, A, B, you know. He got away with the chords because he had the personality and a good singer and he got away with it. He didn't like some of the music we played and he used to come on stage and walk behind the band. Don't forget in those days there were valve amplifiers and open valves and not covered in and he used to step on the valves and say, "Oh sorry about that boys". This happened a few times or broken, leads, you know, sabotage is the word. Fun sabotage. (Alan Campbell.)

The Teenbeats were not about to let the 'fun' stop there. At Cloudland we had a room at the back there where the entertainers just sit there and have a few each. Allan Reed used to like drinking a lot. He'd have his beer and go on stage. So one night we thought that we'd get

back at this bloody Allan Reed. So he drank his beer and went on stage and we were waiting for our set, so we decided to wee-wee in the bottle didn't we. And put the cap back on again. Fixed him up. He never did it again. That's the end of Allan Reed sabotaging our gear. It was fun. Clean fun. (Alan Campbell.) (*It was only Rock'n'Roll*, Geoff Walden.)

Given the *Bee Gees'* success and worldwide fame, it is also interesting to assess their competitive natures as the new rock music was advancing:

Darryl Wright remembers the Saturday afternoon talent quests that were held at Cloudland in 1959 with the *Hucklebucks* and the original *Dominoes* providing music. The brothers Gibb entered the quest one afternoon.

A friend of mine was standing near the stage at the time when they did their first appearance. Of course, the twins Robin and Maurice, were very young at the time, and Barry about 14 or 15. They went on stage and the local promoter said to them when they came off the stage, "That was a pretty good act fellas, but Barry, next time you come up here, make sure your little brothers wear shoes". They actually went on stage in bare feet. (Darryl Wright.) (*It was only Rock'n'Roll*, Geoff Walden.)

The new lads on the block... Barry (12); twins Maurice and Robin (9), in 1959, as the *Bee Gees*, promoting a rockabilly song. Picture: Jim Fenwich.

Courier-Mail.

At the end of 1959, Easter dances plus one on Tuesday, April 24th, at the Bowen Hills dancehall were advertised as a gigantic rock'n'roll 'rally'. The bands, *Gold Tones*, *Hucklebucks*, and the *Dominoes* were to assist in the proceedings. Similarly, the talented *Damsna Twins* were featured as harmony singers. Rock and roll was certainly here to stay at Cloudland in Brisbane!

BUDDY HOLLY AT CLOUDLAND

If people are going to like me, they'll just have to like me with my glasses on.

Buddy Holly

Buddy Holly with his guitar.

On Tuesday of January 28th, 1958, Buddy with the Lee Gordon tour finally left for Australia for a supposed six day tour, following an 'aborted' earlier attempt "when the engine on the plane (portentously perhaps!) failed":

Lee Gordon (born Leon Lazar Gevorshner, March 8th, 1923, died London, November 7th, 1963) was an American entrepreneur and rock and roll promoter who worked extensively in Australia in the late 1950s and the early 1960s. Gordon's jazz and rock'n'roll tours had a major impact on the Australian music scene and he also played [quite] a significant role in the early career of pioneering Australian rock'n'roll singer Johnny O'Keefe...

In February, 1958, Lee Gordon had promoted yet another ground breaking tour starring Buddy Holly & *The Crickets*, Jerry Lee Lewis and Paul Anka. By this time the old *Brisbane Stadium* had been demolished: but, its replacement, *Brisbane Festival Hall*, was still under construction, and the only venue suitable was the famous Cloudland Ballroom, which was located on top of a high ridge in the hills behind the city.

Buddy Holly and *The Crickets* commenced a twelve date, seven-day 'Lee Gordon World Hit Parade' tour of 'Down Under' upon Thursday, January 30th, along with Paul Anka, Jodie Sands, Johnny O'Keefe and the very scintillating Jerry Lee Lewis. They had performed two shows at the Sydney Stadium: one at 6 p.m.; and one at 8.45 p.m.

Buddy Holly and *The Crickets*.

it. His standard use of two guitars, bass and drums, would influence such bands as *The Beatles*, Bob Dylan, *The Hollies* and *The Rolling Stones*.

A poster advertising Mr Lee Gordon's Australian tour.

Buddy Holly and the Crickets had been around the music arenas since 1957. *That'll be the Day* and *Oh Boy* were two of their hit songs. Buddy had been in a quartet with Jerry Allison on drums, Joe B. Maddin on bass and Nick Sullivan on guitar, before he temporarily left the group at the end of 1957, just prior to the Australian tour. He was the first Caucasian rocker to ever produce his own material as well as perform

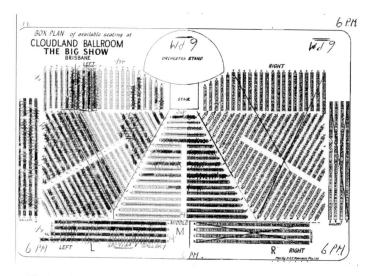

The Lee Gordon 'Big Show' Cloudland floor plan, February 3rd, 1958.

A poster for Buddy's Australian tour.

Paul Anka.

Jerry Lee Lewis, who was from Farriday in Louisiana, had been around since 1957. His hits included *Whole Lotta Shakin Goin On* and *Great Balls of Fire*. The latter was topping the charts at the time he was recording with the Sun label. Paul Anka was the teenage Canadian heart-throb on this tour, with a profile much like Justin Beiber's is today. He'd just started recording at this juncture. He is a singer/ songwriter—so very rare way back then. He had signed up with *ABC Paramount*, having his first world-wide No. 1. hit with *Diana*. Anka had toured with Buddy before on the *Big Show of Stars* for their September, 1957, tour. He also wrote the single *It Doesn't Matter Anymore*, a best-selling single after Buddy's death in 1959.

Jodie Sands (born Eleanor Di Sipio) was also a popular American singer. She hailed from Philadelphia. Jodie had achieved only one major hit, *With All My Heart*, which reached #15 on the Billboard 'Hot 100' chart in 1957. One other recording of hers, *Someday (You'll Want Me to Want You)*, had barely made the 'Top 100' chart the following year (i.e. of the Lee Gordon tour), reaching #95, but it did better in the United Kingdom where it reached #14. Jodie also appeared in the film *Jamboree* in 1957. Her song *Love Me Forever* was a 1958 favourite.

Jodie Sands was also on the Lee Gordon tour.

As for Johnny O'Keefe, it was early January of 1958, several weeks before Lee Gordon's tour commenced, that he recorded the song that would not only give him his first hit, but also the first Australian record to hit the Australian 'Top 40' charts. A song that would give him a name to be remembered for years after his passing was *The Wild One (Real Wild Child)* which Jerry Allison recorded after Buddy heard Johnny perform it during these Lee Gordon shows of 1958.

Johnny O'Keefe, out front of the Sydney outfit, *The Chains*.

Australian Senior.

On this 1958 tour, Johnny O'Keefe would always open the shows (even at Cloudland) along with Jodie Sands, Jerry Lee Lewis, Buddy Holly and Paul Anka who had closed the shows. This particular tour was the second for Johnny O'Keefe and the *Dee Jays*, as they had also toured with the Gene Vincent / Little Richard / Eddie Cochran show in October, 1957.

On Friday, January 31st, the tour moved on to perform just one show at Newcastle Stadium. (The first performance was cancelled owing to poor bookings.) Pat Barton had interviewed Buddy backstage in Newcastle for *Radio 2KO*. On the following day, Saturday, February 1st, the tour snaked back to *Sydney Stadium* for another set of performances—at 2 p.m.; 6 p.m.; and 8.45 p.m.

After a rest day on Sunday, 2nd February, following the tours to both Sydney and Newcastle, the group moved on to perform at the Cloudland Ballroom for two shows at 6 p.m. and 8.45 p.m. on February 3rd. As usual, Jodie Sands and Johnny O'Keefe and the *Dee Jays* were also featured alongside Buddy, Jerry Lee and Paul Anka at Lee Gordon's 'World Wide Hit Parade' at Cloudland. There were some reports that the Everley Brothers were with them, but that was not the case. It may be said this was one of the main sets of acts to ever grace Cloudland's stage. Perhaps it should also be recalled that this date, of February 3rd, 1958 was exactly one year before Buddy played his last concert and died; so there is now yet another reason, in Brisbane's case, to mourn the day 'the music ended'.

On this memorable night of Buddy's concert in 1958, an audience of 8,000 people paid between nine to 29 shillings for a ticket, Tim Moroney "got lucky" and somehow managed to score a free entry to the spectacle. Tim couldn't afford to pay for the 6.00 p.m. show as he was a mere apprentice at the time. His best friend, John Connelly, attended the early show with some of his workmates. Tim's idea was to meet up with John following the first show.

As Tim and his friend Billy Alviers arrived, a big crowd was lining up for the second show. Pat Hill, the Brisbane Stadium referee, who was in the line-up, suggested Tim and Billy copy others and enter through an opened window. John Connelly greeted Tim and Billy and all three agreed to try their luck.

lifted through the window. Tim managed to conceal himself as security men had looked out of the windows for other miscreants as the queue of people laughed hysterically at the entire proceedings. John also managed to get back inside the venue and undergo the privilege of seeing this incredible line-up of talent perform.

"Causing a stir…Jerry Lee Lewis performs at Cloudland, February 3rd, 1958".
Courier-Mail.

Cloudland's stage (in July, 1959) as Buddy's group would probably have seen it (in 1958), along with its very spacious interior.
Department of Public Works, Qld.

Jerry Lee Lewis greets his fans in Brisbane.
Courier-Mail.

Bill gained entry first then the security fellows frogmarched John out of the door as he was being

Around the city of Brisbane, Jerry Lee Lewis greeted crowds; and kept up the momentum of his popular new genre; as well as the promotion of rock'n'roll when he toured here.

On the 4th and 5th February, 1958, the 'Big Show' had appeared in Melbourne, leaving for North America on February 9th. Overall—

> ...the Australian tour was a success with sell out shows in Sydney, Newcastle, Brisbane and Melbourne...For this Brisbane show special seating plans were devised and both shows were sell outs despite the difficult access on a steep hill. Buddy was undoubtedly the star on the tour which even Jerry Lee Lewis said...in an interview with these stars out at the *International Hotel* in Broadbeach prior to the shows in Brisbane...

The (now retired) Catholic Archbishop of Brisbane, John Bathersby, vividly recalls the Cloudland concert and the entire 'Lee Gordon' event. On the night of the show in Brisbane, John and a pal had a break from their theological studies to see the all-star cast at Cloudland. Buddy's song, *Peggy Sue*, still enters his mind to this day.

Johnny O'Keefe owed a lot to Buddy's Aussie visit and his recording of *Real Wild Child*— formerly the Australian veteran's *Wild One*. On Wednesday, February 19th, 1959:

> Jerry "J. I." Allison recorded this song under the name of Ivan with Buddy playing lead and singing background along with *The Roses*. The song was written in Australia and Buddy and J. I. "discovered" it while touring there. Johnny Greenan writes, "Dave Owens and I were the saxophonists for Johnny O'Keefe's band, the *Dee Jays*. We wrote the song after one of our dances ended in a brawl one night in 1958. After a couple of bourbon and cokes or two, we then wrote the song.

O'Keefe recorded it a few weeks later. His name was on as co-writer because he was the front man, as often happens. He had also added a couple of things when he sang the song. It has been in about nine-to-ten movies. David Bowie liked the song. That is why 'Iggy Pop' recorded it. The greatest moment was and still is the use of it in the soundtrack of "Pretty Woman". Unfortunately Dave Owens and John O'Keefe have now passed on and are playing in the band in the sky. We toured Australia with Buddy and the *Crickets*. They were great blokes. We kept in touch when they went back to the U.S. We were all so very sad when Buddy was killed. It seems like yesterday. He was the one who took the song and published it in the U.S. So I owe a lot to our Buddy. Without him, the song would never have gotten out of Australia. It was released on September 26th, 1958. Two takes of *Real Wild Child* were bootlegged in June of 1995.

The Roses of David Bingham, Robert Linville and Ray Rush.

This tour in 1958 was the one and only Australian tour that Buddy Holly ever made, not forgetting a visit to the UK a month later. There was even talk of Buddy now coming back Down Under for a second 'Lee Gordon' spectacular, but details had not been discussed in 1958.

As we had learned later from the 'Movie-tone' News segment at our local cinema, the rock world received a shock in February of 1959 when rock'n'roll stars Buddy Holly, 22; Richie Valens, 17; and the 'Big Bopper' (J. P. Richardson, 28), died in a light plane crash. Their chartered *Beechcraft Bonanza* plane had crashed in Iowa after take-off on a flight from Mason City, Iowa, to Moorehead, Minnesota, in bad weather. Most observers said it was the 'night that the music died'. A reference would again be made to this dreadful episode in Don McLean's wistful song, *American Pie*. If only the group's tour bus hadn't kept breaking down, none of these performers would have flown; and no doubt their yet-to-be-recorded music 'would have lived'!—

The small Beechcraft Bonanza took off from an Iowa airstrip just after midnight on February 3rd, 1959.

The 1947-built plane had three passengers and the pilot on board.

In the snowy, windy darkness the pilot, inexperienced at flying by instruments, became confused and flew close to a farmhouse.

The house occupant turned on the porch light, hoping the pilot would see it and pull up.

The plane gained altitude but shortly afterwards one of the wings hit the ground and was torn off. The rest of the plane had then slammed into the ground, killing all four aboard. (*Courier-Mail*.)

Apparently, the pilot was licensed only to fly by visual reference and should not have agreed to fly in the forecast weather conditions.

The Clear Lake, Iowa, poster of Buddy Holly's last concert, 2nd February, 1959. It was his 11th show on tour.

The plane crash which killed Buddy Holly, Richie Valens and Jiles *The Big Bopper* Richardson.

Ironically, Buddy Holly died *precisely* one year and six or so hours after those two memorable concerts at Cloudland on February

3rd, 1958. Although it's over 50 years since Buddy's live voice has been 'silenced', Troy Lennon in the *Courier-Mail* suggested his influence was still far too widespread to ever completely die down.

> The young rocker had left a stack of recordings that would be released posthumously.
>
> Holly would also influence so many musicians who followed.
>
> *The Beatles* are said to have partly derived their name from *The Crickets* and John Lennon often wore Holly-style horn-rimmed glasses.
>
> ...Leo Sayer, John Mellancamp, Bruce Springsteen, Neil Diamond and Led Zeppelin have all covered his songs.

As an instrument, Buddy's Fender Stratocaster guitar gained quickly in popularity, with such rock heroes as Jimi Hendrix and Eric Clapton.

Whatever his contribution, there are still people alive today in Brisbane who remember Buddy's Cloudland concerts. In the 'wash-up' of details about Holly's death,

it is interesting to note that he was, in fact, only 22 years of age; and had been a recording artist for 18 months. Interestingly perhaps, a rare minor planet was named after Buddy Holly, christened '16155 Holly'. The late 1950s—following Buddy's concert at Cloudland— culminated in a 'Post Office Ball' on June 25th 1958; *The Troubadours* (a swing/big band), along with Johnny O'Keefe, Betty McQuade and the very youthful *Bee Gees* were on the bill.

A Fender Stratocaster guitar set alight by Jimi Hendrix in 1967.

PRINCESS ALEXANDRA'S VISIT TO CLOUDLAND

In 1959, Princess Alexandra arrived for a tour of Australia. She made a special trip to Queensland for the State's centenary celebrations, 1859-1959. During her stay, Princess Alexandra of Kent gushed over a koala in a "specially constructed

gum leaf area" at the prestigious State Reception held at Cloudland Ballroom on Tuesday, August 18th, 1959. It was discovered that four koalas were transported all the way from Lone Pine Sanctuary for the occasion at the Princess' own request. This particular fellow was called 'Alexander'.

The Reception for Princess Alexandra, 1959.

Princess Alexandra gets up close and quite personal with 'Alexander'.

Courier-Mail.

Cloudland Ballroom, July, 1959.
Queensland State Archives.

The Princess at the Cloudland Ballroom, 1959.

Neil Wiseman, in his *Sunday Mail* column, 'The Way We Were' had this to say of the Princess' visit:

Princess Alexandra, a cousin of Queen Elizabeth, came to Queensland in 1959 as part of the state's centenary celebrations, and so successful was her visit that the hospital was renamed after her. On that Australian visit she had a song written for her, *The Alexandra Waltz*, performed by Gatton-born country singer, Gay Kayler. It was written by Queensland composer Clyde Collins but his more enduring contribution to the centenary musical merrymaking was the amiable anthem (*Life is Great in*) *The Sunshine State*.

Brisbane crowds were so impressed with the Princess during 1959 that the *Princess Alexandra Hospital* at Wooloongabba was not only named after her, but to this day it still carries her name.

Two further views of Cloudland Ballroom's interior—July, 1959.

Queensland State Archives.

8

THE PALACE ON THE HILL

I always thought of myself as an ugly duckling

Until

I became a graceful dancer

And discovered

I was a proud swan.

May Fooks, *Bebe's Story*

RECORD HOPS AND PRE-CLOUDLAND DAYS

During those 'teen' years in the 1950s, growing up in Brisbane, leading up to our Cloudland days, our idea of fraternising with girls, boys and courtship was definitely— at one end of the spectrum—of the Rock Hudson-Doris Day variety; but also at the other, of the more earthy 'Me Tarzan-You Jane' type of coupling. We also gained snippets of information from the newspapers, radio, cinema, films and observations from our school, home or all around the local neighbourhood. I had also glanced earnestly at the adult magazines at '*Trevor's Barber Shop*' in the city.

Our early teens and any adolescent years were supposedly a period of tremendous new feelings for both boys and girls, but I seemed to be self-conscious about the opposite sex, and this feeling was engendered by my gangly appearance and overall lack of coordination. I never resented girls as some boys my age did. I graciously accepted their continued presence on the planet; and had hoped that my lack of knowledge in this area would, inevitably, soon sort itself out. After all, following years of segregation, where the prevailing message appeared to be that girls were somehow taboo; and that some were unattainable, I had a lot of growing to do in 'the girl department'.

I found that the girls of 13 or 14 were far more physically and emotionally mature than I was. In addition, they also seemed taller and so heavier. One of the really 'grown-up' girls of my own age group in our street wore stretch Bermudas in purple and black check, a big Lurex jacket, with some pink accessories, and iridescent socks over winkle pickers (long pointed shoes). I used to see her going to town on Saturday mornings, but never had the courage to converse with her. I'd heard about 'widgies' like her—and 'bodgies' in black stove pipe trousers—mentioned in Australia and its sister nation, New Zealand; but regrettably in those days such people became associated in the press with an earlier term—juvenile delinquent.

We only grew to know the girls formally through supervised functions. Societal rules and personal etiquette were norms to which we strictly adhered. Any person who did not copped a 'mouthful' by those in charge of the activity.

I had once danced with a girl who was wearing a strange outfit referred to as a type of 'igloo dress'. The igloo dress—named for its shape—had a plain top and below the waist there was a bunching of material in a criss-cross fashion. The skirt sort of resembled a covered hoop.

The full waltz-length skirt and the lavish use of material in the 1950s.

At one of the real dances in my teens, a record hop, we had to saunter down to the back of the hall to choose our partners. Boys stood at one end and then the girls sat demurely at the other. Sometimes, after most of the choices had been made, the tallest girl and the shortest boy ended up together. Likewise, if there wasn't any- one left to dance with them, a quite fat kid would dance with a really skinny girl. According to our parents, they played 'real artists' for the music at such gatherings: Jo Stafford, Perry Como, Doris Day, Eddie Fisher, Dean Martin, Pat Boone and Rosemary Clooney. There was no sign at that time of rock'n'roll at these functions.

Originating in England, a later rite of passage still for several young Australians, the regal and most distinguished *Debutante's Ball*.

It was around this time that I learned about girls' hands. Several had really soft hands; others wrinkly, cold and ugly ones; still others smooth and sweaty; or a few with dainty fingers and neat hands.

There was very little heartfelt vigilance at these dances. There was no essential purpose of presenting girls to find a (later) match of suitable social standing, similar to the 1930s and 1940s. Our parents were supposed to supervise on these occasions, but they usually smoked outside or chatted among themselves in a corner of the hall. Outside, the 'fast' kids swapped or sold *Ardath* cigarettes at 2/7d. a packet and talked more intimately with the girls. I observed all this, but

was too naïve and hesitant to really take part.

One of the cigarette brands kids smoked as teenagers.

Soon after going to these dances regularly, my friend Michael and I felt it was time to try our first cigarette. We used Dad's "Drum" cigarette papers and tobacco we had found on a wild tobacco tree growing within the neighbour's yard. I tried to show off to a girl down the road about my new-won drawback skills; but, given the strong potency of those unprocessed tobacco leaves, I merely turned a shade of sea green and looked a real 'ninny'.

As for the formal 'dating' by our older siblings, no one could go beyond this particular gem:

Making a date: boys always do the asking.

Arrival: never, ever honk the horn outside. Go to the door and meet her folks.

'Lighting up' at a dance.

CLOUDLAND AS A DANCE VENUE

Love happens to be an astonishing state, a state in which

all of us are astonished.

Poet **Edward Hirsch**

It is easy to gain the impression that Cloudland only catered for rock'n'rollers, especially since the late 1950s, but that notion was far from the truth. The traditional forms of set-piece dancing—such as the *waltzes*, *foxtrots* and the like—also held sway at the ballroom. In its heyday, folk travelled from many corners of the State to attend the functions at Cloudland. Hems would twirl, arms would fling and partners would sashay as the mirror ball spread shards of light into various corners of the room. So, Brisbane then has a great history and visual record of dances, from all of their war and post-war brides meeting prospective spouses at the traditional dance halls which dotted the city—to the iconic Cloudland Ballroom; and the currently heritage-listed *City Hall*.

All of these grand venues had hosted many memorable balls, dances and competitive dance events over the years.

Miss Marie Vaughan and Mr Bill Thurman, ready for a big night out up at Cloudland.

To many Brisbane citizens, Cloudland was also a mixture of high angst and shrieks of happiness: dances, balls or exams…Once the 'testing' was over for yet another year, Cloudland Ballroom returned to its most important of social functions—to being the 'palace' to meet that special someone, just as it had been for my family, relatives and others locked back in the post-wartime era. 'Billo and his Orchestra' or 'Warren Cox and *The Sounds of Seven*' were presenting all manner of music genres from early swing and jazz favourites, to *Beatles*' covers (in the 1950s and 1960s) and current 'pop' tunes. Couples would glide over an initially slippery floor to *jazz*, *jive* and *quickstep*. It was a keenly organised, active environment free of "stray cigarette butts" or the "odour of alcohol"; and, if you were lucky, you'd come home with a photographic record of your night at the dancehall.

My sister, Mrs. Lesley Annette Tissington [nee Lergessner], in the late 1950s, with Ben Mellon, Cloudland Ballroom.

For one satisfied patron, Cloudland was "it":

It had chandeliers, hard timber floors, elegant curtains, domed skylights…and decorative columns. The upper level had seating so you could keep watch down over the dance floor, this being another drawcard for its growing popularity to hold concerts…and a handy viewing deck to spot potential beaus.

Hugh Lunn's observations about the cheery dancehall were most fitting. His memories reflect upon the wonder of this venue; fabulous evenings of dancing and musical interludes; trams offloading bevies of girls in outfits designed by mothers or relatives; and the dance floor undulating and supposedly rising on its springs.

Rosewood couple, Barbara Sellars and Jack Johnston, Cloudland Ballroom, 1950s.

According to Hugh, fellows would also arrive in cars, utes and cabs on either side of Montpelier Hill. Love reared its head and romances blossomed, despite many folk not possessing a telephone at the time.

As for the 'dance rituals' themselves in at the ballroom, here's what one 'insider' confided:

Like any crowded entertainment facility Cloudland could be an uncomfortable place in the hot weather. Therefore, the really big crowds were more likely in the Ball Season during the winter months. On crowded nights, with well in excess of a thousand dancers, couples could escape to one of the balconies which overlooked the hall or even into the vestibule. Most patrons, however, took their chances crammed into the big alcoves where the ladies sat in a state of barely disguised anxiety, waiting for the man of their dreams to appear, and the men stood around impatiently waiting for a dance bracket in which they could [offer] some degree of confidence on the slippery, heaving floor.

Though unthinkable today, in those less liberated times it was customary for the men to offer a lady a lift home at the end of the night. Because fewer women had their own cars they tended to arrive as part of a group in taxis and, therefore, the offer of a lift home not only spared a lady a long wait for a taxi at the end of the evening but was a sign to her friends that she may have found an agreeable partner who now was not only gallant enough to escort her home but willing to ask her out on a date during the following week.

Couples very rarely 'first dated' at Cloudland. In quiet, provincial Brisbane, that meant a night at the movies, a restaurant date at one of the half dozen or so decent eating establishments across the city or, more likely, a 21st Birthday party. If things didn't work out, each of them could return, as a single, to Cloudland at the next opportunity to continue the quest for true love. At the height of the 60/40 ballroom dance craze, there were even midweek dances for those who were truly committed to the task of finding love.

It's hard to recall those 'good old years', when boys sometimes looked like statuesque wax department store 'dummies' in 'tux', suit and bowties while girls were dressed up to the 'nines'.

I think it was our mother or my sisters who informed me of tales about Cloudland, of the girls in lengthy white gloves and cream organza dresses waltzing on top of Cloudland's hill.

Cloudland (Luna Park), 1950s.

But all was not a bed of roses on the hill at Bowen Hills. June Adamson had recalled these years at Cloudland in her book *Don't Rock the Boat* with a hint of unhappiness—

I was never comfortable in this dance venue [of Cloudland] until I learnt to jive. I first visited with friends from the MLC and had a terrible time. It was a male paradise with the boys outnumbered by crowds of well-groomed young girls lining the walls or just standing waiting to "be asked" and many of us just sat and waited all evening. The boys I did see were not my type at all and I was certainly not theirs. They were serious and conventional—in other words boring—for I was in the traditional ballroom dancing area where stylised steps, straight backs, sports coats and ties partnered taffeta, high heels, and seamed stockings. In the cooler months a hand-knitted pale pink or blue angora wool bolero fastened at the neck with one pearl button was donned as a concession to the season and male partners in dark coats hated these garments. Boys decided it was like dancing with a Persian cat as they picked at clinging strands of loose angora on sleeves, collar and coat front; [the] only thing worse than dancing with angora, they'd say, was to see the girl home and try to have a few private moments that didn't leave any evidence.

BOOZE, BOUNCERS AND FOOD

A 1919 approach to young peoples' temperance.

It is easy, in retrospect, to examine this strange image and chuckle over its 'seriousness'. But, the reality of the matter at the dancehall on the hill was that abstinence was required, with very little room for tolerance. Cloudland was, for many years, a quaintly alcohol free 'no go' zone, where you may be able to buy an interesting variety of light fruit punch beverages. In the very crowded vestibule, beneath that unusually corrugated iron arch, serious-looking doormen would 'vet' each patron, refusing outright the admission of any person seeming to be 'under the influence':

Since 1954 the six o'clock swill had been replaced by [a] 10 p.m. closing and alcohol was not allowed within the vicinity of the dance halls, although some boys boasted of the flask tucked inside a sock. (Rules were that 21 years was the age at which hotel bars could be frequented).

Many boys had a routine of not turning up until after 10 p.m. when the hotels closed so were carrying a full load when they did arrive. We always knew who'd walk in the door about 10.10 p.m., who'd be almost legless, who'd morph into an uninhibited comedian singing a parody of Marty Robbins such as *A White Sports Coat and a Pink French Letter* or who'd just be turning up for the last dance and chance of a girl to take home and greeting their mates with "Ya gettin' any?"

Drinking and driving were common; seat belts were unknown and I never lost a friend to a road accident though I did travel in a vehicle with another passenger who refused to sit in the front seat while carrying the portable radio on his lap as a friend of his had been doing that when a collision occurred and the radio was embedded in his body. I guess so many of us survived as vehicles were not high-powered and roads were not as crowded. (June Adamson, *Don't Rock the Boat*.)

Needless to say, any alcohol you may require on the night, to fortify your 'Dutch courage' for the evening that lay promisingly before you, had to be consumed speedily—or "furtively" from a liquor flask—down in the ill-lit carpark, before you emerged at the front entrance or took the stairs to the ballroom.

When alcohol was ultimately served at the dance venue, our present Police Commissioner, Bob Atkinson, recalled one rather memorable night he spent at Cloudland. At the time—1968—Bob was interning as a police recruit, ending up as a volunteer to wait at the annual Police Ball held at Cloudland that particular year. He wasn't successful at this task, recalling that the folk he'd waited on at their tables weren't probably getting value for money.

Adding to the solemnity of his evening, the loudspeakers at the venue announced that the then Premier of Queensland, Jack Pizzey, had died.

Cloudland personnel monitored much more than just alcohol. Inside this charming dance palace, floor supervisors ambled among the jiving or ballroom dancing couples, organising the 'horse-shoe formation' for the evening's *Progressive Barn Dance*. Stern bouncers, at this juncture, often asked serial smokers or 'over-amorous' pairs, to vacate the floor. In these more conservative times,

'try before you buy' was hardly on the 'cards'; in fact, the motto of most adults and of some younger people was 'no ring, no ding' in reference to 'sedate' manners:

Because Cloudland had a long association with traditional pattern dancing, it is generally considered to have attracted a different clientele to the suburban halls generally associated with rock'n' roll within the late 1950s. Physical violence then was not normally associated with the venue at this time. However, according to John Bell, the venue had its share of trouble. Although John had an interest in rock'n'roll from a [very] early age, his life-long direct involvement with the movement started as a result of John Stuart's escapades at Cloudland. Stuart had been causing a major problem by 'bashing up' all and sundry, including the police, in his efforts to gain entry to the dances. John Bell was a boxer at the time and was contacted by [the] Cloudland management asking if he could handle Stuart because everyone was terrified of him.

And again:

John Bell took on the job as bouncer in the late 1950s and was successful in restricting Stuart's access to the venue. His method would not bear scrutiny today however.

I was the bouncer up there to stop Stuart and these other lads getting into the place. That was my job and I was the only bouncer. I used to walk around the Cloudland hall and do outside with the cars— all the louts playing up with the cars. We used to stop that going on if we could. There was a fellow called John Hannay that (sic) was employing the band at that time. We did lots of stuff at Cloudland and some [real] terrible things that you would never get away with today. You could get away with it those days because in the old days you could bash people and all that sort of stuff—you [just] would not be allowed to do it now. (John Bell.)

John was very strict on both their behaviour and dress. He felt that it was important for parents to see that everything in the dances was being run in a very controlled manner.

We were very strict and [do] you know, people couldn't get on the dance floor and yahoo and carry on. They were pulled up straight away and if there was any trouble they were thrown out straight away, barred for life or whatever. (John Bell.) (*It was only Rock'n'Roll,* Geoff Walden.)

Cloudland Ballroom's 'Supper Setting 2' dining area, July, 1959.
Queensland State Archives.

Although alcohol was absent for a time at Cloudland, anyone feeling a bit 'peckish' could avail themselves of some 'fodder' or 'nosh'. The food critic, Peta Hackworth, especially recalls the standard menu and the reasonable meals served at the venue. She did not mind the 'white' or 'brown' meal choices either: chicken fricassee or a spaghetti bolognaise. Generally, such dishes were presented on white oval chinaware with 'splades', and the accompanying bread and butter (or margarine spread) would be shaped in small, neat triangles.

Those who missed out on Cloudland's nightly fare usually wended their way off to Pat Monahan's Takeaway Café, *The Windmill,* on Petrie Terrace. Pat was a very affable Irishman. Later it became *Harry's Fine Food* Snack Bar from 1964. It was then run by Harry Nicholas, a chap from Cyprus—the 'Godfather' of takeaway food.

Bentley's sketch of *Harry's* iconic 'fast food' Petrie Tce. outlet. *Sunday Mail.*

CLOUDLAND'S ICONIC DANCE FLOOR

No one ever likes to dispel myths, least of all those regarding the extraordinarily constructed wooden dance surface at Bowen Hills. Roy Bonney says his father, Earnest, nailed down the floor using hand-made nails.

As Alistair Gow recalls, Cloudland—

…was famous for many reasons, not the least its spectacular 'sprung wooden floor'.

Jitter-buggers, rock'n'rollers, & students sitting exams, indeed anyone who [had] ever set foot inside Cloudland always remembered the springy floor.

Not everything, though, was as it seemed with that floor.

I recently received a letter from Alistair Gow of *Alex Gow Funerals* in Brisbane.

"I have agonised over many years whether to let the mystery and the legend continue or to speak out about just what was beneath that floor", he wrote.

"If you are of a melancholic disposition and like your remembrances left the way they are, don't read on. If not, it's best to let Alistair tell his own story.

"As a young man [back] in the late 1950s, I was a ballroom dancer on the staff of Mr Bill and Fay Johnston's *Dance Studio*", Alistair later confided. "The Johnstons had arranged with Hans Apel, the owner of Cloudland at the time, to use the ballroom on Saturday afternoons for our training. In return…we would, after training, blow up 500 balloons which we would suspend above the old dance floor in a large net ready for the regular Saturday night dance. Many, I am sure, will remember.

"Being an apprentice carpenter and aware of the spring in the floor and also being aware of the reputation of Cloudland's 'sprung' floor, I was interested in seeing the construction beneath.

"One Saturday afternoon, Mr Apel opened the little door at the back of the stage, which was the only access to the area beneath the dance floor, and allowed me in.

"To my disappointment I found that the construction of the floor was just a standard bearer and joist arrangement sitting on stumps and similar to that used at the time in most timber-floored buildings, including your main average residential dwelling".

And again:

Why, then, did the floor have its unique springing action? Alistair has a four-pronged theory.

"Firstly, it was built around 1940, at the time when long lengths of Queensland hardwood were abundantly available and the bearers (which sit on top of the stumps) stretched in one piece from one side of the dance floor to the other", Alistair said.

"Similarly, the floor joists were in long lengths and the joints were staggered over the bearers, as good carpenters would be expected to do.

"Secondly, the floor, which was a two-layered timber floor, was very strong and was obviously very tightly cramped when it was laid.

"Old, experienced carpenters who worked with tongue-and-groove floorboards will know that if you over-cramp a floor, particularly over large open areas, you can cause the bearers, floor joists and floor in the middle of the area being laid to rise and lift off the stumps.

"I believe it was this principle that [had] assisted in allowing the dance floor to flex and gave the impression that it was on springs.

"Thirdly, the bottom layer of floorboards was just a standard four-inch-by-one-inch (100mm by 25mm) dressed tongue-and-groove board.

"On top of this was laid the dance floor that consisted of narrow boards approximately one inch and a quarter (32mm) in width and laid in a rectangular pattern. I don't recall nail holes being visible so it is likely that these floorboards were 'secret nailed' and could have been quite thick.

"And [then] finally—and most importantly—the stumps beneath the dance floor had sunk into the ground.

"Hundreds of dancers simultaneously thumping on the floor above in dances like the *Boston Two Step*, and the *Conga* and the like over many years had taken its toll", Alistair said.

"The long lengths of timber used for the bearers and the floor joists, combined with the strength and tightness of the floorboards, caused

the middle of the dance floor to be suspended in mid-air after the stumps had been driven into the ground by the combined weight of the dancers".

As Geoff Walden in *It was only Rock'n'Roll* argues, Cloudland's special dance surface underwent renovations in the mid-1950s:

During the war, Cloudland was leased by the Americans and when they came in, according to Jim Burke, "so did the termites". One of the most notable features of Cloudland, as far as dancers were ever concerned, was the 'sprung floor'. Jim Burke states that this floor was added in 1955 when Cloudland was patched up and a new floor was constructed which was capable of bouncing up and down like a waterbed. As traditional ballroom dancing went the way of many other pre-war cultural pursuits, so the structure, as a centre for dancing, was doomed with the introduction of amplified music. Cloudland and its management were able to adapt for a short period to new expectations but not without some struggle.

DEBUTANTE BALLS

John Brack's *British Modern* (1969), oil on canvas.

In both Ireland and Australia, the 'coming out' of young girls was referred to as 'debs', or the debutante ball. In some countries the event was called the high school formal; and the "prom" was now wholly a North American phenomenon. Perhaps as proof of the Americanisation of the world, the prom, meaning a formal 'dress up' celebration of the final year of high school, or the ball, caught on in

England, then big time in its 'colony' of Australia.

According to the debutante ball's strict rules of engagement the celebration was a rite of passage for every Australian teenager. Pat Zalewski, who trained more than 10,000 young people for deb balls, advised that when she made her debut "a deb was a deb…she never went to dances or parties before she made her debut…then, at the ball, she really came out into society".

[So] the debutante ball was a holdover from colonial times, borrowed from the Mother Country where the daughters of aristocracy came out by being presented to the monarch thus marking their official debut in society.

In provincial Australia, the person who received the young women might be a mayor or member of parliament. In the small communities in the big country west of the [Great] Divide, it might be the wife of a prominent grazier who did the honours. In a large cultural grouping of, for example, people of Scottish descent, it would be the chieftain of the town's *Caledonian Society*.

Cloudland could be a welcome and exciting venue during the ball season. For those who did enjoy the night, and set out determined to do so, there was a pairing off of couples; an invitation to unattached girls so no one would be left on the 'sidelines'; a pre-Ball party (with alcohol); as mentioned, no alcohol was served at this time at Cloudland; and fruit punch at the dance venue often tasted quite 'unusual'. Throughout the night, attendant mothers, like ardent fairy godmothers, helped to transform the deserving Cinderellas and see

to their every whim and fancy. As deb balls generally occurred on a Saturday night, the Sunday morning newspaper, the *Sunday Mail*, displayed couples on show in their social pages, with a suitable, accompanying paragraph.

My sister, Mrs Lesley Annette Tissington [*nee* Lergessner], dressed for a ball at Cloudland, late 1950s.

Not everyone looked forward to the big night. In fact, June Adamson was one who still 'blanched' at the very thought of attending a deb ball at Cloudland:

…demure debutantes [all] head-to-toe in virginal white were presented to pompous dignitaries before they "came out" while [their] proud parents sat watching in the balcony; during the Ball Season it was a busy venue and each Saturday night it came alive with romantic ballads and up-tempo blasts from

Billo Smith and his Orchestra. (Don't Rock the Boat.)

June Adamson also depicted the effect on girls brought about by the ball events at Cloudland:

Cloudland was the main venue for the ball season and pairing off meant much more than just going to a dance. Couples going steady naturally [did] and an invitation to an unattached girl from a greatly desired young man set the pulses racing as who knows, perhaps it would lead to something more, maybe a diamond, something permanent?

Generally, I felt the opening of Ball Season was a little like the opening of the duck-shooting season but without those overalls and waders. These fragile hunters pretended a sweet and feminine softness from the top of their piled curls to the hem of floating tulle disguising a steely resolve to get their bird; even Annie knew the danger of relying on the gun alone. A [most] modest décolleté supporting the obligatory corsage carefully chosen to enhance the colour scheme was much more effective.

Furthermore:

Of course it was a challenge to the beau to pretend an interest about the colour[s] [selected] in plenty of time before the big occasion; to ensure by casually asked questions that the blooms in his corsage fitted the picture and did not bring his partner to tears.

Competition was intense as parties of the same social set [all] competed and the number of balls attended was notched on the bedpost. The social rating and surname of the partner as well as the occupation of his father was of foremost importance as was the label on the florist's box.

After the ball I heard chatty gossip in the lunch room of who had worn what, who had partnered whom and exactly what had happened at the private pre-Ball Party where champagne had flowed. Alcohol of course was banned from Cloudland itself, but somehow the fruit punch was spiked and expected to be spiked, with nearly every male putting up his hand in cheeky admission of being the culprit. (*Don't Rock the Boat.*)

In Brisbane, in 1939, the *Courier-Mail* reported that 'Girls Make Bow to Archbishop: Fifty Debs at Catholic Ball'.

Palms and pot plants flanked the stage where the debutantes were presented to Archbishop James Duhig by the matron of honour, Mrs M. J. Eakin.

The girls entered by a side door, filed across the floor and mounted the steps to the platform and after the presentation (a curtsey by the deb, an acknowledgement by his Holy Grace) [they] had formed a semicircle on the floor facing the dais.

Following on the good archbishop's address the girls and their partners participated in the *Debutante Waltz*.

Matching Early Victorian posies were carried by all the debutantes, and one of the most popular materials for their frocks was fine silk net, mount-ed on either gleaming satin or rustling taffeta.

Frocks of filmy white chiffon were also ones favoured by a number of girls.

The platform party included the great, and good of the Catholic community—Windsors, Biernes, Macrossans, Macgroartys, and the McKillops and their ilk.

The Masonic lodges had an equally impressive turnout later in the year.

"Coming out...and gracing the stairs at Brisbane's Cloudland Ballroom, these twenty-five youthful ladies...presented to Archbishop James Duhig at the *Young Catholic Workers and National Catholic Girls Movement Debutante Ball* in 1955".

Courier-Mail.

One participant-observer at this formal function wore a tuxedo with an accompanying bow tie; and the girls all wore long dresses, gloves and carried a posy *a la* all previous debutantes.

...a girlfriend asked me to be her partner for a Debutante Ball, for her "coming out", the quaint term of the time, meaning entering society. We had to rehearse the *Debutante Waltz* over a period of several weeks prior to the event. On the night, the girls were dressed in their absolute finest, including a corsage bought by each male for his partner. The boys wore dinner suits, and if my memory now serves me correctly, a pair of white gloves. We had to escort the girls as they were introduced to the dignitary of the evening (I'm fairly sure that it was the Anglican Archbishop of Brisbane), and then we all performed the waltzing before the rest of the attendees joined in. I recall that I was hopeless during the rehearsals for the waltz. They kept clashing with my many football matches, so I missed a few. The ones I did attend didn't go well either—I kept making mistakes, much to the annoyance of my girlfriend who was so keen for all to be perfect on the night. Fortunately, when the evening had finally arrived, I performed magnificently for her—didn't miss a step, so she was very pleased with me. Following that event, I remember attending several balls at Cloudland—always a ton of fun, too. All of that is history but, far more importantly, whatever future Cloudland may have had as an entertainment venue has been destroyed along with the building.

This young lad's experiences in mastering dancing reminded me of Michelangelo, who, speaking of his art, once said: "If people knew how hard I had to work to gain my mastery, it would not seem so wonderful at all".

Although balls at Cloudland might feature pretty pastel dresses, Peta Hackworth was one who departed from tradition: she purchased an elegant black wool sheath number decorated with black fur. In those days, no one ever wore black outfits to balls. (She later cut off the bottom of her dress, making it into a hat and neck muff.)

Though Peta sought to be different, even apart from the crowd, she recalled that period at Cloudland as one of such good-natured consideration and of refined manners. Dressing quite appropriately, as well as offering a lady flowers, was the norm in those precious days.

June Adamson also found the dress 'sense' of rivals at Cloudland balls created 'commentaries' in her particular workplace:

> My drummer had a different beat but I listened with fascination in the lunch room as cliques of Old School girls carefully looked [all] around the room and if the coast was clear, lowered their voices and [then] verbally tore apart the expensive gowns of their new rivals and questioned the skills of the chosen dressmaker; funny how they were so frank in front of me.

> After all the secrecy, the careful choice of design, the expensive tailoring, the tracking down of co-ordinated accessories in [some] elbow gloves and dancing shoes, it was considered bad form to wear the outfit more than once. Where do second-hand ball gowns end up, I wondered? Do these girls have a special closet stuffed with satin, lace and memories? Or does Christian generosity and charity mean that [the] poor peasants in China are forced to paddle the paddy fields clad in these odd castoffs? And why are exotic flowers sacrificed for one brief night of glory?

> On the Sunday morning there was another challenge to face. There were Brownie points to be earned by featuring in the *Sunday Mail* social pages where couples were on show with an accompanying paragraph. On Monday morning at work the [pages] were read aloud and if the journalist had been inaccurate or less than effusive, the target's brows were lowered and a black look was worn for the rest of the day while their genuine friends commiserated. Satisfied and secretive smiles from all the jealous ones left out said, "Ha Ha'. (*Don't Rock the Boat*.)

Girls and their partners of Greek descent and also some Australian couples, presented to Mr Bill Herbert, the State Government Minister during 1965 at Cloudland. *Note the dress styles. George Poulos and the Kythera-family.*

Photo courtesy Chris Goopy.

ISABELLA DE FALLA'S STORY

There is no remedy

for love but to love more.

Henry David Thoreau,
(1862) US writer.

Someone once remarked that if you want to be happy for a day, buy a new car. If you want to be happy for a weekend get married, but if you want to be happy for a life time, be a ballroom dancer. So it was with my fictional character from New Farm, Isabella De Falla.

In my earlier book, *From Olive Grove to Eucalyptus Tree: An immigrant family in baby boomer Australia*, I set out, in fictionalised form, Isabella De Falla's 'brush' with dancing and her debutante balls at Cloudland. Here she takes over the narration of her numerous experiences.

Isabella De Falla tells her story:

Despite my mighty efforts to socialise and be noticed at Debutante Balls, for example, those at Cloudland, I was stuck with a continuing problem. I was now five feet nine inches tall and apparently still 'climbing'. At my usherette and other moonlighting jobs in the city, I was continually left open to taunts and moronic comments such as 'How's the weather up there?' When the same people found out my friend Avra was really short, they were a little more gracious in the daily references. They good-naturedly referred to us as 'Long Sal' and 'Little Evie', the latter because of a song made famous by *The Easy*

Beats. My ongoing life, though, had become a retail agony. Clothes were too short; heels were too high; and I suffered back problems with seats, counters and tables that were too low.

To add to these 'traumas', my short girlfriends made off with the tallest dancers. For a time there, it seemed these young men all liked pocket-size, smaller women. With my height, no bona fide "Nureyev' was ever going to hoist me into dance orbit, perhaps try as I might. As the saying goes, you can't make a 'silk purse out of a sow's ear'.

Any dances that I had gone to turned out to be quite a nightmare. The smallest boy would zero in on me, until I stood up. Either they'd make a beeline straight for the exit, shooting off like a Bondi tram, gabble something incoherent, or else stay dancing quite motionless, transfixed with their head buried loosely in my chest. If the latter was the case, they would keep turning up wistfully for subsequent dances, a bit like Banquo's ghost in Shakespeare's *Macbeth*. Albeit the idea of the 'Deb' or Debutante Balls later came under scrutiny in the 1960s, But for girls like me in the 1950s, such events were the way we would soon 'come out' in society. Even Papa approved of this 'tradition'.

I wanted to wear a shortened, mid-length skirt to my initial formal, with matching patent white leather shoes, much like a rock'n'roller; but Dad rejected 'any such thing'. He explained that it was my first official dance. I was seen by him and others as being too young and way out of touch with the conservative-looking and long-flowing, full-length debutante gowns around this time. What's more, he argued, why wear something so 'provocative?' While my dad's advice was sound, my brother Gino then stated that I was old enough to wear whatever I fancied. Unfortunately, Gino's observation fell on deaf ears.

In the finish, Dad picked out the material for the debutante dress. I had been taught sewing at a private school and I carried this skill on at New Farm State School. By the mid-1950s, this sewing in my formative years had stood me in good stead and also kept me up with current fashions. With my Austral sewing machine I purchased with Papa's assistance, I would cut out patterns and busy myself with 'notions' (selecting the thread, zips, catches and elastic) to make up my outfits. Once, when I entered the *Courier-Mail*'s Home Dressmaking competition, with a 'nifty little

number' according to Dad, I earned myself £50.

A woman's usual chores involved sewing. An advertisement current within the 1950s employing a smidgen of humour.

I made my first piece of clothing, a rock'n'roll outfit, from a pattern in a *Women's Weekly* magazine. From there, I seldom looked back with my Austral sewing machine and dressmaking, often buying a length of printed cotton material on a Thursday or a Friday, cutting it out; and then sewing it for a Saturday to wear when Avra and I went to Cloudland or a local 'hop'. By then, of course, I was going to work as an usherette and sometimes changing at work before going off to the local dances. In any case, in the end I had the nous and wherewithal to complete my deb outfit to my family's satisfaction.

After one or two 'knock-backs' from my asking, father picked out a very tall lad that I liked. Dad believed the boy wanted to ask me himself, but was far too shy to do so. At least, that's how Papa put it. Thankfully, I 'came out' with other debs at a ball at Cloudland. With the orchestra playing in a corner of the room, I had absolutely no fears about being a 'wall flower'. After all, I had my beau, Jon, to chat with on the night. I was no longer caught out, as was usual, having to make small talk with short strangers. Then, if Jon requested a dance, I obliged. I can still picture it in my mind's eye, with all of us lining up on the dance floor of Cloudland in the late 1950s.

Clad in our fine silk, neat frocks, gleaming satin, taffeta and white chiffon dresses, we curtseyed to our partners and then commenced the *Debutante Waltz*. It's hard now to believe, after all the fun I had at my first formal event, that a *Sunday Mail* article, with an accompanying story, had announced in 1962, '***Debbery ...Debbery Goes into Decline'***.

FANCY DRESS BALLS

Besides the deb balls, schools and other organisations put on the fancy dress balls held at Cloudland. According to Di Bingham:

Every year, the school had a fancy dress ball at Cloudland Ballroom and Mum slaved at the sewing machine making Rod, my brother, a pirate or me a little Dutch girl. We would ride up the steep hillside at Bowen Hills in that open tram/train (which ran to the "back" entrance) and walk into the cavernous ballroom with its specially sprung floor for dancing; and alcoves for sitting and the place would be [just] full of shrieking kids and clenched-teethed parents and teachers. There was always an official photographer; and in one year, Rod and I were immortalised in our fancy dress personas, my hair a mass of very unnatural curls. Unhappily, in 1982, this icon from my childhood went literally under the developer's hammer and it took just 60 minutes at 4 a.m. one morning to demolish our memories. The site is now covered in a modern luxury townhouse development and not the great arched entry way that dominated the skyline on the north side for over 40 years.

In reference to another school 'do' there, this other observation was made:

> ...at primary school in the '60s we had our annual folk dancing and ballroom dancing night there ... in all your [very] best clobber, your olds came along...the floor was still [all] waxed to perfection... no hard shoes allowed...sliding in socks was awesome...the outside promenade to check out the city and the river...kissing your grade six GF...and getting bagged by your mates for doing it...and then taking an emotional failed king hit swipe at them with one arm.

A former Mitchelton State primary school student also has a similar story to relate when their annual fancy dress ball was held at Cloudland. He recalls that the 'sprung floor' during the *Boston Two*

Step encouraged enthusiastic, if not graceful, bouncing.

A conga line—with some in fancy dress—snaking its path along towards other Brisbane happy revellers.
Courier-Mail. Picture research: Gwen McLachlan.

To the sound of "Let's all form a circle for *Auld Lang Syne!*", on New Year's Eve this traditional rendition of parting would resound about the Bowen Hills suburb at Cloudland on the 31st of December each year. People gathered at the dances, got together a 'party' of people—some were in fancy dress—and they sang on the surrounding streets to ring out the old year and to ring in the new. In Brisbane, resolutions were made and strangers kissed. It was the one occasion during the year when it was said "anything goes".

DANCE COMPETITIONS

Leslie and Dorothy Allen *c.* 1957: Dorothy's gown is emerald green with red poinsettia flowers and darker green leaves; all hand-made including the hand stitched sequins. This was her first competition gown.

Courtesy of Dorothy's mother.

The [dancer's] art is in heels and toes, stiff pleats and arms swing in unison, a vicarious war of good manners and style.

An anthem's art is the equivalent sung: two strangers side by side can do it and imagine common ancestors watching over them like parents inspecting their young, making every-one else a foreigner not quite good enough to belong.

Craig Sherbourne

Dancers in motion... "light filters in through the windows during a ballroom dancing festival at Cloudland in 1952".
Courier-Mail. Picture: Bob Millar, Jnr.

Brisbane suburbs had hosted social dancing on Friday or Saturday nights before folk were able to venture out to the palace on the hill. Variety has always been the spice of life for dance competitors since then at Cloudland. "It was

ballroom dancing, not so much for all of the fanciest footwork"—albeit that blithe steps were surely now in evidence—but for the *"slow-slow-quick, quick-slow* pacing", according to one commentator.

Capturing a competitive moment in time... "music, movement and the post-war spirit is captured at a Ballroom Dancing Festival, 1952, at Cloudland".
Courier-Mail. Picture: Bob Millar, Jnr.

A *Courier-Mail* article of 1962 described in great detail the precise moves partners would need to use for competition events:

The dancers bowing and curtseying to their partners were in conventional pairs but not for long. "Although they outnumbered the boys 3-2, these girls were not just like wall-flowers", *The Courier-Mail* reported.

"The boys just took an extra partner and they danced in threes".

"The method was simple. The boy put one arm around the waist of the inside girl and held the hand of the outside girl. The outside girl put her hand on the shoulder of the inside girl, who put hers on her partner's shoulder".

Famous dance pair, and now retired garden partners, Norman and Nancy Berg, were the Australian Ballroom Dance Champions in 1952; and performed around Australia, including venues like Cloudland.

"The couple's later marionette show was a big hit in Japan and won them many awards".

Australian Senior.

As dancers, Norman and Nancy performed alongside famous entertainers such as Frank Sinatra and Nat King Cole; and were familiar faces on Japanese television shows.

Ballroom dance 'comps' at Cloudland were a pretty serious affair, as this Melbourne report confided:

BALLROOM DANCING
Promoters eager to
book champions
By Alan Grant

Promoters are usually pretty quick off the mark to book the winners of the Australian Championships for a professional engagement, but they were quicker than ever this year in signing up the 1950 champions, Jack Bosley and Joyce Morris.

To make sure of being "first in" with the new champions, the management of "Cloudland " Ballroom, Brisbane, had an agent on the spot at the Melbourne Town Hall the night the championship was decided.

An attractive contract was all ready for signing as soon as the result was announced and not long after they left the floor in the final, Jack and Joyce had signed on the dotted line.

Then had followed a hectic week of demonstrations to all the Brisbane audiences and judging of the competitions regularly staged by the "Cloudland" management.

Jack and Joyce do tell me they were greatly impressed by the ability of Brisbane's top amateurs, who defeated representatives from Sydney and Canberra in a three-cities' challenge.

Jack and Joyce are cricket fanatics and were longing to turn up to the first England-Australia Test. I'm told they'd have made the trip for a bunch of bananas, so the "Cloudland" engagement was doubly attractive to them.

ALF DAVIES and Julie Reaby, worthy runners-up in the professional championship are also often "in demand". I hear that Alf has received an offer that would tie him up for a long season.

I learned of nothing "officially" of their chances, but in my opinion

Alf and Julie, after their brilliant showing in the championship, should be "certainties" for inclusion in any "test" team of dancers we may send abroad to represent Australia..

As he now does not want to miss his chance of inclusion in the team, Alf is not committing himself to any prolonged Australian contract. A wise move, I would say.

(The Argus of December 16th, 1950.)

Even square dancing made its appearance on the hill. Square dancing was an adaptation of the traditional American style and dances were performed to the folk music of the past. Taking up the square dancing 'challenge' at Cloudland meant that real mental and physical work had to be learned—especially with entire dance movements; changing dance movements without notice; and keeping up with the callers. The men wore long-sleeved shirts and string ties; the women chose skirts with frilly petticoats and shoes with leather soles.

'Twirling the girl' kept square dancers up on their toes at Cloudland. *Senior News.*

CLOUDLAND'S QUAINT ALPINE RAILWAY

The Cloudland Funicular Cha-Cha

Black shellac solid vinyl scratches sounds for a time when the whole world wore hats. I am counting the stars above Newstead and doing the funicular cha-cha. And jive was for juve delinks/ be bop/ here we go

~ blue note and Billie's nocturne lay a flow. A gal in a Lindy satin skirt & mohair top berserks *Go, cats, Go!*

Voodoo / trance / dance dance.

In Sammy's Late Night Cafeteria musical hysteria ~ Clayfield Clarry roars *That Viper can blow!* and he'd be a bloke deep in the know playing [upon] a different bandstand every night up with the gods like the Billo Smith Band/ be bop or CLOUDLAND CLOUDLAND CLOUDLAND where you just might go crazy with our altitude's air.

Be bop / bobby sox / here we go! *Slip us the lubricant! Hey, you hoons, don't break those chandeliers: put those shivs away.* Be bop/ way back/ way back in the ether when the whole world wore [those] hats that same gravel-voiced DJ intoned *here's a little tune you just might know*. Black shellac solid vinyl

To that mating ground of the lusty free here we go!

CLOUDLAND CLOUDLAND.

Robert Morris

The cover of poet Robert Morris' *The Cloudland Funicular Cha-Cha.*

Cloudland's alpine-style railway.

The world's oldest continuing example of the kind seen from the 1940s as the Luna Park (Cloudland's) 'alpine railway' was the Scenic Railway, at Luna Park, Melbourne. The funicular project was completed in the early 1940s, probably close to the time on October 26th, 1940, when Melbourne's last cable car went on its final trip.

This photograph of Luna Park, by Charles J. Stehlik, is of Luna Park (Cloudland) in World War II. It displays the entrance to the "open air alpine tram type arrangement". *Note the turnstile on the right.*

The architect of the railway project imagined the location as an alpine resort and used a funicular railway, based on a European design: to convey its patrons from Breakfast Creek Road to the top of the hill at the 'grand entrance', where Cloudland was situated. Evidently, the trip took 2½ minutes to make the journey from the vicinity of the bus or tram stop. There were two 'cars'—one moving in either or different directions at all times—and carrying 30 passengers up a steep (approximately 110 yard) climb (i.e. 100 metres).

Two other views of the 'funicular railway'.

As one patron who used the 'alpine' facility recalls:

In much earlier times, the dance hall complex had boasted a cable car to ferry patrons from the tram stops... By the time my contemporaries and I had begun our Cloudland careers, the cable car had ceased operation although its tracks were still in place. There was a car park on the Sandgate Road side of the complex, while those without any cars arrived either in taxis or by train to the old Bowen Hills station to be followed by a steep walk up to the entrance.

During the 1950s and 1960s (to 1969) 'Cloudlanders' additionally travelled by tram from Fortitude Valley to the large dome on the Brisbane skyline.

The 'Alpine Railway' finished its operations, closing in 1967; then the Cloudland Bus Service was introduced to 'ferry any visitors from Breakfast Creek Road. In time, Hans Apel and his sons drove patrons up the hill in a VW Combi van. The space which the funicular railway occupied was then turned into a venue car park.

The funicular railway in its operational days.

The funicular railway pictured after its use-by date.

Courier-Mail, November 8th, 1982.

Spectacle from atop the funicular railway, pre-1967.

Apel family collection.

The entrance to Cloudland Ballroom.

Apel family collection.

Front entrance into Cloudland, pre-1967.

Apel family collection.

9

IVAN 'DAISY' DAYMAN'S CLOUDLAND, 1960s

THE 1960s

The beginning of the new decade—the 1960s—was marked by various conflicts around the world:

It was the end of a significant year—1960 was racked by the birth pangs of a dozen new nations in black Africa; nationalists revolted in Algeria, Abyssinia, Laos, Nicaragua, Costa Rica and Turkey; John F. Kennedy was elected United States president; Russia had recovered three dogs, alive, from space; then the Americans recovered three mice; and Princess Margaret was married to Anthony Armstrong-Jones.

For us in Brisbane, though, the early 1960s was a period of freedom and of peace in our own corner of the universe. Very few had it better than Lou Reed: 'Hey, babe—take a walk on the wild side'.

Speaking for myself, the '60s was 'the decade'. It was a teenage period as the post-war baby boomers were now moving towards their own adulthood. The old rigidity, repression and political conservatism of the 1950s (with its relatively strong Westminster base) had dominated our lives for the past thirteen to nineteen of so years. This grey-flannelled era was now quite vigorously opposed by an equally rapid and fast changing

lifestyle and moral system, where the familiar and stoic British values we had known, loved and grown up with comfortably, were presently up against the American derivative: rock'n'roll, plus radio and the TV culture.

During the era of the 1960s, the entire family could now all enjoy a breath-taking and a widening range of luxurious consumer goods.

As the '60s unfolded, beat generation author William Burroughs, with his divisive novel, *The Naked Lunch*, had tested American obscenity laws, softening censorship in both the United States and elsewhere. There was *such* a sustained and liberating *joi de vivre* concerning the new decade, that in Britain someone referred to it as 'The Swinging Sixties'. The world was instantly linked loosely by a global-type mentality of pop culture (TV, music, fashion, partying and enjoying oneself) which threatened to run haywire. It was little wonder then that the three principal passions of this whole decade for baby boomers were drugs, sex and rock'n'roll.

In this charged climate, the baby boomers moved to present themselves openly and pragmatically. They exhibited anti-establishment attitudes; self-fulfilment; a fashion consciousness; laughter, whimsy and optimism; and hedonism; experimentation; instant gratification; and faddism. They also embraced pop culture, shouted slogans, revolted against parental authority, and protested against the war while 'doing their own thing'. It was, indeed, an *Age of Aquarius.* As the entertainer, Johnny O'Keefe, summed it up for us all: 'I drive myself hard, then suddenly some'. No wonder we all sang along with *The Who* in 1965 when they advised: 'I hope I die before I get old'.

Merle Thornton, mother of actor, Sigrid, and a pioneering radical feminist who had lectured in women's studies at St. Lucia's

Queensland's University, affected Brisbane's social history. During 1965, she and Rosalie Bognor chained themselves to the bar of the *Regatta Hotel* in Toowong. At this time, women could not drink in any public bars in Queensland. Fortunately, the occurrence sparked intense debate and the archaic law was changed soon afterwards.

Injustices of racism and dis-crimination during the mid-1960s had inspired Aboriginal activists in their struggles for change.
What's On Inside Qld –Feb-Mar. 2012.)

The old Regatta Hotel.
State Library of Queensland.

Merle Thornton and Rosalie Bognor as they chained themselves to the *Regatta Hotel* bar.

CLOUDLAND, 1960s

There's nothing like a dream to create the future. Utopia today, flesh and blood tomorrow.

Victor Hugo (1802-1885),
French author-playwright

Even by the 1960s, when other local dance halls had begun to lose their 'glitter' and 'allure', Cloudland was still a 'crowd-puller'.

David Gibson reminisces about the dancehall's former place in Brisbane's skyline:

You'd sit up there on Machinery Hill [at the Exhibition Ground in Brisbane] and you would look

behind you, and there was the magnificent neon ribbon around this extraordinary portico. In much the same way that the television towers on Mount Coot-tha now are all the 'porch-lights' of the citizenry of Brisbane, that neon rainbow was [such] a comforting and a reassuring part of the Brisbane skyline.

If you were looking over towards Cloudland's illuminated arch, in 1961 *The Shirelles'* hit song *Will You Still love Me Tomorrow* posed an eternal question; and patrons inside the venue would later be dancing the 'twist' and the 'pony' to the beat of Chubby Checker. If you tuned into the local radio airwaves, Elvis

Presley's *Little Sister*; Del Shannon's *Runaway*; and *Where the Boys Are* by Connie Francis might be lulling you this very same night.

Cloudland's grand entrance—the "impressive and imposing interior of the original ballroom", 1960.

Courier-Mail Archive.

Dorothy and Leslie Allen, at Cloudland, 1959/60.

Getting prepared for an old time dance item, Cloudland in 1961.

Dance night at Cloudland, 1961.

Apel family collection.

THE SUNSHINE GROUP AND IVAN H. DAYMAN

In 1962 the Panorama Room was added to Cloudland's activities by Hans Apel. Within the same year, a Northern Command Ball was held at the ballroom venue.

For most of the '60s decade, Cloudland was used regularly by Australian bands. It was also a central location for the Sunshine group. This organisation was headed by the (soon to become) Brisbane entrepreneur and promoter, Ivan H. Dayman, of Dance Promotions Pty Ltd., who had travelled originally from Adelaide. He leased Cloudland Ballroom from H. R. Apel in February, 1964, although Hans Apel was to still own the complex, with his hand steadily on the tiller, until 1968. Dayman's lease, however, supposedly ran into the year of 1978.

Ivan Dayman.

State Library of Victoria.

In Queensland, Dayman shored up his Brisbane interests:

In the early 1960s it [Cloudland] was a major venue for his Sunshine group, which had opened a string of dance halls and clubs around Queensland and [music/circuits/venues] in Sydney and Melbourne. The Sunshine organisation included artist management, booking agencies, and a string of music venues in major cities and towns (most called "The Bowl"). Dayman also set up Sunshine Records [in late 1964 with Paul Aulton and Nat Kipner]—whose roster boasted top 'beat' bands including Tony Worsley & *the Blue Jays*, Normie Rowe, Ronnie Burns and Mike Furber.

How Ivan found the time and energy (in the 1960s and 1970s) to work as a record producer and band manager; and also look after the local pop 'legends', like Normie Rowe, is anyone's guess.

Ivan was most eager for his new protégé in Rowe to reach success:

The head of Sunshine records, Ivan Dayman, also Normie's manager, ran a long-established string of national venues. He knew the art of promotion. Legend has it that the security guards he hired to protect Normie from his enthusiastic fans were also under instructions to trip the singer or push him off the stage into the arms of his fans, ensuring those 'riots'. These venues were also crowded beyond capacity, resulting in fans fainting from more than Normie Rowe worship. However it had happened, it all made for great pictures and headlines in the newspapers. The hits kept coming.

Normie Rowe and his group *The Playboys* became the star attraction of all the Sunshine tours, which criss-crossed the eastern coast of Australia. Normie was on a bus with all the rivals for his crown as Australia's No. 1 King of Pop—Tony

Worsley, Mike Furber—anxious to upstage him.

Ivan Dayman's 'Dance Promo' for Sunshine Records, 1963.

Normie Rowe.

There was hardly ever a dull moment or a time to 'slacken off' for Ivan Dayman, as he managed Cloudland Ballroom including its accompanying *Panorama Room*'s day-to-day operations, including a restaurant. Evidently, the *Panorama Room* was based on one constructed in Redcliffe in the 1940s; and it had featured details of its trade for weddings, dances and parties in a local 1949 advertisement. H. R. Apel, the owner prior to Ivan's leasing of the venue, had initiated its original operations at Cloudland.

Dayman's Sunshine Group didn't just stop with those 'beat' band signings listed previously:

Cloudland's front entrance.

> Among the [other] acts signed or managed by Ivan Dayman were... Peter Doyle, *The La De Das* while they were in Australia, and *Mother Goose* in the late 1970s. Dayman signed the *Bee Gees* early in their career, but only managed them for a brief period of limited success before they had departed for England.
>
> Dayman owned multiple venues within his territory, for instance, the Cloudland Ballroom in Brisbane (leased from H. Apel around 1964), *The Bowl Soundlounge* in Sydney, and the *Op Pop disco*. By having a stake in both the bands and the venues, he was able to monopolise his area of audience.

Ivan's partner, Nat Kipner, (with Toni McCann, Col Joye and Robin Brompton) at a cocktail party in Sydney.

Nat Kipner's liaison and partnering with Ivan (and his crucial role in signing, promoting and recording each new 'beat' act) was a close one, bonded through the former's close interest in, and expertise about, various music genres:

> Nat's introduction to the recording industry came via a business partnership with Ivan Dayman... In late 1964, he and Nat opened another dance hall in Sydney, and started the Brisbane-based record label called Sunshine Records. Nat's first productions for Sunshine were on Normie Rowe's 1965 hit LP, *It ain't necessarily so*. One of the highlights of the LP was *She used to be mine*, a song written by Nat and his son Steve. Nat's production tasks for Rowe then extended to a No.1 single, a most scintillating cover version of Johnny Kidd and *The Pirates' Shakin' all over*.

CLOUDLAND'S PANORAMA ROOM
Overlooking Brisbane

The 'Panorama Room', 1960s

In June of 1965, Sunshine released another of Nat's productions, *My baby/No* by Toni McCann and *The Fabulous Blue Jays*. Although it wasn't a hit, the record in now regarded as one of the finest of Australia's early punk singles.

One of Normie Rowe's Sunshine Label 45 rpm covers.

Over time Pat [Aulton] linked up with Adelaide promoter, Ivan Dayman, who was still in the process of building up his Sunshine music mini-empire, which included artist management, a chain of venues in several major cities including the fabled Cloudland Ballroom, and the Sunshine and Kommotion record labels. Pat's duties were not just confined to Dayman's Cloudland operation:

...Ivan Dayman whisked me away from the *Clefs* and Barrie (McAskill) did a sterling job as my replacement: The Norwood Ballroom with Neville Dunn's *Planets*, The *Hi-Marks* plus a couple of other bands were my day-to-day work until Ivan decided to invade Melbourne so I relocated and worked at Town Hall dances some being Preston, Canterbury, Ballarat and Bendigo.

For his Sunshine releases by Normie Rowe, Pat taught himself how to produce records—a skill at which he was obviously a natural—and he also produced nearly all of the highly successful recordings of this whole creative period, including Normie's landmark double *A*-side "Shakin' All Over"/"Que Sera Sera", which is believed to be the biggest-selling Australian single of the 1960s. He also produced several singles for the short-lived Kommotion label.

Around the beginning of 1967 Dayman got into serious financial difficulties. Kommotion folded, Sunshine was taken over by Festival and Pat discovered that as a director, he was liable for part of the debts Dayman incurred. As a result he had his car and furniture repossessed and was out of work until Fred Marks of Festival came to his rescue, offering him the position of staff producer, concentrating on the pop artists. Luckily for Pat, this coincided with Festival's move to new premises in Pyrmont and the upgrading of its studio with new 4-track equipment.

Bill Casey, the pop culture historian, blames Ivan Day-man's questionable business practices for Sunshine's demise as well as the contributing circumstances of the financial strain of Normie Rowe's extended overseas tour.

Two views of Cloudland Ballroom, ca. 1960s, Bowen Hills, Brisbane. They depict the *Panorama Room* to the *right*.

DAYMAN AT CLOUDLAND

Irrespective of some of his financial woes, discovering a 'jewel in the crown' of his operations in Cloudland Ballroom was to be Dayman's saviour.

Pat Aulton's 'introduction' to Dayman's pivotal operation in Brisbane—Cloudland—was a little 'bizarre':

Ivan Dayman, who was a promoter and…my employer, and he was a nice bloke. Very straight and very loyal and I was loyal to him. We did Adelaide, we did Melbourne. Melbourne was terrific because we opened Preston and Canterbury. Then Ivan said, "We're going to Brisbane". I said "OK. What are we going to do there?" He said, "I think I'll take over Cloudland". So he came here and we saw Hans Apel who owned Cloudland and he leased it to Ivan. It had an office out the back and a huge ballroom which I used to sweep every day apart from work at night and we built the crowd up from 1250 with Bernie Kempster. I must go back to this story because it is a lovely story. We walked into the hall on the first night, Ivan and I just standing there looking at these people, and it was like going back 30 years because they were all ballroom dancing, *foxtrot*, etcetera. There was a list, a white list at the front, all backlit and it said *foxtrot, quickstep, foxtrot*. It was all in a little box and it was right in front of Bernie Kempster who was the piano player of the 16-piece orchestra and Bernie had the [task] of replacing these sleeves. The next might be a *polka*, etc. The end result was we kept looking at Bernie and I said to Ivan, "He hasn't got his teeth in". I looked at the charts and they were 1932 Jimmy Lally arrangements. It was a time warp. He seemed just out of control. I just couldn't believe it because having come through all the rock'n'roll system, we had walked into the place and said, "Ivan, we need a good broom here". Ivan had also spotted it and as observant as he was, we just walked in and did it. It was [really] wonderful. (Geoff Walden, *It was only Rock'n'Roll*).

Pat Aulton.

At Cloudland, following Ivan Dayman's 'invasion' of Brisbane, Pat Aulton also "became the emcee and the singer with three bands working the ballroom and during the day—[he] was also the cleaner". Pat Aulton and Ivan Dayman kept a tight rein on Cloudland's working musicians:

In order to work regularly, Alan Campbell had to be a member of the musicians' union. "If you weren't a member of the union you could not play at Cloudland Ballroom".

When Ivan Dayman was running the venue, the *'no ticket no work'* rule was strictly adhered to. Tom Day remembers Bill Robertson visiting at a mid-day record hop Dulcie was running at The City Hall. She had hired the *Planets*, which presented a [big] problem for Bill. "Righto Dulcie, get your cheque book out. If you don't I'll shut you down. They're not yet in the union". Dulcie wrote out a cheque and bought all the band members union tickets. Tom was totally unaware of any situations where the union had actually shut any venue down—"it was all bluff".

Rick Farbach.

To bring some added stability into stage proceedings, Ivan Dayman had also hired Rick Farbach as his band leader at Cloudland. Rick stayed three and a half years, writing and making many commercials; writing scores for two movies, as well as playing them; and completing numerous arrangements for theatre orchestras then conducting them.

Some of the 'resident' band groups Paul Aulton had something to do with from the late 1960s included *The Sounds of Seven*, *The Highmarks* and *Seasons of the Witch*. The dance format in this decade covered old time '60/40' through to high standard rock'n'roll. *The Sounds of Seven* featured John Lye on the drums and Jeanette Burke on vocals.

Ken Campbell took over as [their] guitarist in *The Sounds of Seven* in 1968 and was responsible for arranging all of the music the band played. During busy times Ken played up to fourteen nights straight. All of the musicians had second jobs and those long nights made for some sleepy days during their day jobs.

Vince, Chas and Ken agree[d] that the acoustics in Cloudland were fantastic. He treasured his time on top of the hill where the view inside was just as good as the view outside.

Ross D. Wylie.

Bill & Boyd; Mick Hadley and *The Purple Hearts*; Rev. Black and *the Rockin' Vicars*; Peter Doyle and David Greenwood also worked at Cloudland for Ivan Dayman. Julie Paris recalls:

> ...we moved to Brisbane, and I was just 16 years old. I got in touch with Ivan Dayman who booked me to sing at some dances at the old Cloudland Ballroom, and I also performed at Mersey City (Festival Hall) alongside Ross D. Wylie and *The Kodiacs*, Tony Worsley and *The Fabulous Blue Jays* and David Greenwood, who was also an announcer with radio station 4IP. In those days I called myself Julie Paris (the Paris was compliments of Freddie, but I had just thought that Julie went well with it). Most of my music was from Helen Shapiro, Connie Francis as well as a lot of male vocalists such as Neil Sedaka (*Hey, little devil*) because I have quite a deep voice, so I did a bit of country rock as well.

Peter Doyle.

Julie 'Paris'.

Bill Cate of Bill & Boyd fame, with his two talented children, Melanie and Matt.

The *Gold Tones*: Marcie Jones; Toni McCann; *The Librettos*; *The Atlantics*; Tony Cornwall and *The Knights*; Ricky and Tammy; Jonnie Sands; *Wickety Wak*; *The Cookies*; *The Playboys*; Julie Paris; Ross D. Wylie and *The Kodiacs*; Tony Worsley and *the Fabulous Blue Jays*; *Running Jumping Standing Still*;

Mike Furber's teaming up with *The Bowery Boys* at Cloudland was clearly not one of Ivan Dayman's greatest moves:

> A lot of blame can be rested firmly at Ivan Dayman's feet. He was already middle-aged and he knew nothing about rock & roll. He continually pushed Furber while leaving *The Bowery Boys*

out of television appearances and interstate tours. It's strange now to imagine, but we all think that Furber was a solo star and *The Bowery Boys* were a bunch of patsies who were just paid up to back him. This, of course, is false, but it was exactly what Dayman wanted everybody to think. Well, he had succeeded even though the guys from *The Bowery Boys* still thought of themselves as part of the whole box and dice and not only just Mike Furber's backing band.

This occurrence had left the late Dean Mittelhauser marooned from his own band, with Mr Dayman grooming him as a solo act, almost like a Normie Rowe clone.

Mike Furber.

Mick Hadley of *the Purple Hearts*' oddball 'teaming' with Ivan at Cloudland may also be recounted here:

The King in sign and disband of Sixties Brisbane was Ivan Dayman. Rolling in quids from his 60 /40 dance operation at Cloudland, Ivan 'Daisy' Dayman was Father (a smidgin of Sam Giancanna as well as Colonel Tom Parker) to the Brisbane Music Scene. The blond, six-foot, & tanned Mick Hadley, with a nose making him far more rugged than pretty, was soon in the sights of Dayman.

Hadley's response that singing and his harmonica playing was just part

of the band package, had Dayman still sign the [*Purple*] *Hearts* to his Sunshine Label but surely confused his management style. What does it mean if the plunk is more important than the look? So while Normie [Rowe] flew solo to whatever will be, Mick wailed that he was the fool who dropped right out of school. He had the loyalty to never see any of his fellow *Hearts* as dead weights to a career.

Mick Hadley and *The Purple Hearts*.

Another of Dayman's tour group to Brisbane's Cloudland was Peter (John) Doyle:

By the time he was sixteen, Peter had obtained a recording contract with Ivan Dayman's *Sunshine Records*; he had secured four top 40 singles and an album called simply *Peter's First Album*; he performed regularly at Melbourne's Festival Hall and toured around Australia with other nationally acclaimed stars, for example, Colin Cook, Marcie Jones, Normie Rowe and *The Playboys* and Tony Worsley. He made regular appearances on TV, including the *Go Show*, Graham Kennedy's *In Melbourne Tonight* and *Sunny Side Up*. Popular, shy and retiring, Peter never pushed himself but his voice and musical abilities were so great that he could not fail to be a star.

Tony Worsley's input to Cloudland in particular, and the Brisbane rock scene in general from 1959 to 1967, should never be devalued:

Tony was born Anthony Asheen Worsley in England in 1944 and emigrated with his family from his hometown of Hastings to the sunnier climes of Brisbane when he was 15. Tony had already set his sights on a show biz career. As a lad he won several amateur talent quests in England including one judged by Lonnie Donnegan and Tommy Steele, which carried first prize of a Decca recording contract. Needless to say, his parents' decision to leave for Australia right as this point didn't go down well with the ambitious young singer—"I didn't get on with my parents too much on the ship for the first few weeks!"—but he was determined to fulfil that new dream in his adopted country. By day he worked as an apprentice rigger in the Brisbane dockyards, but at night he patrolled the dance halls, waiting for his big chance to get up on stage.

Peter Doyle 1949-2001. He later joined the *New Seekers*.

The band featuring Tony Worsley and *The Fabulous Blue Jays* was a very exciting and accomplished addition to Cloudland's line up:

Tony Worsley (vocals)

backed by

The Fabulous Blue Jays:

Original line-up (1959):

Frankie Brent (guitar, vocals) 1959-?

Bobby "Spider" Johnson (drums) 1959-60, 1964-66

Chris Lawson (guitar) 1959-?

Doug Stirling (keyboards) 1959-?

Later members:

Laurie Allen (keyboards, guitar, vocals) 1961-63

Jimmy Cerezo (lead guitar) 1965-66

Mal "Beaky" Clarke (rhythm guitar) 1963-67

Johnny Cosgrove (guitar) 1960

Ray "Screamy" Eames (lead guitar) 1964-65

Alan Easterbrook (sax) 1959-64

Doug Flower (guitar) 1963

Malcolm Hope (bass)

Ray Houston (bass) 1960-62

Royce "Baby" Nicholls (bass) 1964-66

Paul "Bingo" Shannon (sax, keyboards) 1964-66

Graham Trottman (drums)

Denis Tucker 1963-4?

The New Blue Jays **(1966)**

John Bellamy (bass)

John A. Bird (keyboards)

Paul Fox (bass)

Vince Maloney (guitar)

Phil Manning (guitar)

Brian Patterson (guitar)

Brian Saunders (bass)

Jim Thompson (drums)

Tony and *The Blue Jays'* record for the Sunshine label.

Tony Worsley.

Ivan Dayman's offer to Tony Worsley via Nat Kipner was hardly going to set him up on 'easy street':

In 1964, there was another who wanted to organise the back up and sell of Tony Worsley.

Ivan 'Daisy' Dayman, retired at 40, an Adelaide gravel pit owner, was

gouging enough shillings out of his Cloudland Ballroom lease to dream of a national circuit of Swingers Clubs from Cairns to Broome. In conjunction with ex-Gold Coast Real Estate Salesman, Nat Kipner, also being organised was the Sunshine record label.

Worsley was taken on the roll.

"Dayman had offered me £35 a week (10 times Tony's sail-maker's wage) with limos, hotels, the whole bit thrown in if I'd front Melbourne band *The Blue Jays*". I was 21 and didn't want to put a deposit upon a block of land, you know. Sounded like good times to me so I was off whooska right in sweet".

It did not take long for Worsley and *The Blue Jays* to hit their 'beat' musical 'straps' with Ivan:

After teaming up at the start of 1964, Tony and *The Blue Jays* had immediately set about creating a dynamic stage show, based around Tony's brash but appealing tenor voice, a rough'n'tough stage presence and cheeky, boyish good looks. Backed up by one of the tightest and the most competent bands in the country and *The Blue Jays* trademark "fattish" sound, blended-sax-and-guitar, in a potent lead instrumental assault, giving them a much heavier attack than many of their contemporaries. From this most recently acquired Brisbane base... Dayman had promoted the group on his popular "Bowl" dance circuit package extravaganzas, and Tony & *The Blue Jays* quickly earned a reputation for upstaging the main acts.

(Speaking of his 'all or nothing' approach to performing, Tony Worsley had quipped: "You, too, might see blue shadows in the night if a career as a Beat star had you remembered for the Ballad—*Velvet Waters*".)

Bentley's sketch of Cloudland's fabled arch.   *Sunday Mail.*

10

MUSIC FOR EVERYONE'S TASTES

EVENTS FOR THE 'PUNTERS'

Many a male baby boomer at Cloudland may remember the Saturday nights there. They would have a few ales at the local 'watering hole', such as the *Waterloo Hotel*. Most young folk presented themselves well—couples were neatly dressed. The 'standard attire' for most young blokes was a shirt, and a tie with neatly-pressed slacks. Most young girls wore the fuller type skirts.

June Adamson declared herself a bit of a 'rebel'; and took to a daring 'hoop' skirt. Her attire of choice was—

> ...a cane hoop guaranteed to keep fashionable billowing skirts from collapsing and grasping at legs for support, hindering movement and spoiling the effect.
>
> These were my teenage years of jive and rock and roll...Now I was determined not to go looking like a country cousin so [I] stocked up on the latest fashions. I thought I had all I needed until in a...shop I saw THE HOOP! So of course I had to have one.
>
> Swirling skirts over my starched half-slips were what I was used to,

but this outlet promised that the hoop was far superior. It was made from light cane and was suspended by tapes from a cotton waistband and was, of course, quite flexible. But you just try to sit in a milk bar with a rigid hoop beneath your skirt. You try to board a crowded bus with this odd fashion accessory. It was strictly for standing around in, and, of course, never caught on. I was probably their first and last customer.

Oh yes, the bus. Getting on was the first problem; trying to pass through the entrance door was a major obstacle until I turned the hoop temporarily onto its side. Trying to obey the instruction to "Pass on down to the back" was the next, as each time I was pushed against other standing passengers the hoop raised itself either front or back, exposing skinny fake-tanned legs and I hate to think what else! Other passengers seemed to find it so hilarious in a very good-natured way and I could only grin back in a pretence of good humour. The only escape was to push myself and my hoop out to the footpath where I loosened its tether and stepped out of its embarrassing embrace. My previously puffed skirt collapsed, my ears and cheeks were burning and I almost ran. There was one thought of consolation; at least no-one knows me here. I dumped the hoop and left it behind for ever. I wonder now what became of that ghastly fashion mistake.

As David Moss also recalls about the 'Cloudland girls:

I have memories of Cloudland and the fabulous girls that had a lot of class, the days when us as young blokes could actually dance with and close to a girl. Now the guys have no romance, just a case of will you or won't you. No respect and today's girls are too fast for the likes of me.

Within these times, the "women were [often] wooed and courted, couples danced together… in unison with the music of the big band".

By the 1960s, our conservative clothing of the 1950s had also given way to much more colourful garments. A few of us had started to wear our hair long, like *The Beatles* and other rock groups. Some of the girls even had prim hairdos, held together with pins and hair spray.

The standard attire for Cloudland— a full skirt.

By 1964, besides *The Beatles*, we also had the 'Mods' and 'Rockers' with which to contend. About this time, though, Brisbane had experienced all the bodgie and the widgie 'beat speak' of 1958 and beyond. This was 'cool', 'cat', 'Daddy-o', 'pad' and 'square'. On humid nights, we had danced ourselves into a ball of sweat at Cloudland. By then, the various Mod and Rock bands were easily accepted as the norm.

The Beatles performing in 1964.

Yet another of Cloudland's admirers remembers how she met her future husband there:

My memories of Cloudland are in the '64 to '68 era. We would go there often.

Most of our 'courting' was done there, In that era you weren't 'legal' to go to the pubs til you were 21 and apart from the movies and private parties there wasn't a lot to do.

One memorable night I went out with a nursing friend. While there we saw the boy we had met at a friend's party the week before. My friend [then] pointed him out and we brazenly approached him. Being the gentleman he was he danced turn about with us and I whispered to my friend, "We should be right for a lift back to the nurses' quarters".

So about 11.30 I said, "We have to go soon as we have to be back by midnight". The reply was "Oh, well, good night, I am sorry I don't have a car". Well that resulted in a great dash down the hill to make it back to South Brisbane on time.

A happy ending to the story, is that we did continue to see each other and will celebrate our 40th Wedding Anniversary this December.

We attended many balls there as well as all the Saturday night dances.

One young lad recalls his initial experience at a more formal event at Cloudland with mixed feelings:

By the time I reached dancing age my own early experiences of Cloudland in the mid-Sixties were ambivalent ones. There was the Teacher's College *Welcome Dance* of 1965 where, as a 16 year old boy from out of the bush, I was way out of my league among the broad shouldered men and sweet smelling women who [had] glided in pairs across the floor which, I was reliably informed, floated on springs.

Kath McGrath had fond memories of joining a band for its 'gigs' in the 1960s:

For Kath McGrath, the Cloudland Ballroom was more than a dance hall: it was the training ground for a career.

It was the early 1960s and the big band was playing popular jazz and swing songs. All they needed was a pianist.

"I was meant to be filling in for a month and when it ended I went to work in pubs. Three days later I got a call saying all the boys wanted me back", Mrs McGrath, 78, said.

Mrs McGrath, who lives in the Ipswich suburb of Goodna, spent a "wonderful" 18 months playing piano at the popular venue in Bowen Hills, before moving to Melbourne for a career in theatre.

"It was a different era, a lovely time musically, and there was something quite special about our Cloudland", she said.

"There were so many funny things that had happened there during the balls, the dances and the debutante balls". (*Courier-Mail*.)

Within the late 1960s Roland Ott took over as the ballroom's manager; and on September 12th, 1968, both the exterior and interior of Cloudland were painted, and a new ticket box installed.

'FUNKY' DANCE CRAZES

By the 1960s at Cloudland, many dancers had moved away from foxtrotting to 'frugging'. The 'frug' was a '60s dance craze which had evolved from the 'Twist', like the 'Swim' and the 'Monkey'. During 1962, the 'Mashed Potato', the 'Loco-Motion', the 'Frug', the 'Bump', the 'Monkey', the 'Swim' and also the 'Funky Chicken' were now popular dance forms, and seen with various degrees of expertise at Cloudland. The 'Twist' and 'The Stomp' also gave rise to intricate gyrations and frenetic leg motions. In essence, this baby boomer phase had a taste for the quintessentially adolescent—*The   Beatles,   the*

(Volkswagen) *Veedub*, the mini, the twist and the discotheque (plus Elvis Presley purple).

Eventually, the stomp had succeeded the twist in Australia. Little Pattie's song, *He's My Blonde-Headed Stompie-Wompie Real Gone Surfer Boy* reached Number Six on the 'Top Twenties' record list in Brisbane in 1963. With its reputation for having a highly 'sprung floor', the dance surfaces at Cloudland were not dealt any favours when the stomp craze was popular!

The twist is in evidence at the *Arthur Murray Studios*, Brisbane.

This odd dance craze—of the stomp—emanated out of Maroubra Beach, Sydney. It can be traced back to the singer 'Little Pattie' in 1963; and was a dance fuelled by the local beach scene in Australia in the 60s. It was much simpler than the twist.

A form of 'Go-go' dancing sometimes graced the dance floor at Cloudland:

> Go-go girls were an essential part of the 'furniture at '60s discos before the word became synonymous with permed hair, giant mirror balls and the sequined jumpsuits, a la *Saturday Night Fever*.
>
> The look involved a bunch of dancing girls all dressed in miniskirts and knee-high boots, with any tendency to blush from embarrassment hidden by a thick layer of foundation, bright lipstick and mascara.
>
> At first it was considered scandalous behaviour, particularly since British supermodel Jean "The Shrimp" Shrimpton had only recently [in 1965] scandalised our Australian society at a Melbourne Cup week function by wearing a mini that had ended slightly above her rather lovely knees.
>
> But it wasn't long before the go-go girl became almost as respectable as Jimi Hendrix. Then Andy Warhol and others pushed back the boundaries of what was deemed acceptable faster than a go-go girl could shimmy, shimmy, and shake. (*Sunday Mail*.)

An exhibition of 'Go-go' dancing.
Courier-Mail.

'CATACLYSMIC' CHANGES

Enjoy when you can, and endure when you must.

Johann Wolfgang von Goethe (1749-1832), *German author.*

By the late '60s, during the Vietnam War, the drinking age in Australia was lowered to 18 from 21 on the grounds that if 18 year olds could be conscripted to fight in the army for their own country, they should have the right to vote and drink. As a result of this drinking age being lowered, Cloudland was then able to serve alcohol to its patrons and young males did not have to resort to a City or Valley hotel in order to get up 'Dutch courage' for their outing at Cloudland.

Quite a lot of couples met at Cloudland; and it's safe to say that, prior to the pill's introduction, some of their offspring are only here because of that majestic place with its splendid setting. In fact, although it may be a slight exaggeration—and I am only 'joking'—I believe about one-quarter of the people of that vintage conceived in Brisbane were really the children—or by-products—of Cloudland!

Much earlier, the contraceptive pill and its arrival in Australia from

1961 revolutionised just 'how far a girl could go' after meeting a fellow at Cloudland.

Contraception has been around in various forms for millennia, but it wasn't until the US government approved the Pill in 1960 that it became so popular, so liberating.

The contraceptive pill works simply; it delivers two key sex hormones that trick the brain into thinking the body is already pregnant. It revolutionised the way women approached sex within the 1960s and was regarded as a great blessing to men who hitherto had been responsible for contraception.

Women felt invested with a new sense of ownership of their bodies. Many even improved their control over family planning; others welcomed a new sexual openness.

But the Pill had, and still has, its detractors. The Catholic Church banned it from use by its congregations and some women did not like the side-effects, accusing the pharmaceutical industry of mass exploitation. (*The Australian*.)

Up at Mount Coot-tha, after a big night at Cloudland, star-struck couples would often stop to admire all the stunning sights of the twinkling city lights. Within this picturesque setting, some blokes' sole intention was always to try to 'score'; but they'd often wonder if the girl was on the pill—although at this stage of our lives some of us were still avoiding the sex act.

One night, my friend Michael came across the nubile, alluring, and confident, Margo. He couldn't get her underwear off for the life of him. Somehow, the step-in and suspender belt had become 'skew-whiff'. The clips in the belt had left the stockings at odd angles and made the step-in ride up. Frustrated, Michael always checked on successive evenings if the girl he was with had too much 'box and tackle', by examining the fold lines under her clothes. If it looked like an 'Everest' job, Michael gave the game away.

Besides moral issues, for example, using the pill or not, the means of travel to Cloudland was also an issue. Before cars, north side gents, say, had asked a girl where she lived. If she said 'south side', they'd give her no more attention; and then seek another dance partner at Cloudland. As people now recall, these were times when it was safe for folk to walk home from the ballroom.

Changes to the way people travelled to Cloudland more or less steered 'Cloudlanders' towards using private vehicles or taxis. Most of the baby boomers would recognise the term "three on the tree" (a three-speed, column-shift gear change) automobile common around this period; and owned by many males.

As the iconic 'Alpine Railway' had been shut down in 1967, the Cloudland Bus Service was quickly introduced to bring the numerous visitors to the hilltop from the Breakfast Creek Road. On April 13th, 1969, Cloudland patrons were further inconvenienced when the last tram was taken off the Brisbane streets to much opposition.

SNIPPETS FROM A BABY BOOMER'S DIARY

All human actions have one or more of these seven causes: chance, nature, compulsion, habit, reason, passion and desire.

Aristotle (384 BC-322 BC).

In my book, *Snippets from a Baby Boomer's Diary*, I wrote extensively about the palace up on the hilltop at Bowen Hills. Fortunately, the work has achieved a kind of 'cult status' in Brisbane circles, with its humorous recounting of the 'growing up' years in Queensland's much-loved capital city. Set out below is a memorable section of this book…

The majority of baby boomers like me remember Cloudland warm-heartedly. It was the iconic music and dance venue of Bowen Hills which provided work for those in the entertainment industry for over 40 years. Cloudland provided a venue for the Brisbane community and so many baby boomers have vivid memories of its numerous functions.

Most boomer males opted to arrive at Cloudland by 9.30 p.m. or thereabouts for the *Progressive Barn Dance*, thereby perusing all the 'talent'. The 'standard attire' for local men was a tie, white shirt and slacks.

In the 1960s, Cloudland Ballroom changed dramatically from a place where the girls had worn gloves, formal dresses or full skirts and stoles during the 1950s. Sedate, traditional, big band music at this venue and the City Hall in Brisbane had given rise at one time to "pattern' dancing: *The Barn Dance, The Pride of Erin, The Gypsy Tap* and *The Canadian Three-Step*. Between 1957 and 1963, when Elvis Presley and 'bodgies' and 'widgies' were in vogue, this was bound to have a dramatic effect upon all of the staid musical offerings at Cloudland. We'd been to see the film *Jailhouse rock* starring Elvis Presley and thought it was tremendous.

From my earliest memory of 1957 onwards, into the 1960s, Cloudland had featured rock and roll as well as ballroom dancing at its Saturday night dances. With its dimly-lit balconies and its view of Brisbane's kaleidoscope of colourful lights, many young couples found romance at this hilltop dance palace. Cloudland was a magnificent looking place, especially in the evenings, illuminated and colourful, with well-clothed folk arriving in big American cars with their whitewall tyres.

As we grew older at the end of our teenage years, Ray, Alan, Michael and I would head off to Cloudland on a Friday night. It was somewhat like the reconnaissance mission on which the suspected

American 'spy', Gary Powers, had agreed to over Soviet Territory. I always washed my hair with Mum's 'Lustre-cream Shampoo of the Movie Stars'. I would put on a snow-white, drip-dry shirt (that Mum washed; and hung in the shower for me), and sharp tight-pegged black trousers that I had wished and begged her for years; and a thin belt. Then I'd polish my brogues with Kiwi shoe polish so Mum could see her reflection in them. I'd also slick my hair back with Brylcream or Californian Poppy just like Little Richard. There was never any real thought that, like James Joyce's schoolboy, I should see myself 'as creature driven and derided by vanity'. In fact, my potential had no ceiling. I was guided by the Latin proverb: 'He who loves himself best need fear no rival'.

The author dressed up for a big night out at Cloudland. On this odd occasion my favourite Marlon Brando jacket was missing, substituted for a suit.

Making oneself a little more attractive to those of the op-posite sex: an advertisement for some 'Imperial Leather' toiletries.

'Brylcream, a little dab'll do ya', I would sing to myself and to the mirror. 'Now, how about finding me a good sort, for one good sort?' I would add for luck, checking my duck's tail at the back and then teasing my forelock at the front. 'One like Tania Verstak [the gorgeous Russian girl who defected to our country; and became Miss Australia]'.

Then, if it was cold, I'd pick up my snazzy Canadian lumber jacket (which Mum loathed) and then drape it over one shoulder, just like I had seen Elvis or Marlon Brando do in the cinemas like *On the Waterfront*. Dad would invariably turn up at the front door to take a 'squizz' at me as I was about to leave and he'd acknowledge my appearance with a grunt of disdain.

A young Marlon Brando.

'Surely, *he's* not going out like that, Edna?' Dad would ask, 'Aren't you going to wear braces with those trousers?' he'd say turning to me directly.

'It's only a phase that he's going through, love', Mum would reply, as Dad would go meekly back to his *Telegraph* newspaper. 'He'll get over it'.

For transport purposes, I had a second-hand car at this point in time—my rear-engined *Fiat 600*. I could not really afford a *Mini-Minor* like some of my mates had (that was *the* car), but it got me 'from A to B'; and enabled me to take along my friends.

Before I hopped in the car, Mum would always lecture me in the same way every time.

'I know you're older now, Jim', she would explain, 'but don't you get too carried away. You'll only regret the results. Be home early'.

In the 1960s, Cloudland featured amplified guitars and modern-style orchestration. We would dance upon the springy floorboards to *The Gypsy Tap* as the band played *It's a Sin to Tell a Lie*; and then glance around the pillars at the girls on the seats, passing time for the rock and roll segment to commence. We'd get an orange soft drink or a cup of coffee and a biscuit and then look around for a possible dance partner.

At the music breaks, we'd often 'lair up' outside in front of small groups of girls by lighting our cigarettes and striking wax matches upon the outside walls. Occasionally, a girl was sufficiently impressed to make stilted conversation. At the time, we really did believe we could accomplish a great deal regarding girls with a big, toothy grin. Some may find that idea a bit disturbing, but to us that didn't matter in the least.

In those days, girls wore so many outfits it was hard to keep up with them. Several of them were quite simply dressed, wearing white frilly blouses, with lace and milkmaid sleeves, cardigans, box-pleated tunics, an Alice band in their hair; neat patent leather shoes or soles with elegant, spiked heels. A few wore dainty twin-sets in either pale pink or chartreuse Orlon (or cotton) with small pearl buttons. The odd 'renegade' wore a full skirt with a starched, rope petticoat so that the skirt would whirl out. They predominately had petite waists, slender hips and sizeable, fully-developed firm-looking busts.

Audrey Hepburn's 'beehive'.

Iconic 'meter maids', Gold Coast.

Others, according to Michael, looked 'common'. They wore tight mini-skirts and had beehive hairdos which were teased to an immense height, smoothed (to prevent any 'caving in') and then lacquered with Gossamer Hair Spray. Generally they were quite 'cheaply' dressed, like our Gold Coast 'meter maids', according to some of our mates.

'See that tarty looking 'bird in that mini-skirt with that frizzy blondish hair, heavily made-up white face and licking an ice-cream?' commented Michael as he carefully perused the 'common' girls.

'Yes. Over there, you mean?' I replied.

'Well', Michael went on, 'she looks just like a decoration on a Christmas tree'.

'Aw, gee, that's a bit much'.

'Let's see if she wants to see herself in lights up at Mt Coot-tha?'

If, in the dimly-lit room you had asked one of *these* kinds of girls to dance by mistake, people looked at you both wondering if you were 'potty' or 'Beauty and the Beast'. In most cases though, if you couldn't have what you liked, you learned to like what you had.

Whenever we 'won on' at Cloudland and met a girl, we normally drove to Mt Coot-tha in the western suburbs. Sometimes, if we were lucky, and the police didn't arrive and shine a torch on us, we were able to 'pash on' *ad nauseum* with our enthusiastic partners.

From Mount Coot-tha, during twilight, on a crisp evening, you could clearly see panoramic views of the Brisbane metropolis; as far as Moreton Bay on the Pacific Ocean and outwards to the Great Divide inland. The meandering Brisbane River, like the Rainbow Serpent of its Aboriginal Mythology, looped and bent just like a twisting silvery snake towards the bay. Soft lights danced on the river amid the glow of sub-tropical skies. In the growing darkness, all the gums, iron barks, box trees, ash and wattle appeared imperious, grim and determined. Down below us, the verdant gully that gave rise to the city, spread out before us. A hint of breeze might billow in the bush about us, encouraging a twitter from a lone bird.

Should we ever 'win on' or be successful with a girl, and pick up another date, we would feel like the wily American astronaut, John Glenn, blissfully orbiting planet earth. If we didn't, we'd lie like all heck. Michael and I boasted to each other how we had gone with a particular girl; and we would supply all the 'intricate' details. Mindful of the American poet, C. K. Williams in *Love Beginnings*, some folk at Cloudland might take a rejection to heart: 'The old, sore heart, the battered, foundered, and faithful heart, snorting again, stamping in its stall'. Once my best friend, Ray, ran

off with a lass I'd met at Cloudland. Gee, I missed seeing him around for a time!

Picasso's *Le Baiser* (The Kiss, 1969). His painting reminds me of carnal pleasures at Cloudland.

Approaching girls at Cloudland's dancehall was an exacting, delicate, yet strategic exercise. Ostensibly, the boys were attempting to get the girls to do certain things; and all the girls were naturally trying to prevent them. More than once, my friends were asked if they were members of the '*Wandering Hands Society*'.

Parties were also a feature of our growing set of nocturnal activities. We'd turn out all the lights when the 'oldies' went out; and turn them all back on before they arrived back home. The twist was a real favourite at outdoor parties. However, at around 10 p.m. or so, we'd press our bodies together and dance as close as we possibly could while still drawing breath. The girls were far more relaxed on these occasions. They usually wore *muu-muus*, open sandals and uncomplicated hairdos. The boys usually wore jeans.

In the 1960s, little shifts and muu-muus, as glamorous versions, made the trans-ition to 'after five' frocks.

green expanses thinking of nothing specifically, except girls in general.

The *Breakfast Creek* Hotel built in 1889 to showcase the French Renaissance style.

On some dry, or thirsty afternoons, we'd make our own entertainment. We'd drive to a North Brisbane hotel like the *Breakfast Creek*. It would be in the 'Brekkys' fine beer garden, where several Marilyn Monroe blonde copycats attracted glances at the brightly painted wire and wooden tables. We would often sit out on the grass enclosure, beneath the leafy

If we were in a more active mood, we'd go to the *Blue Moon Skating Rink* at South Brisbane and roller skate to music. We'd also play the juke box or the pin ball machines, while we drank a 'spider' with *Coca Cola* in it. One of my favourite records at this time was Lucky Starr's *I've been Everywhere*.

But mostly, if we had little to do, we would just cruise in Michaels FJ Holden and drive with the music blasting. Maybe, on the odd occasion, we might even see Rock'n'roll George. The mere feel of sniffing the city's breezes, with the car windows down, energised and relaxed us both.

THE DECLINE OF DEBUTANTE BALLS

From the start of the 1960s in Brisbane, the idea of a formalised and big-scale 'production presentation' for young women came under close and careful scrutiny. As I've previously mentioned, the *Sunday Mail*, in a 1962 report, was very quick to pronounce that: **"Debbery... Debbery Goes into Decline".**

> Even five years ago, making her debut was a must for almost every girl whose parents could afford it and for most of those whose parents could not.
>
> Now most girls prefer to come out at a private party. (Neil Wiseman, 'The Way we Were'; *Sunday Mail*).

That same year there would be no debs present at the Post Office Ball at Cloudland: "We can't get enough girls from the Post Office to make it worthwhile", the organising secretary remarked. "There just isn't the interest in it anymore". Moreover, the All Hallows Ball, which 15 years earlier had boasted more than 100 debs, was down to 15. Contrast this trend with such events as the 1947 Post Office Ball at Cloudland which provided participants with a souvenir telephone directory. With what may have been a clue to the demise of formal balls, by the middle of the decade both sexes came under fire for their general behaviour in society:

In June, 1966, the Brisbane *Courier-Mail* 'turned a feature writer loose upon the subject of etiquette for males: much criticised by newly liberated female Brisbanites'. He reported that—

> In the opinion of professional social advisors, the outgoing, quite socially conscious Australian fits into one of three categories: [very] few realise the benefit of the art and try to perfect it; others have heard of the term but consider its theory so very unmanly; most have never heard about 'etiquette' and so know nothing about it.

One *Courier-Mail* nostalgic columnist continued on the etiquette and social standards debate by confirming that much of our past, acceptable behaviour was in danger of being 'consigned to history':

> The *Australian Women's Weekly* weighed in with a 1966 supplement dealing with the vexed question of which were the correct pews to seat two ex-wives at the funeral of a bloke who was [most] probably [so] relieved to be allowed to then rest in peace; ruling that the constant interruptions of a talkative neighbour 'may be a sign of a mental illness', which seems to be a rather harsh diagnosis; and reassuring a novice drinker that although the olive in a martini was usually 'poured' into the mouth, picking it up with thumb and forefinger and then eating it 'was now not an adjudged hanging matter'. Such advice was a valiant but a doomed rear-guard action in the face of [such] overwhelming odds. The sexual and social revolution was gathering pace and it was only a year later that the *Summer of Love* [and the whole Hippie movement] spread on psychedelic ripples to swamp the world.

In this 'modern' era of the 1960s eschewing etiquette, the hope in some quarters was that girls would still witness the survival of such formal functions:

Jewish Guild secretary Mrs R. Beeck said: "It doesn't seem we are going to have debs this year. The girls definitely are not as keen as they used to be".

Commercial artist Merrilyn Leagh-Murray, 19, said of debutante balls: 'It's a lot of tommyrot. It's just an excuse to get a white dress. It was all right in the old days, when the idea was to launch you in the marriage market and some handsome hero would dash up to carry you off…"

But the Mater Hospital Ball Society president Mrs G. P. Carroll would have none of that: "We have no intention of dropping the presentation. We feel it's a wonderful occasion for the young people—something for them to remember".

Marriages so similar to this one in the 1960s were no longer tied in with the former notion of 'deb balls'.

CLOUDLAND AS AN EXAMINATION CENTRE

In spring and summer, the delicate lavender of the jacarandas reveal themselves in a brilliant flash and display of colour. When these familiar blooms of the jacaranda commenced to appear around Brisbane's suburbs, most people's thoughts began to turn to the more 'testing' time—examinations.

In the words of one observer, the arrival of the 'purple' flowers—jacaranda *mimosifolia*—are almost symbolic for the city and our identity:

A city's character is the sum of its unique parts—its people, its climate, its architecture and its geography. In Brisbane's case part of that character starts to bloom at about this time of year, as right across the city countless thousands of bare brown branches burst into life with their brilliant sprays of purple flowers. It is a heavy heart that fails to be somewhat lightened by the vibrant jacaranda display that signifies not only the change of season, but for many also the beginning of exams, the start of the beach season and the time to dust off the cricket gear. They're bright and new, a lot like Brisbane itself;

and in their own unique way are not just a signpost, but also a part of who we are.

Another commentator about the qualities of the flower recalled splendid times at Cloudland:

Traditionally, the jacarandas in Brisbane started flowering about six weeks before uni exams, so the beautiful sight of the jacarandas beginning to flower has never been welcomed by uni students. The by-now demolished Cloudland ballroom was used as an exam venue for uni students, and I remember sitting in an exam, gazing down on the magnificent vista of hundreds of [such] beautiful jacarandas [all] flowering below, promising myself that if I ever had my own house and garden, I would never, ever plant a jacaranda tree! Cloudland was one of the best dance and concert venues in the country. It hosted thousands of dances and concerts from the 1950s to the early 1980s, including some [of the] very famous events—e.g. ....concerts by Buddy Holly on his only Australian tour in 1958. Cloudland saw many romances blossom—my husband and I arranged our first date during a *Progressive Barn Dance* there. Although its architectural and cultural significance was so unquestionable, Cloudland's prime hilltop site made it a highly desirable target.

Notably, for the education of Queenslanders, Cloudland remained an examination venue from around 1964 to 1974 for the University of Queensland and also the Queensland University of Technology. In 1966, Sue Peterson was crowned Miss Queensland one evening, then was brought back down to earth the following day by sitting for two three-hour English papers at the same venue.

Children from primary schools sitting their final examinations at the Cloudland Ballroom.
The Queensland Newspapers.

One former University of Queensland student recalled how anxious the examinees became:

Cloudland was also the venue for sitting university exams within the '60s, as the University of Queensland did not have sufficient large open areas for such requirements. In tightening economic times when wages drop and jobs are scarce, people [often] return to education. So maybe the new Cloudland will once again soon become an exam[ination] venue.

Because high school students were required to sit external exams, the night-time revelry regularly would change complexion during the day as worried students worked their way through curly questions set by their University of Queensland lecturers.

My own memories of Cloudland and the University of Queensland are conceivably somewhat 'tainted' as, initially, I also ventured there, too, as a hapless university student, to sit for my exams from time to time. All of us students sat in solemn rows, wishing music would start up like the Cloudland Ballroom we all knew and loved. But alas! We were observed by some stern supervisors, much like the crescent moon at Cloudland or the weird plaster statues that graced the tops of the surrounding pillars at the university.

Another observer of university life remembers:

Those were the days when University examinations were held in the ballroom each November. My peers and I sat for Annual Degree Examinations in subjects like English Literature, Political Science, Australian History and Psychology at desks placed on the very [same] spot where, of a Wednesday, Friday or [a] Saturday night, couples would *foxtrot, jive* or *gypsy tap*. For a week or two each November, the coloured lights, mirror balls and brassy music would [all] make way for desks, clocks and an array of signs saying **Silence Please**.

On November 1ˢᵗ, 1971, there was quite a mob scene in Queen Street, Brisbane. It was held outside Newspaper House at 11 a.m.—

…hundreds of excited teenagers mobbed *Telegraph* Newspaper trucks and disrupted traffic in a scramble for papers with the Junior Examination results. Seven hundred and fifty papers were [all] snapped up in a few minutes.

The accompanying picture, taken in January, 1971, for a late edition of the Brisbane afternoon newspaper, the *Telegraph*, shows the rush for the paper's first edition that day.

"This was the scene in Queen St. outside Newspaper House at 11 a.m. today as hundreds of very excited teenagers mobbed *Telegraph* trucks and disrupted traffic in a scramble for papers with the Junior (year 10) examination results", the paper reported.

'When the first truck approached, these young people surged out and surrounded it, all with the same thought—to be first.

"Seven hundred and fifty papers were snapped up in a few minutes".

(The results took up twenty pages in the tabloid *Telegraph*. About the only people who regret the switch from the newspaper results to, at first, a phone-in recorded system, and now the net, are newspaper circulation managers. Exam results did wonders for all their figures in the post-New Year holiday doldrums.)

And, breathlessly: "Young girls were even seen standing in the middle of Queen St. oblivious to traffic, looking up results. The scramble was so great that any pedestrian traffic on the Newspaper House side of the street was disrupted. Some students were really excited that after having found good passes they leapt in the air and tossed papers over their head".

At the Bowen Hills headquarters of Queensland newspapers, hundreds of students and parents all waited outside the publishing dock: "Delivery boys were mobbed as they carried out bundles of *Telegraphs*".

Many of the students sat their exams at Cloudland. The dance hall (demolished at 4 a.m. on a Sunday in November, 1982, but that is another story) was used so extensively in the days of big public examinations for school and uni students.

For example, in 1966 University of Queensland students tackled their [very] first English paper at old benches set up on the sprung timber floor of Cloudland where, the previous evening, a dance band played for a ball held for the crowning of Miss Queensland. The Miss Queensland winner was Sue Peterson who, coincidentally, sat two three-hour papers in English at the same venue the following day.

Cloudland was a [far] more comfortable venue than the Sheep Pavilion at the Ekka showgrounds, where an overflow of 600 students sat their exams: "at the end of the day they bitterly criticised the seats provided...the low seats and high trestle tables made writing an ordeal".

The Junior examination of 1971 was the last of a system introduced almost 100 years earlier.

In closing, Tim Moroney remembers his last attendance at the Cloudland Ballroom which was for his 'Introduction to Law' examination in 1974 when he was still attending the University of Queensland.

"University degree examinations – as students tackled their initial English paper in Brisbane. This picture was taken at the Cloudland Ballroom, at Bowen Hills. There, so many hundreds of the candidates were accommodated".

Courier-Mail. Picture taken by Gerry Jasiulek.

The 'mad rush' at Newspaper House.

Courier-Mail. Picture: Geoff McLachlan.

Scott Hutchinson and his dad, Jack (*right*), with a replica of Rock'n'Roll George's FX Holden—
prominent around Cloudland, 1960s-1970s.

Courier-Mail. Picture: David May.

11

THE FADING OF A 'STAR': CLOUDLAND IN DECLINE

THE 1970s IN BRISBANE

The past is a foreign country; they do things differently there.

The Go-Betweens' L. P. Hartley

Whereas the 1960s had been looked upon with affection, during the '70s times had changed. The 1970s almost passed us baby boomers by like errant Rip Van Winkles. For most of the new decade, we became locked up in a rose-coloured time warp, fuelled by means of an ever decreasing youthfulness. Although I only jest, we seemed to possess none of the ongoing problems experienced, say, by an ever struggling young Rocky Balboa—aka Sylvester Stallone—in his bout for the world heavyweight title in the 1976 movie *Rocky*.

By the time the 1970s reached us, many of our hopes of the 1960s had been fully realised; the optimism and idealism of that decade had come to fruition. The 1970s saw the large, talented baby boomer generation reach an intellectual peak and Australian life took on a new look of maturity and resourcefulness.

From the 1960s, Australian 'nationality' had assumed its legal status and official recognition. There was no greater example and reflection of this new-found reserve of national feeling than in the process of 'Australianisation' which affected our youth as well as ageing baby boomers themselves. The love of the British Empire which had epitomised the Menzies rule was lost forever. In the 1970s, when US cultural historian, Christopher Lasch, published *The Culture of Narcissism* in 1979, he set in motion a huge debate about the state of American society. Taking Lasch's lead, we boomers no longer sought to survive now in the daunting vicarious shadow of the UK and / or, the USA. We displayed independence, inventiveness and creativity, pride and patriotism. Admiring the home-grown product, we no longer accepted everything from overseas without question. For one thing, we were all sporting Mexican-style 'Zapata' moustaches!

Germaine Greer at a women's liberation march in Australia in 1972.

1970s hairstyles.

By the late 1970s we were disco dancing. Similarly, we still grew our hair long and straight, as we had suffered from the pangs of conscience over women's rights, the Vietnam War and apartheid. We were told we were growing 'out of ourselves'. But around this time, we had 'other fish to fry'. "I'm so full of love I could burst apart and cry", we crooned with *Jefferson Airplane* in our lounges: "*Take me off to a circus tent/ where I can easily pay my rent/ and all the other freaks will share my cares*" might be nearer to what we were experiencing.

We boomers were also the truth and beauty seekers of the 1970s: of opposition to conscription, our Australian participation in the Vietnam War, and Apartheid. We even helped out with the cleaning up during the 1974 floods when, by the 26th January, 1974 (Australia Day), some 14,000 homes were flooded in just one weekend. This was a worrying time in the State, especially so for teachers, who, about this time every year, fretted about getting to school for the start of term, particularly if they were transferring to a new job. Now everyone was affected! Our rollicking larrikin image had also been forged by our hostility to the ongoing south-east Asian conflict and by our need to fight adversity (such as floods and droughts) in a harsh, ruthless continent. We still possessed an innocent and proud land. However, that American culture which I spoke of was still knocking increasingly at our doors without respite.

By these turbulent times of the '70s, Janis Joplin had crooned: *Freedom's just another word for nothing left to lose*, on eight-tracks across North America. Bell-bottoms, peasant blouses, and tie-dyed anything were the emblems of 'Flower Power', a term coined by Allen Ginsburg in 1965 to promote non-violent demonstrations and passive resistance, so now both the fashion and politics of this era presently formed the most powerful culture of all: *youth*. Today, the latter still fight for their rights…and win.

DISMANTLING THE BELLE VUE HOTEL

The end of the 1970s witnessed a general hue and cry over the destruction and desecration of a public building. To some people in Brisbane, this event involved as much heartache and anguish as they had known during the 1974 floods.

After midnight on Saturday, April 21st, 1979—perhaps as a portent about the 'things' to come in 1982 with Cloudland—and despite protests from the people of Brisbane and an enormous public wake, the Bjelke-Petersen government moved the Deen Brothers' wreckers in to demolish an historic city landmark of Brisbane called the *Belle Vue Hotel*. It took up to seven days. The Anglican Dean of Brisbane, The Very Reverend Ian George, alleged the Premier had acted 'like a thief in the night'. Joh responded only by saying: 'It's the usual thing to knock buildings down at night'.

Belle Vue Hotel, 1933.   *State Library of Queensland.*

Two views of the excavator, site of the bulldozed *Belle Vue Hotel*, April, 1979.

A multitude of protesters turned out to witness this destruction; and several wild brawls erupted, even though people were mostly just there to simply and quietly put their case. Seven people were arrested by the police guarding the site. But it was impossible for any of the bystanders to save the historic building.

'It's a bloody disgrace', effused an elderly gentleman in a straw hat, as onlookers stood by helplessly on the footpath. 'To think *I* had once voted for this government and then defended it against my friends— in fact, against every one. Bjelke-Petersen's just a dictator, similar to Adolf Hitler. He should go on back to Denmark or wherever he came from'.

'We should get the Deen Brothers to demolish Bjelke-

Petersen's property up at 'Ten Mile' during the night, just like he has done here', some folk returned. 'See how he'd like it. As far as I am concerned, this is our cultural heritage, our history, he's destroyed'.

A relic recovered from the *Belle Vue Hotel*. A secret report confirmed that two million dollars would be needed to restore the old building; and forty thousand dollars for its demolition.

No one could imagine the sense of loss we felt that night. *The Belle Vue*, with its ornate cast-iron, lace verandahs and curved corrugated iron roof, had been constructed in the classic style of Queensland hotels. The *Sydney Bulletin* described the *Belle Vue* as 'a glorious colonial pub, its old starched lace skirts properly picked out in white, its corrugated rooves curving down as plumply as a nineties belle'.

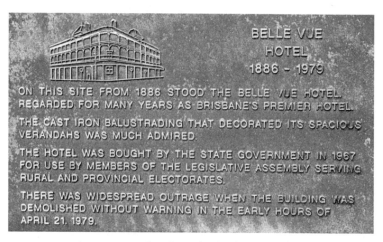

A commemorative plaque for the *Belle Vue Hotel*.

The ornate *Belle Vue Hotel* was bought for the Queensland government in 1967 by the then State works Department. In 1974, the Department tore off its verandahs and removed its iron lace decorations. At some point these items simply just 'went missing' from the hotel's George Street site. The Queensland Government, it appeared, had wanted them for some other purposes. However, this brick and timber building was also riddled with West Indian termites. By 1979, the Queensland Government, almost by fiat, it seemed, had recovered the entire site. A major and historic landmark of Brisbane had promptly disappeared from the horizon. It would be sadly missed; and, as yet, has not been replaced by another structural landmark.

THE 'AGEING' OF A GRAND OLD ICON

"We're all just drawing in the dirt with a stick. All you can hope for is to leave something. You maybe get to be king of the glove compartment for a while. King of the fishbowl. And then you are gone".

Tom Waits, US songwriter

By the 1970s, the crowds at the Cloudland venue had progressively dwindled, giving some ground to discos, pub music and nightclub entertainment. Yet, rock music still held sway for the fickle former dance crowds. As the decade unfolded, ballroom dancing was becoming unpopular, being replaced by "filthy rock concerts"; and such events were becoming the norm, and the only occasions upon which to adorn Cloudland's floor. It seemed now as if a 'new wave' of skinhead and punk rock 'anarchy' was beginning to appeal to a sizeable proportion of Brisbane's youth.

Rumours were certainly circulating in 1972 that the Cloudland venue would soon close its door in 1973. Some said a gigantic home unit enterprise was about to be built on the site. Joh Bjelke-Petersen was not helping with these matters either by reporting that he was considering purchasing Cloudland Ballroom as a cultural and recreation centre. Peter Kurts purchased the Cloudland site from the previous owners, H. Apel and Sons, in June of 1974. A Sydney developer, he paid $700,000 for Cloudland, a great price for 6½ acres of hilltop land three kilometres from the heart of the capital city of Brisbane.

In 1976, Kurts' preliminary plans to redevelop Cloudland Ballroom into a multi-million dollar home unit complex were shelved. Apparently, Perimeter Investments Pty. Ltd. did not proceed with its proposal to rezone the site. The idea was to construct terraced high-rise unit blocks, a bowling green, and a car park as well as a restaurant. Kurts had planned to demolish Cloudland at this juncture, but the property and development boom had busted, forcing him to shelve his plans for a period.

Following the news that the 'springy' floor of Cloudland had collapsed while a big crowd was stamping out a *Gypsy Tap*, the new owner of the ballroom 'sprang' into action. In 1976-77 he spent $100,000 on some restoration work, including $14,000 to eradicate white ants; and repainting by the Baker Brothers. One important measure he took was to strengthen Cloudland's iconic dome as it was sinking into the ground. The pink-domed building now stood like a 50-metre high bisected pink toadstool.

Kurts took up his new role at Cloudland with considerable aplomb and relish. A 60/40 dance ran on Wednesday nights, complete with a big band sound, redolent of the 1940s. An adult disco, called 'Silva Palm' was also run in the Panorama Room on Thursday and Friday nights, to capacity crowds.

On Friday and Saturday nights the ballroom was also booked for balls, conferences, conventions and indoor sport events. If it wasn't booked, a teenage disco was also conducted.

Dancers again swirl through the ballroom.

The Panorama room's Saturday night 'Top 40 Disco' was subsequently established as an entertainment attraction for young people. Leading bands provided non-stop dance music, and a free Cloudland bus collected juvenile dancers at the City Hall Square at 8 p.m. and 8.30 p.m. Tony and the *Blue Jays, The Easy Beats, The Mixtures,* Jay Payton and *The All Stars, Clockwork Strawberry, Vanity Fair, Hush, Air Supply, Troubadores, AC/DC, Sounds of Seven* and *Seasons of the Witch* were a few of the bands who entertained the youthful patrons at the venue.

As a way of reinvigorating their public's somewhat flagging interest in ballroom dancing, in May of 1976, the Cloudland management instituted changes to their weekly schedules; regular disco dances began at Cloudland; and the 70 metre by 53 metre by 23 metre dance floor had gradually filled up since that time.

Mick Medew who fronted the band, Mick and *The Rumours*.

Courier-Mail.

In September of 1977, 950 Caledonians put the so-called 'Canadian redwood-sprung floor' to the test. They had it jumping 9.5 c.m. off its supports. The old Cloudland custom of a traditional barn dance was also revived most dance nights at 10.00 p.m.; but an effort to fully re-establish the usual 60/40 dances on the hill met partly with failure. Merv Rowe, Cloudland's property manager, lamented the fact that 200 people were not enough to be visible upon Cloudland's huge dance floor. So people were flocking to the RSL or bowling clubs—to smaller venues.

The Easy Beats.

But, with new management policies soon in harness to now

counteract its competitors, the 500 to 600 people attracted to Cloudland were now fitting comfortably in to the venue, whereas previously there were four circles, with dancers unable to move properly. The dances were now being held between 8.15 p.m. and midnight; and patrons were being charged $3.50 a head to hear two bands and to dance. At this time, Saturday night dances were attracting more people at Cloudland than anywhere else in Brisbane. With the 'success' of the Saturday events, Friday dances commenced within October of 1977, to the rock beat of James Elliot and friends.

But, overall, 1977 was not a really good year for Peter Kurts for many reasons. In fact, it was a low ebb. Everything Kurts attempted flopped. By this same year, he was also unlicensed to serve alcohol. Then it was up to the ball committees to obtain licences for their functions. The way such events were progressing, Kurts only held 28 balls in this particular year.

Between 1977 and 1979, Kurts' Panorama Room also received a face-lift. A rumour circulated that white ants were the cause of this refurbishment, which had included new chairs and some other furniture. By now (1978), Ege Snook was installed as Cloudland's manager.

During 1978, Kurts planned to spend another $100,000 to bring the Cloudland structure back to its original condition.

Kurts lopped off the tree tops in front of the sky dome, so patrons could see for kilometres around the site—especially the rainbow lights pulsing in the dark, night sky; and he stopped the roof leaks when it rained. Then the roof was changed from a 'cottage' style to a 'lean-to' model. The royal blue and gilt ceiling was repainted as well. Despite the diminishing returns and the dwindling crowds, Kurts decided to carry on relentlessly with the running of the dance hall, though it was tempting to lease out the premises to another manager to carry out its day-to-day operations.

In the interim, as perhaps a temporary measure, Kurts planned to keep the ballroom going for only one year and then build two 19-storey home unit blocks and eight blocks between eight and ten storeys. By the mid- to-late 1970s, the cracks' that had now begun to appear within Cloudland's former breathtaking interior and exterior would simply not go away.

Discover Perfection in Catering

WEDDINGS, PARTIES, CONFERENCES, LUNCHEONS, SEMINARS, FASHION PARADES & SOCIAL CLUB FUNCTIONS —— PHONE 52 1511

An advertisement for the Panorama Room.

In the '70s, Merv Rowe wanted to bring Cloudland back "to the good old days".
The Australian, October 8th, 1977.

Another happy couple posing at Cloudland, ready for a fun night of dancing.

Greg Holmes and Ege Snook also had plans to "revive" Cloudland.

At an extravagant Queensland State Reception on March 9th, 1977, Queen Elizabeth II, escorted by Queensland's premier, Joh Bjelke-Petersen, had entered this 'wondrous fairyland' of Cloudland. To avoid the Queen's looking upwards, there was a canopy of red, white and blue which covered the flaking ceiling and the ballroom's dilapidated dome, as they badly needed painting. A display of orchids in one corner of the room was designed to divert the monarch's attention— so were big blow-ups of the new State Government crest covering the pillars upon the dance floor. Similarly, the Queen walked on brown and gold-flecked carpet borrowed from the Railway Department—generally used for any carpeting of the State's air-conditioned railway stock.

Mrs Ngaio Dayman, at the front of Cloudland's giant arched dome, hoping the Queen would not look up.

Sunday Mail, 27th February, 1977.

Queen Elizabeth II meets the crowds at King George Square, Brisbane.

Courier-Mail. Picture: Roman Biegi.

As a regular performer on the music scene one local musician could also see that a bit of the writing was on the wall by the '70s and '80s:

> At the time I was playing my rock music, another bane for Joh and the boys in blue. In the late '70s and early '80s music venues within Brisbane were closing almost quicker than they could open, so if opportunity was to ever knock for me—a budding songwriter and guitar player with his own band—it would [just] have to be on a door somewhere far afield.
>
> I left town [during] 1984. A friend mine once quipped I'd done the Brisbane exit thing before it became fashionable.

Perhaps, then, as a signal of the 'grand lady's' demise, or re-configuration, a 'Market on the Mountain' opened at Cloudland Ballroom on June 11th, 1978. Between 8.30 a.m. and 3.30 p.m. about 5,000 people had bought goods from 110 stalls about the ballroom dance floor. Items included clothing; jewellery; paintings; furniture; plants; toys; and antiques—ranging in cost from 30 cents to $300. Carol Needham remembers the markets 'as a new thing at the time, where you could buy almost anything'. The market manager was Mr J. Edwards. (It was operating until December, 1980; and was then later re-opened and active until 1982.)

Crowds appear at Cloudland, but this time not to dance, but to shop.

Weekend Australian, 11th November, 1978.

THE PANORAMA ROOM

By February of 1979—with the ballroom's operations somewhat winding down—work was nearing completion on a $30,000 project to fully renovate Cloudland's wedding facilities. The *Panorama Room* was entirely refurbished with some new wallpaper, wall mirror tiles, a mahogany bar for its newly-returned liquor licence and new carpeting. The area was now able to seat 250 people who could sup upon the standard or exclusive gourmet menus.

The Cloudland Centre, 1970s.

For instance, car dealers used the ballrooms' massive dance floor to launch new models to the general public. One of Cloudland's several advertisements carried the following enticing prospect.

Get your message across as
CLOUDLAND BALLROOM does
with a P.A. System
from
D'ALTON JOHN
39 AGNES ST, TORWOOD
Phone 371 3707

Advertising helping to promote the Panorama Room at Cloudland.

An advertisement to make known Cloudland's multi-functional public offerings.

The brand new foyer en-trance, at Cloudland Ball-room, with the Panorama Room to its (*right*). *JOL.*

The extravagant dance floor at Cloudland prepared for a Mitre 10 hardware convention. *Sunday Sun, 2nd October, 1977.*

Viewing the "panorama" from the re-developed Panorama Room.

Under the direction of Peter Kurts and his team, the *Panorama Room*, as a viable annexe to Cloudland ballroom, also catered for trade displays and cabarets.

From 1978 to 1979, Clan Mackenzie Balls were also featured at Cloudland. By this same period, 'cabaret balls' were all the rage at the dancehall. Patrons could wine and dine at elegantly presented tables, while artists went through their intimate music routines.

Happy debutantes take to the floor with kilt-clad escorts. Clan Mackenzie Ball, 1970s.
Sunday Mail.

In 1979, there was apparently a fire at Cloudland [in September],

and an unconfirmed story that an RAAF-dropped flare might have been the cause. Following complaints by its neighbours, the decade of the '70s at Cloudland also ended on a sour note when the venue's liquor licence was cancelled.

A typical 'cabaret ball', Cloudland Ballroom, 1970s.

ʼAN EMERGENCE OF 'OUT THERE' ROCK BANDS

The 1970s also witnessed a much younger brigade of music acts than Ivan Dayman's 1960s bands (although the *Purple Hearts* were still playing now), and they had taken vigorously to the Cloudland stage. A whole new era of Cloudland "devotees" was being spawned, especially for 'live' music concerts.

According to one reliable source:

[There were the] *Purple Hearts* with their Lobby-powered innovation slant on city blues, and *The Five*,

a tight R & B tinged covers band in daggy, unmatching clothes. The majority of the then Brisbane working rock bands were still from that old mould of tidy, uniformed instrumental combos with separate singers out front for a few songs in each set lots of Cliff and *The Shadows*. Hair length was gravely controversial then. At best you'd be picked on, at worst nearly arrested. There was immeasurable respect to be gained from the fans by sporting long hair. It was clear evidence of your being a professional rock musician, since you would not be accepted without a short back and sides in any other field. Yep it was definitely an indication that you'd arrived.

The late Mick Hadley, who had formed *The Purple Hearts*. He passed away at the Robina Hospital, on the Gold Coast, 25th October, 2012.

Split Enz promoting *I Got You*, 1980.

The Saints.

The 1970s and early 1980s saw an array of Australian bands at Cloudland, when Brisbane had a thriving rock underbelly; viz: *Split Enz, XTC, The Sports, Cold Chisel, The Stray Cats, The Saints, Australian Crawl, Echo and the Bunnymen, Midnight Oil, UB40, The Go-Betweens, The Clash* and Richard Clapton.

One lucky 'punter' relives those times:

...later in the '70s we went there [Cloudland] for all the great rock shows...even went to the last one.

I met the most beautiful girl in the world at a Graham Parker and *Rumour* concert...her friends had deserted her...she came from out of town to the friends' b'day night...they had lost her... "we" took her on home...to my mum and dad's where the bunch of us would regularly crash out on a big night out, boys and girls...they'd cook brekky for us all...my room entered into the kitchen...so I then brought this green eyed girl out to breakfast...having pointed her towards the spare room earlier... which she coyly refused with an eye flutter...sigh... (YaY!!) light bottle green eyes...the like I've never seen again in two trips around the world...I'll never forget them...

An audience at Cloudland for a concert event, 1970s.

On offer, also, at the venue in the 1970s was the 'Toadshow light show' by Ross Philip; the *Delltones*, after they played on the last *Bandstand* programme that day (24th July, 1972); Toowong School's Fancy Dress Ball; the Annual Musician's Ball (*Panorama Room*); *Railroad Gin*, nationally known and successful; Ex-*Little River Band*'s Graham Goble's own show (14th January, 1976); Graham Parker and *The Rumour*.

In 1979, *Matchbox*, with its hit, *Rockabilly Rebel*, appeared at Cloudland; *The Agents* (1979); *Strange Tenants* supported by *Furious Turtles*; Richard Clapton (18th May, 1979); *Razar Band*, *The Angels*, *The Sharks* (30th June, 1979); Jo Jo Zep and *The Falcons* (6th July, 1979); *Split Enz* with *Riptides* and *Dr Feelgood* (13th July, 1979); *XTC* supported by *Flowers* and *The Numbers* (28th July, 1979); *The Sports*, *Humans*, *Aliens* (18th August, 1979); *Go-Betweens* (10th

November, 1979); Graham Parker and *The Rumour*; and Jimmy and *The Boys*, supported by *Razar* (Christmas, 1979).

There was currently still quite a selection of leisure time dancing for people of all ages on offer at the dancehall; i.e. Wednesday nights (Modern); Thursday nights (Mater 60/40); and Saturday nights (mostly jive), as well as a few balls and concerts during the winter months.

Youth dancing on Cloudland's 'springy floor, 1970s.

Couples in various attire still enjoying close dancing up at Cloudland, 1970s. *Note: all the roped areas separating "waltzers" and "jivers".*

Courier-Mail.

Two couples at a Teachers' Welcome Dance at the Cloudland Ballroom in 1973.

Courier-Mail.

As the 1970s unfolded at Cloudland, after the 'mini' of the 1960s came the 'midi' and 'maxi', as female patrons to the venue had decided they could now wear whatever they desired. As a matter of fact, the halter-neckline 'frock' became a fashionable style for evening dance wear.

According to one regular attendee at Cloudland:

During the 70s, my entire family would often go to Cloudland upon a Saturday night. We would dress up in our long dresses and all my brothers would wear good shirts and long pants.

We would dance the night away to the music of two popular bands— *Sounds of Seven* and *Seasons of the Witch*. One band provided music for *The Gypsy Tap*, *The Pride of Erin*, *The Progressive Barn Dance*; and other such dances. The other band would play more modern music for jiving.

It was a magical time. The large 'disco' ball that revolved from the ceiling and the soft 'ultraviolet' lights created a wonderful atmosphere for a fun evening.

My entire family (parents included) would go home at the end of the night feeling quite contented with the evening as there had been music and dancing to satisfy all ages.

Happy memories indeed!

Another patron has this quaint memory to relate about Cloudland during the floods in Brisbane in 1974:

Every person who had ever become a Cloudland 'regular' would have special memories or stories to tell. For me it was the night of the 'flood'. A humid Brisbane January night erupted in a tropical downpour during which water poured onto the floor, and across a number of the alcoves. The dancing carried on with supervisors taking care to steer the waltzing couples away from the deeper end of the floor.

AC/DC had played Cloudland on November 30th, 1975. Kath Christie's daughter, Donna, recounts here how her mother went into 'damage control' the night that the lads were performing:

My mother worked at Cloudland for many years. She was a secretary to Ivan Dayman who was an artist manager (including managing Normie Rowe and Johnny O'Keefe) and the long-term lessee of Cloudland. She would come home with stories of the "famous" people she had met and the stories fascinated me and my sisters.

One in particular was when a band was performing for youngsters and she was horrified to hear the "f" word coming out of the speakers. She was in her office but Mr Dayman wasn't there this particular night so she telephoned him at home. He said, well, Kath, just go pull the plug and that is exactly what she did. The singer was screeching into the microphone when suddenly silence...

The band just happened to be AC/DC...I wonder if they remember being silenced for using foul language by a little old lady at Cloudland. My sisters and I were so embarrassed at the time when she told us what she had done.

Mum had a wonderful time working at Cloudland and, although she had retired, was devastated to hear about its demise.

Her name was Kath Christie and known to lots as "Kathie".

Sadly, now, in retrospect for the late singer, when Bon Scott realised at a young age that "it ain't no fun waiting 'round to be a millionaire", he had set his sights on singing after earlier stints as a drummer.

Bon Scott, original front-man of AC/DC. Before he'd joined them he was once employed as a 'postie' in Perth.

A number of other rock bands, including (the aforecited) *Angels*, graced Cloudland's stage in the 1970s:

My friends and I 'grew up' at the one-and-only Cloudland...1978-1982 or thereabouts.

Student nurses living in-residence at the nearby Royal Brisbane Hospital, we saw every live band who performed there...in particular I remember *Split Enz* in their earliest days, all made up; *Cold Chisel* when Jimmy Barnes was young and wild and crazy. *The Angels*...the sprung dance-floor was also quite an experience with hundreds of us dancing *en masse*!

Socio-politically, those were unfortunate times with all that political corruption, and the trashy glitzy, greedy 'progress'.

Ironically, future rock 'legends', *The Saints*, had also run afoul of Cloudland's dancehall management, while backing the very popular, but quite eccentric group, *Mother Goose*:

The band [*The Saints*] was offered a spot supporting AC/DC (who were back on a return tour of Australia, after being confused with punks themselves in England and Europe) at the Miami Hall on the

Gold Coast. They duly played to an empty theatre. *The Saints* had already been told they would never work in Brisbane again following a support slot to *Mother Goose* at Cloudland Ballroom. Likewise, AC/DC's diligent road crew now were affronted by *The Saints'* general 'lack of professionalism'. The hostility and the resentment *The Saints* generated was most extraordinary. As Ed Kuepper has noted wryly, *"The Saints* were never highly regarded as musicians".

The Saints' 1976-1978 album cover.

Mother Goose.

Conflict did not only occur between bands and management at

Cloudland in the 1970s. Bill Kelly, a keen amateur photographer, spent time during a *Jimmy and The Boys* concert taking photos of the large police contingent at the venue. This could be risky at the best of times in the Bjelke-Petersen era: and a plain clothes detective confiscated his camera film.

Jamie Dunn was the Brissie band Hands Down's drummer.
Courier-Mail/Sunday Mail; in *Our Queensland*, 1970.

By the late 1970s, veteran broadcaster and entertainer, Jamie Dunn was touring with his band at that stage. He described Cloudland as being in its "twilight" days, the place itself was "looking a bit tatty", and "the dance hall was growing old with attitude and worn edges". Jamie can still recall the edifice's smell, which "he [likened] to [that of] his grandad".

Every Wednesday night, from 1978-1982, the *Rythmaires* (including Cliff Field, bass guitars, drums, vocal, M.C.; and Wayne Close on sax) and the *Bowcatts* (Bill Bowcatt on drums) played at Cloudland. (On Saturday nights, the band *Sounds of Seven* also performed there). Permits were required to sell liquor at Cloudland in the 1970s and ball licences were distributed at a rate of up to three permits per year. With 300 people turning up regularly to the Wednesday night dances, Cliff Field sought a liquor licence for every week his band performed. He used his and his wife's name on the permit and then approached Father David Anthony of the Woodridge Anglican Church for his assistance. Father Anthony had worked out a scheme whereby all profits from Wednesday night liquor sales would now be spread across various church associations in his parish, e.g. a youth group; men's club, etc. This same Anglican priest helped Cliff fill out each permit application. Then Cloudland's manager, Ege Snook, gathered up the takings for the night's liquor sales, putting aside the venue's expenses with profits going directly to the said church.

One night, Cliff and his wife heard a knock on the door. Two burly Liquor Squad policemen entered Cliff's house and accused him of selling 'sly grog'. When Cliff explained that he was a non-drinker and that his liquor permits were above board, the men said they were serving him with a notice to appear in court, despite the fact that they approved of Cliff's ingenuity. Oddly, in retrospect, Cliff believed the court may have been presided over by none other than Jack Herbert, the 'Bagman' of the later Fitzgerald Inquiry and another person who also fronted the inquiry. The court lauded Cliff's effort

to forward liquor-sale profits to various "charitable" and worthwhile social groups. They informed Cliff they would henceforth amend the current liquor registration to allow for such new and socially commendable changes.

(Cliff Field also claims he played one of the final concerts at Cloudland on the evening of Wednesday, 2nd November, 1982, five days before the dancehall's demolition.

On July 19th, 1980, rock music came to Cloudland with a scream and a wail. Jimmy Barnes and *Cold Chisel* played there to a riotous reception. The set list for the gig was as follows:

1. *Standing On The Outside*
2. *I'm Gonna Roll Ya*
3. *Home & Broken Hearted*
4. *My Turn To Cry*
5. *Best Kept Lies*
6. *Shakin' All Over*
7. *Shipping Steel*
8. *Never Before*
9. *Ita*
10. *Juliet*
11. *Rising Sun*
12. *My Baby*
13. *Choirgirl*
14. *Four Walls*
15. *One Long Day*
16. *Conversations*
17. *Khe Sanh*
18. *Cheap Wine*
19. *Star Hotel*
20. *Don't Let Go!*
21. *Merry Go Round*

Encore:

22. *Georgia On My Mind*
23. *Breakfast At Sweethearts*

24. *Tomorrow*
25. *Knocking On Heaven's Door*
26. *Wild Thing*
27. *Goodbye (Astrid Goodbye)*

Cold Chisel: Jimmy Barnes: Ian Moss; Phil Small; Don Walker; & Steve Prestwich.
The Daily Telegraph.

12

CLOUDLAND'S "DEATH KNELL" IS SOUNDED, EARLY 1980s

'GENERATION ME'

> You as *you* may not matter to anyone in the world, but you as a person in a particular place may matter unimaginably.
>
> **Agatha Christie,**
> **The Man from the Sea**

Number one on the list of famous last words is 'It can't happen here' according to David Crosby, the US rock singer-musician. Well it did in Australia! The new decade had begun upon a sour note when a baby, Azaria Chamberlain, had disappeared on a family trip to Ayres Rock in August, 1980. It was believed that she was taken by a dingo and police started a hunt to find both the child and the offending animal.

By the 1980s, baby boomers had tamed all their radical streaks of the 1960s and 1970s; and had settled down to enjoy the wealth and comfort of their advancing years. Comfortable within a high income bracket, this 'Generation Me' was now to be permeated with

self-absorption and the concept of self above personal sacrifice. Clearly, a person's potential had no ceiling. Of course, many in our nation blamed 'Wall Street'—the symbol of gross consumerism—together with the 'Gordon Gecko 'greed is good' wealth accumulation mentality of our US allies for our sudden inward turning approach to personal economics. Work stress and financial pressures, cumbersome mobile phones, as well as selfishness, began driving the nation of Australia and many Brisbanites on towards the 21st century. These were all the dire effects of the 'Generation Me' rush of the 1980s. Evidently, this was a decade that was finally putting the boot into the Rubik Cube, or *Duran Duran*, Cabbage Patch Kids and the mullet haircut.

As author, Susan Johnson, revealed:

> I am a baby boomer, a member of that lucky economic race who had

the time and money to sit around in cheap flats while attending university for free. We didn't know we had it easy; the government paid for everything, from a year off on the dole lying around reading books to a free tertiary education. Then after we travelled the world for a year or two, and worked for several years more, we bought houses in inner-city Brisbane for a song.

Everything seemed so possible then. Youth is usually a flame-proof experience, a time when we do not yet understand that people grow old, much less believe that we ourselves will die. But our particular youth was of an especially self-indulgent kind, so impossibly easy...

We believed we [had] invented the sexual revolution, feminism, [plus] anti-consumerism and the new world order. We were the first girls in the world to grow up with the Pill; and we were determined not to live lives like our mothers. Baby boomers were the first generation in our human history to grow up in the belief that self-definition was a birth right. (*The Weekend Australian*, July, 2008.)

However ironical nowadays—and in somewhat of a reversal of all her initial ideas—Germaine Greer had also written in a similar vein for her first book, *The Female Eunuch*:

Whole women would have been restless, aggressive, unpredictable, curious, lustful, imaginative. They might have been adventurers, artists, inventors, explorers, revolutionaries, but they wouldn't have been mere housewives... and housewives were what were wanted.

In the 1980s, besides the change in boomer thinking, the woollen 'jumpers' and double-breasted suits which marked baby boomer apparel in the 1970s was most definitely

out now. A new svelte, 'space-age, skivvy' fashion was emerging.

The casual male uniform of the early 1980s in Brisbane.

In the early 1980s, at Cloudland, Princess Di's romantic dresses and evening gowns had set a trend for women; and colours such as fuchsia, sea greens, purples, royal blue and bright red shimmered in silk and other less natural fabrics.

Linen was another of those '80s fads which are somehow forgotten:

We were mad for it in the '80s, mad, despite the fact that you would spend hours at painstakingly ironing your linen suit, & carefully working your way around the giant gold buttons, then you put it on; and for a moment, look like the most well-groomed woman on Earth.

Then you would move and the whole thing too would crumple like an unmade bed, and by the time you got to your car you may as well have been wearing a roll of used cellophane. (*The Australian*.)

'Power' jackets with shoulder pads had also appeared on young girls in their twenties:

> It was the '80s, and, if you were not around then, to give you an idea of just how popular they were, I was chatting to a friend, Michelle, the other day and she told of lovingly placing a pair in her backpack for her 1982 trek around the Greek Islands.
>
> Yes, there she is in every photo—in front of the Acropolis, downing [some] daiquiris at sunset on Santorini—sporting a pair of shoulders Lote Tuqiri would be proud of.
>
> Shoulder pads were so huge; they used to sell shirts with Velcro already attached to them so you could pop your pair on with ease, and if there was not Velcro available girls used to tuck them under their bra straps.
>
> Less lazy girls used to safety pin them on their straps, but I, of course, never did, which is why all my shoulder pads would often pop out during *Hungry Like the Wolf*, landing like little fillets of sole on the dance floor. (*Courier-Mail*.)

Despite the appearance of these somewhat outrageous fashion trends, the surfacing of 'punks' and 'skinheads' at Cloudland's rock concerts in the early 1980s gave rise to a considerably more grungier look as the decade progressed.

CLOUDLAND IN THE EARLY EIGHTIES

Tell all the Truth but tell it slant—

Success in Circuit lies

Too bright for our infirm Delight

The Truth's superb surprise

As Lightning to the Children eased

With explanation kind

The Truth must dazzle gradually

Of every man be blind—

Lest we blind those whose vision we wish to correct, we must be careful with the truth, for it is, indeed, both bright and dangerous.

Emily Dickenson

In the 1970s Cloudland refused to be beaten when the floods had ravaged Brisbane in 1974. However, by the early 1980s, Peter Kurts, the owner (from 1974-1982), advised the Brisbane public that the old 'Cinderella' ballroom was in a structurally deteriorating condition, leading inevitably towards a terminal state as a viable building. Needless to say, the 'old girl' was not even 50 years old, relatively 'young' for a building of its kind. Peter lamented that the improvements needed to make the building safe were simply not cost effective.

'The hard truth' of Kurts' warning about the decline of one of Brisbane's iconic structures was an example of those phrases decorating the front of nasty news, bitter disappointment, economic recession, belt-tightening and pain—especially the idea that the 'old grand dame' may have had a fatal disease and would ultimately need to go under. The actual truth was that Peter Kurts was now giving out mixed messages by the early eighties—that he had a buyer for the 'old girl'; and that his company wanted to build a residential development on the spot.

The Brisbane developer and yachtsman, Peter Kurts (1924-2005), who had sadly sailed his final voyage.

Yet, for the moment, Cloudland was continuing its current operations. It was used as a flea market in the early eighties. But the 1970s and the 1980s had also ushered in a younger brigade of band acts to the Cloudland stage, so a new breed of Cloudland devotees quite different from other decades was spawned. Some of these groups opted for original songs with a decidedly 'Aussie' flavour. Others made do with cover versions of any popular tunes of the era, **viz:**

Rock of Ages '80s hits included:

Just Like Paradise – David Lee Roth

We Built This City – Starship

Nothing But A Good Time – Poison

I Wanna Rock – Twisted Sister

Too Much Time On My Hands – Styx

Renegade – Styx

Oh Sherrie – Steve Perry

Hit Me With Your Best Shot – Pat Benetar

Don't Stop Believin' – Journey

Heaven – Warrant

The Search Is Over –Survivor

The Final Countdown – Europe

As the early 1980s hit Cloudland, more or less the same rock groups which appeared at the venue in the 1970s returned once more: *Split Enz, XTC, The Sports, Cold Chisel, The Stray Cats, The Saints, Australian Crawl, Echo and the Bunnymen, Midnight Oil, UB40, The Go-Betweens* and *The Clash* took to the venue's principal stage.

Peter Garrett, the Federal Minister for the Environment, Heritage and the Arts—as well as the famed front man for the legendary rock band, *Midnight Oil*—recalls Cloudland being a grand rock venue, near the greatest in Australia during the period of the 1970s and 1980s. He not only performed at Cloudland, he enjoyed watching other live groups there, too. For Peter, Cloudland's change from a dance palace to a type of stadium for any rock acts was just a natural progression: from the ballroom's early musical traditions to a high decibel physical sound.

Fans of Peter and the '*Oils*' and of *The Angels* jumped up and down on the warped Cloudland floor that was made for jumping.

Peter Garret (*centre*); The Deputy Mayor of Brisbane: Cr. Graham Quirk (left); Nigel Chamier (City Hall Revitalisation committee); and Cr. Nicole Johnstone at Brisbane's City Hall. Photo: Mr Tony Moore.
Brisbane Times.

In 1980, Keith Urban, before rocketing to international stardom, began his singing career in Brisbane. While a juvenile, he won "best young male at the *ABC Country Music Show* at Cloudland". As a country music singer and guitarist, Keith went on to win the Country Music Association's 'Male Vocalist of the Year' award three times.

On January 12th, 1980, *The Angels* performed at Cloudland; followed by *Cold Chisel* on July 19th, 1980; and *Dragon*.

At one 1981 concert in the same year as Australian cricket captain, Greg Chappell, had caused a furore when he ordered his brother, Trevor, to bowl underarm to a New Zealand batsman—*INXS* was first up to perform: *Mental as Anything* followed their set; and *The Angels* were headlining. In the same year, *Australian Crawl* were on

their 'Sirocco tour' and also made 'how to make a record'; *Mental as Anything*, supported by *INXS*; *Echo and The Bunnymen* with the local band, *Zero*; *Midnight Oil* played and wrote a song for Cloudland on their 'scorching of the earth' tour (October 8th, 1981); Ian Dury (November 27th, 1981); *Simple Minds* 'Sons of Fascination Tour', supported by *Icehouse*; and *UB40* performed (1981).

Michael Hutchance (*top, centre*) and *INXS* achieved seven US top 10 hits. (Rock'n'Roll, 1955-2005)
Courier-Mail/ Sunday Mail.

Stephen Cummings in his book, *Will It Be Funny Tomorrow, Billy?: Misadventures in Music*, speaks about another (May 2nd) 1981 concert he performed at with *The Sports*. The line-up included the legendary 1970s London two-Tone Ska band, *Madness*; and Brisbane group, *The Go-Betweens*; evidently, *The Swingers* cancelled their gig as a support band:

Cloudland perched elegantly upon a hilltop, like a Greek god overlooking the town's corrupt police force; and Joh Bjelke-Petersen's sinister National Party; and all the machinations that went on below...

One memorable night there in 1981 we had played with London Ska band, *Madness*, and local heroes, *The Go-Betweens*. I think we were on the bill to drag in more punters. *Madness* attracted an odd mix of skinheads and fun-loving popsters; and at night's end the lead singer sidled up to me: 'For old blokes you're pretty good mate'.

The *Madness* line-up, 2011.

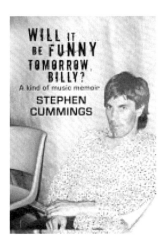

Stephen Cummings with his book about his music career.

Timothy Kelly recalls the same gig in 1981:

It's a cool night in May and my friend Scott and I are about to witness a side of Brisbane we never knew existed. London Ska band, *Madness*, are playing at Cloudland and Scott's older brothers have allowed us to tag along. I sense that they're not too thrilled by having to baby-sit two fourteen year olds at a [rock] concert, but they should have thought about that before they introduced us to those wonderful sounds that exist beyond the top forty. If we were never allowed into that downstairs room with its piles of LPs, 45s and NMEs, then we, like most other fourteen year olds within Brisbane, would never have heard of *Madness.*

The car has been parked half-way up a hill and we follow a darkened road as it winds its way to the top. Soon we all arrive at the large ached entrance of the ballroom. Like most Brisbanites, we are used to Cloudland's exotic shape against an otherwise drab skyline, but this is the first time we have seen it up close. Slender columns reaching up into a blue-lit archway create an illusion of elegance that suggests tuxedos and ball gowns rather than braces and boots.

Furthermore:

We line up with all our fellow concert goers and I am [really] amazed by the number of skinheads and punks making their way inside. You rarely see [any of] these types around Brisbane. I wonder whether they only come out at night. They look [so] dangerous as they raise their arms to be frisked by the bouncers. Scott and I momentarily enter their ranks as we too are frisked.

Once inside, Scott's brothers go their separate ways as the first band of the night, a three piece, plays on the small cave-like stage. When I get older this band will provide a soundtrack to my life and my own band will open for them at *Caesar's Palace*, in Ipswich. Right now, however, I don't even know who *the Go-Betweens* are.

Their set soon finishes up and an announcement comes over the PA that *The Swingers* have had to cancel due to the drummer breaking his arm. We wander all around the dance-floor, waiting for the main support band, *the Sports*, to hit the stage. By the time they come on, the ballroom is full. I can see nothing except Stephen Cumming's head, and that's only when he leaps into the air. They play all the hits including *Don't Throw Stones*, *Who Listens to the Radio* and *Strangers on a Train*. Then they're gone.

And again:

People manoeuvre for position[s] and the crowd starts surging towards the stage. The sound of a fog horn bellows throughout the darkened hall and *Madness* bounce on to the stage [all] holding pineapples [up] above their heads. The upbeat ska rhythms get the entire crowd skanking and then the floor starts bouncing like a trampoline. The speaker stacks on either side of the stage are shaking.

A sickly sweet smell fills the air. It is the first time I smell marijuana. I start to wonder whether I am stoned. Scott seems to be acting strangely. Is he swaying too much? Then he falls back onto two skinhead girls who almost stomp on his face.

Madness finish the set with *Return of the Los Palmas* then leave[s] the stage. The crowd disappears just as quickly but Scott and I have to wait around for his brothers. The lights come on and I wonder how all of the bottles of alcohol [scotch] which presently lie empty and scattered across the floor were smuggled in past the bouncers.

I'll return to Cloudland in a couple of months for Triple Zed's battle of the Bands, but *Madness* never will. On the Brisbane leg of their Australian tour next year they will play *Festival Hall*. Suggs, the lead singer, will finish the show by asking the audience, "Whatever happened to Cloudland?"

When Stephen Cummings of *The Sports* was interviewed by an ABC Radio journalist at the Queensland Writers Festival, Timothy was chuffed that the former front-man referred to this 1981 performance at Cloudland with *Madness* and *The Go-Betweens*. As Timothy said at the time: "Sometimes you wonder if things in the distant past ever happened; it's good to get corroboration".

'PIG CITY'

Most nights during the summer of 1979 to 1980 punk concerts at Cloudland a more visible police presence was exhibited. There were sniffer dogs in the audience; and plants within the crowd acting as narcs. Bouncers roamed the venue checking out punks and skinheads and trying to show audience members who really was in control.

By the age of sixteen I was taking regular hour-long Friday night train rides from the southern working underclass suburb of Woodridge to the Cloudland Ballroom in Bowen Hills, a majestic venue frequented by [many] generations of dancing Queenslanders. There I experienced the most amazing array of early eighties Australian pub rock bands along with a cavalcade of international acts including *The Clash* and Ian Dury and *The Blockheads*. Dury was warned that if he sang "Spasticus Autisticus" police would storm the stage and arrest the band. They played the track during the encore and nothing happened, however the suspense was fabulously nerve-wracking. One thing was always assured at Cloudland; everybody had to jump in time to the music due to the 1940s multi cross ply... built dance floor and everybody had to jump to the omnipresent mass of intimidation that was the Queensland police force.

And again:

The British punk movement of 1977 was typically portrayed as politically driven and working class. But this was how the self-important London music press wanted it to be. It is equally [and] so generally accepted that punk in Australia could not possibly have been politically motivated since we in the Lucky Country had so little about which to complain. This is ignoring the fact that the reformist Whitlam government was thrown out of office in 1975, that unemployment ran almost as high in Australia in the late seventies as it did in Britain; and that the Joh Bjelke-Petersen regime within Queensland had banned street marches. Yet, even a band like *The Saints*, despite a genuine and justified streak of left-wing radicalism encompassed a musical revolution before anything else.

These years of 1979-80 were best summed up by a song which emerged as 4ZZZ's anthem; one recorded at a later period by the *Paremeters* in October, 1983, called *Pig City*. According to Rob Lastdrazer—

I'm not really sure why I've written this piece, suffice it to say that when I heard the terms "coming of age" and "Brisbane" and "Pig City" in the one sentence I felt a little aggressive twinge in my lower back. Maybe this is a form of therapy? Maybe I'm venting? Whatever. Here's to all the Queensland refugees who fought the law and got out of town to play another day. I'll be raising a glass and celebrating Brisbane's coming of age from the comfort and safety of a gaffer-taped bar stool in Melbourne. Cheers.

A 'promo' for the *Paremeters*.

For a reaction like that to the term 'Pig city' used at Cloudland during the early 1980s you would have to go back to police in Brisbane, who went on stage at the end of a play in 1969, and arrested an actor for obscene language": F...boong'. Actually it was the play *Norm and Ahmed* by Alex Buzo, a serious examination of racism in Australia. Actor Norm Staines was fined, but on appeal the charge was laughed out of court, all the way to the High Court.

Brian Setzer of *The Stray Cats*, Cloudland, 1981.

and changed early 1980s Cloudland patrons in Brisbane were also played by American outfits, *The Ramones,* and *The Stray Cats.* They seemed to have altered the 'outlook' of many eager concert goers to 'alternative' rock music with their 'revolutionary' zeal.

By the start of 1982, *Australian Crawl, Cold Chisel, Angel City, Split Enz,* and *Midnight Oil* were reaping huge touring profits at the Bowen Hills venue, a sum which would make medium-sized corporations jealous by comparison. In effect, *Australian Crawl* set a new record at Cloudland (in January of 1982) when they grossed a staggering $50,000 by 'taking the door' and drawing 5,000 fans at $10 a head.

During 1981, two other epic concerts which both challenged

THE CLASH

The *Clash* played seven nights in Tokyo, as well as Sydney on their 1982 tour.

As punk rock bands go, *The Clash* was the *crème de la crème* of British rock bands; rock royalty, if you could say that about a punk music outfit. As a one-eyed Australian fan reveals:

> ...*The Clash* were a very important part of my teenage upbringing and exposed me to a whole new world of music with bands being influenced by them in the inner-city areas of Sydney in 1977. While so many people were buying records from *The Wombles*, a disgusting English group that had dressed up in furry animal outfits and sang low grade bubble gum pop, I managed to get hold of *The Clash*'s first album entitled, *The Clash*...it was like a breath of fresh air for a kid

living in the suburbs. It sent me on my way to search out everything that was there to now be explored. RIP Joe Strummer...one bloke, who died too young [in December, 2002].

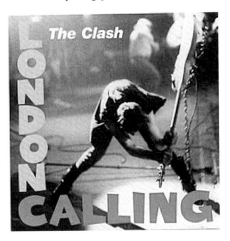

A record cover promoting the Clash's 1979 hit, *London Calling*. (Rock'n'Roll, 1955 to 2005)

Courier-Mail/Sunday Mail.

The Clash performed at Cloudland on Saturday, February 20th, 1982, one of the last concerts at the venue. Here is how one skinhead stood up to the 'redneck' crowd; and, in so doing, he supported *The Clash's* lead singer, Joe Strummer:

I wish to share a story for the record about the 1982 *Clash* concert at Cloudland in Brisbane. I think it was in February of 1982.

Specifically I would like to talk about how I stopped a *Clash* concert in full flight in 1982; and to set the record straight about the incident.

Land rights for Murris and Kooris (indigenous Australians) were in full flight in 1982 and why shouldn't it **(sic)** be...we whities stole their land with no treaty. I was a Punk...That Joh political conservatism era was

now in full flight and police were politicised in the process.

I was most ashamed to be an Australian on that night, when Joe Strummer called a land right activist upon stage to advocate for the land rights struggle about half way through the set.

I listened to the arguments put forward and was on side but the 4,000 odd rednecks in the crowd were not and this poor man was booed off stage. I could actually understand the injustice.

Joe Strummer was obviously not impressed and [he] shouted angrily at the audience...OK YOU WANT IT...YOU GET IT and proceeded with the classic *Clash* song *White Riot* and the crowd went wild.

A Murri guy next to me started spitting at Joe Strummer from the mosh pit and I said to the guy stop spitting on the band and he said do you want to fight me and I responded for the record NO!! I felt Joe was not the person to spit on... the rednecks in the crowd were the obvious target.

With that, the guy grabbed me around the front collar of my shirt and started to twist it tight. I broke the hold and proceeded to deck the guy. "Sorry mate" you should have left it alone and I would have done the same thing to Whitie under the circumstances.

Additionally:

Joe could see what was going on and called for the front of house lights to be put on. It was clear that a lot of damage had been inflicted on this fella from me with splits under his eyes, mouth and blood coming from his nose, not a pretty site **(sic)** and for all my troubles, I split my knuckle in half from the impact. I went overseas the following week to London as I had enough of Brisvegas at this time (with a plaster cast on for my troubles). A white bouncer intervened with the Murri and a black bouncer intervened with me, but it was just restraining us both.

I made a hasty exit through the crowd.

I read in a *New Music Express* magazine about 1982 (in a park in Copenhagen) how Joe Strummer thought Brisbane people were racists and to a point he was right. But I bet the guy I had fought would not have realised I was on his side...life is funny like that.

As punks we were always getting into trouble with the law so I could appreciate the plight of Murris and Kooris and this led to a number of Brisbane punks training in a cell-like group...who were prepared to take on the law...We trained at Darra and were doing Karate training like 50 push ups with bare knuckles on wooden floor boards. We were extremely fit and political. Several say Brisbane punks were the only true punks in Australia. We thought this only proper as our punk friends were being beaten up by bad cops in the Valley area and at the police watch-house at Makerston St., Brisbane...I have since learnt to use the political system for the good of the community and have very sound relationships with Murri and Koori activists.

The Clash on stage at the Cloudland Ballroom, 20th February, 1982.

What had actually happened at *the Clash's* Cloudland concert was that Joe Strummer of *The Clash* had made a reference to 'Pig City', in regard to Brisbane being a 'police state'. *The Clash* then invited Bob Weatherall, the Queensland Aboriginal leader up on the stage. Bob had then danced and 'raved' about the protests over the holding of the Commonwealth Games in Brisbane in September-October of 1982.

THE CLASH
Australian Tour February, 1982.

Feb 11 Capitol Theatre, Sydney, Australia
Feb 12 Capitol Theatre, Sydney, Australia
Feb 13 Capitol Theatre, Sydney, Australia
Feb 14 Capitol Theatre, Sydney, Australia
Feb 16 Capitol Theatre, Sydney, Australia
Feb 17 Capitol Theatre, Sydney, Australia
Feb 18 Capitol Theatre, Sydney, Australia
Feb 20 Cloudland Ballroom, Brisbane, Australia
Feb 22 Thebarton Town Hall, Adelaide, Australia
Feb 23 Festival Hall, Melbourne

By the end of their Cloudland 'gig', *The Clash* had witnessed an immense police presence—somewhere in the hundreds. Joe Strummer taunted them on the night with these words: *When they come knockin' on your door, /How you going to come,/With your hands upon your head,/Or your hands upon a gun'.*

In 1982, the year *The Clash* played at Cloudland, the number of punk rock concerts was three times in excess of the 2,500 maximum placed on these events at Cloudland. Moreover, six people had been arrested for some drug-related offences during the *Clash's* concert. Six cars were towed away by police; and 23 traffic offence notices were issued for illegally parked vehicles. Such occurrences had led the Hamilton Ward Chairman, Syd McDonald, to revoke Peter Kurts' licence to hold rock concerts. McDonald had also argued that the peace and the tranquillity of Bowen Hills had been disturbed by Cloudland's Sunday morning flea markets.

The late Joe Strummer's (and *The Clash's*) political activism in their Cloudland concert of February, 1982, certainly lived on well after his passing:

A friend of Joe Strummer, legendary former front man of English rockers, *The Clash*, [John] Mayall, submitted a rather detailed funding proposal to Strummerville, the British-based charity set up after Strummer's death in 2002 to support projects that helped change the world through music: "Joe was a humanitarian and environmentalist. He would have loved what *Narasirato* was about. I can just see him here, playing his guitar under the stars, enjoying village life".

"We didn't know Joe Strummer', says Manuasi, pulling his Strummerville T-shirt—with its red, green and gold logo—over his head for another band photo shoot. "But we are glad that his spirit is here, helping the world know about us".

Rest now, Joe Strummer of *The Clash*. You've finally answered the call to your Maker. Seeing you live at Cloudland was magic for those who were lucky enough to be there!

Cold Chisel played their last concert at Cloudland on February 26th, 1982. It resulted in 14 charges against patrons. The list of

offences had included: drug-related behaviour; indecent behaviour; obscene language; drunkenness and also drink driving. After the show, local residents near the ballroom in Bowen Hills complained of assaults; bad language; some blocked driveways; and bottles being thrown.

Cold Chisel as they appear today.

During this same year of 1982, the Rover/Ranger Council organised its Debutante Ball. Seven 'Ranger Guides' were presented to the Queensland State Commissioner and the Chief Commissioner for the Scout Association at Cloudland Ballroom. This was probably the last Debutante Ball held before Cloudland disappeared'.

On Friday, May 28th, 1982, around 2,000 people also attended a 'Thirties and Forties' revival ball at Cloudland. It was organised by La Boite Theatre and the Community Arts Network of Queensland. It enabled the ballroom to return to more sedate events than *The Clash* or *Cold Chisel* shows.

The Commonwealth Games Bush Ball, featuring the *Verandah Band, Borderline* and the *QFF Bush Orchestra,* held a dance event, sponsored by the Queensland Folk Federation. It was to be among the very last of Cloudland's shows and events.

On the 6th November, 1982, Peter Kurts confided that Cloudland's big arch had to go, preventing the dancehall's rebuilding. He had ceased trading at the venue by midnight, leaving tables set for the supposed Sunday night trading. Under a veil of secrecy, coiled cables were smuggled into the ballroom's ceilings; squares of tin sheeting masked the chainsaw cuts to poles holding up the iconic arched entry; and 24 police officers met at a clandestine rendezvous point with the Dean Brothers. Everything was now in readiness for Cloudland's imminent demise. All that the 'inferno' left behind was nostalgia and memories.

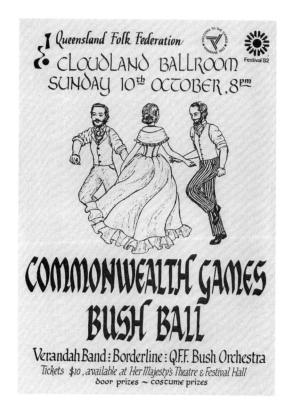

13
CLOUDLAND'S 'HYBRIDS', POST-1982

LITERARY CLOUDLAND

Cloudland's legendary ballroom at Bowen Hills was remembered in Matthew Condon's book, *Motorcycle Café;* Susan Johnson's *Hungry Ghosts* and Venero Armanno's *Romeo of the Underworld* and *The Volcano;* and by several poets such as Robert Morris and Ross Clark.

Venero Armanno, a local Brisbane author, draws heavily on reality for all his unconventional stories. In *Romeo of the Underworld,* a "sultry tale about Romeo's sad love life…Romeo Constanzo returns to his home-town of Brisbane after many years in gritty Sydney, to housesit for an old friend. A near-death experience on a plane kicks off the storyline".

The sudden and controversial destruction of the famous Cloudland Ballroom devastates our Romeo. He finds, much to his chagrin, "that his beloved teenage hangout [has] been replaced with the looming threat of townhouses".

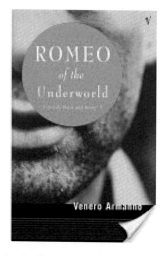

The book, *Romeo of the Underworld*, by Venero Armanno.

For many newly-established Italian immigrants in the 1980s, like Emilio Aquila in Venero Armanno's *The Volcano*, Cloudland and its music offerings are also parallel to experiencing New York's famous Statue of Liberty. It also offers mobility into Australia's social milieu. One day Emilio had asked Mary if she recalled a place called Cloudland. 'Did you used to go there?' She had replied: 'I think I was about 10 or 12 or something when the developer knocked it down'.

In *The Dirty Beat*, Armanno explores the music offerings at Cloudland:

> My new step-father was also an ex-swing drummer and across four decades he'd played shows at church halls, small and large jazz clubs, the City Hall and the Cloudland Ballroom. His main gig had been with an outfit called *Jimmy 'Knockout' Jones and His Incredible Sixteen-Piece Orchestra.* Band leader Jimmy Jones had his entourage together for nearly twenty years and Conney said that [during] their time they'd entertained everyone from debutantes, desperate bachelors and a few discouraged spinsters, Country Women's Associations and Masons, to local political leaders, visiting dignitaries—and [also] royalty—but, to *Knockout*'s eternal consternation, never the Queen of England.

The Dirty Beat by Venero Armanno.

In Susan Johnson's, *Hungry Ghosts*, Margaret Buchan, unhappily wedded to an older man and 'estranged' from her only daughter, seeks some 'solace' in memories of her youthful joyfulness at Bowen Hills in the early 1940s: Cloudland's sprung floor swaying beneath her dancing shoes; and soldier's kisses in the outside darkness.

Teddy Vine, the part-Aboriginal 'hero' of Elizabeth Webb's *Into the Morning*, also finds out that black folk are barred from Cloudland in the 1950s.

To George Baker, the 'patriarch' of Matthew Condon's *The Motorcycle Café*, Cloudland is symbolic of a different repulsion. George is angered when his daughter's initial visits to the hilltop palace appear to be an abandonment of her family.

The poem by Robert Morris about Cloudland's 'funicular' railway endorses, too, memories of Cloudland and its 1950s 'be bop' Billo Smith Band.

Ross Clarke's poem *Escaping Cloudland* salutes his memory of sitting a November examination for the university, complete with an entrapped pigeon 'fluttering [up] against all the upper glass windows'. Ross' supervisors, hoping to keep any disturbance to a minimum, release the frustrated bird after finally opening the windows at the conclusion of the testing. Ross feels that the students and this lone pigeon experienced a common 'captivity' and a 'fellowship' which carried over into 'post-exam celebrations'.

That night, toasting every subject,

Every professor, we raised a glass

As well as to one who strove with us.

ABC AND CHANNEL 7 'DOCOS'

In 1982, a videocassette, *World Peace Tower*, was produced by the ABC and Channel Seven. It examined Brisbane's building structures; and offered documentary-style excerpts from various program broadcasts. It also offered two ABC Nationwide segments from November 8th and 9th, respectively entitled *Cloudland's Demise* and *More of Cloudland's Demise*.

CLOUDLAND (THE PLAY)

Peter Noble and Darien Sticklen's 1983 play *Cloudland* had the stamp of the Queensland Theatre Company imprinted on the script itself. This is interesting as, at one time in its history, the QTC came under scrutiny as an object for demolition, just as Cloudland did. The only important difference was that the QTC survived, and Cloudland was destroyed.

CLOUDLAND: THE MUSICAL

In July, 1995, Craigslea State High School performed *Cloudland: The Musical*. A videotaped copy of *Cloudland* was produced by the Year 11 FTV students. The lyrics and music for the show were produced by Peter, Marianne and Mark Nahusen. This was Peter's second musical. *Cloudland* was set in the 1950s and takes a look at the advent of rock'n'roll, and was based upon Brisbane's famous ballroom—a home to three generations of revellers—which was demolished in the early 1980s.

Even though *Cloudland* premiered at Kelvin Grove State High School in 1994, four other Queensland high schools, including Craigslea, had then chosen it as their 1995 productions.

Members of Cloudland's cast.

Courier-Mail, 9th May, 1994.

'THE DELINQUENTS'

It is indeed interesting how a major feature film, *The Delinquents*, was also connected with the name 'Cloudland' within 1989. The movie is "about a small town in Australia, somewhere in the late 1950s. Brownie and Lola are so very deeply in love. Nevertheless, because they are underage..." (and so on). This film was directed by Chris

Thompson and featured our own Kylie Minogue, Charlie Schlater and Bruno Lawrence. It had screened at 101 minutes, and was classified as a drama/romance. What had made the film nostalgic as well as watchable is that the last scene was shot at the site of the demolished Cloudland. Its vacant land served as a film set.

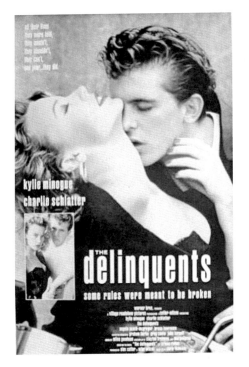

The Delinquents, 1989.

CLOUDLAND 𝒜PARTMENTS

In 1986 the Brisbane City Council gave approval in principle to rezone the Cloudland area for the construction of approximately 180 units. The Emanuel Group consequently paid $2.5 million for the Cloudland site as well as the approved plans in 1987. Then, in 1988, Cloudland changed hands for $4.5 million. It was purchased by Hooker Homes Pty. Ltd. and Mercantile Credits Limited. From November 30th, 1989, the 2.5 hectare property was open to all tenders, along with the aforesaid approved plans for a $35 million residential development.

The new Cloudland plans approved by the Brisbane City Council included forty-seven three-bedroom townhouses, forty three-bedroom apartments in three-storey blocks; and forty three-bedroom apartments in an eleven-storey tower. The townhouses were expected to fetch $270,000 each; the apartments $330,000; and the units $370,000. Around 1994 the initial stage of the apartments was built.

The demolished Cloudland Ballroom site. It still had not been developed by 1991.

The initial stage of Cloudland's redevelopment. Some of the forty apartments start to take shape. *JOL.*

Although Cloudland Ballroom's architectural and cultural significance was without peer, its prime hilltop site also made it a highly desirable land target. Some said it fell prey to rapacious developers; others that it was looking tired and had had its day.

As George Deen remarked: 'something has to go for something else to replace it'. An apartment complex now occupies the old site where Queenslanders once boogied the night away above the bright, twinkling fairy tale illuminations of the city.

Apartments on the site of the old Luna Park (Cloudland).
Photo: Peter Dunn, March, 2005.

A number of the exceptionally sarcastic commentaries about Cloudland's replacement are worthy of mention here:

> Look on the bright side. Instead of magnificent Cloudland, we now have a block of very ordinary units to look upon. A definite improvement to our city scape. I think that was Joh's handy-work too wasn't it?

And further:

> And what did we get instead? A gated complex of town-houses and units. I'm sure they have superb views; and even though I'm now an apartment dweller myself, I didn't welcome their arrival. This is the street view of the entrance to the place...[and] all that is left of Cloudland now is the name that is included in the stylised logo visible above the garage at the front.

Moreover:

> The architectural atrocity that replaced Cloudland can be seen on the Brisbane City Council website. In what they laughably refer to as the 'urban renewal', BCC winked at the illegal demolition and rubber-stamped the redevelopment of the site of Australia's finest Art Deco ballroom, which was replaced by a $20 million, 125-unit private apartment complex of unsurpassed ugliness.

The old concrete steps (to the *left* of the image), perhaps one of the only original bits of Cloudland in existence.

The entrance to *Cloudland Apartments*.

Boyd Street in Bowen Hills.
Photo by Peter Dunn, March, 2005.

Some folk had even referred to the "old lady's" demise, and her substitution with 'flats', as very similar to a description by John Milton of '*Hell*' as '*Pandemonium*'.

Marie, at Cloudland Luna Park Ballroom, in 1956] actually met her husband, Trevor, there during that particular year. In 1997, they couldn't escape their origins and destiny. They had purchased their penthouse, *Cumulus*, upon the residential apartment complex constructed on the former grounds of Cloudland. The pair had felt they have now gone the 'full hog', so to speak—almost like a complete circle. As their first night of their honeymoon was spent in the later-to-be dismantled *Belle Vue Hotel*, there is indeed an ironic twist to their fate.

Marie & Trevor at Cloudland, 1956.

MOVIES

A non-feature length movie, *Cloudland*, was also produced as—

...a collaboration between *Late Nite Films*, 16th *Street Actors Studio* and Writer/Director Nicholas Hammond. This short film version is a collection of scenes from a screenplay written by the famed writer/director/actor, Mr Nicholas Hammond (*The Sound of Music*). The film is set during the Second World War; and is about the relationship between the American soldiers and [our] Australian women during this time. (*Late Nite Films*.)

In 2001, there was an announcement about a new 'Aussie' musical film called *Cloudland*:

...Executively produced by Dean Elijah, this film centres upon the legendary Cloudland Ballroom, which opened in Brisbane's Bowen Hills in 1939 and closed its doors in 1982, after hosting the likes of [both] Buddy Holly and Johnny O'Keefe. Cloudland follows three usherettes who [all] begin working at the ballroom in the early '50s and it follows their lives over the next three decades. Elijah's company *Rising Son Productions* is currently courting Baz Luhrmann to direct, and the *Twentieth Century Fox, Dreamworks, Warner Brothers* and *Village Roadshow Pictures* to get behind the screenplay, which is currently in its third draft.

In 2002, Revolution Rock Motion Pictures further produced a short-subject video entitled *Cloudland* which featured dance music of the time in Brisbane.

A scene from *Cloudland*.

TIM KELLY'S
'A PLACE CALLED CLOUDLAND'

In 2002, Tim Kelly composed song lyrics to honour the venerable ballroom:

A Place Called Cloudland

Well I was just fourteen
Innocent and a little green
But from innocence we all must fall
Me, I landed on a sprung dance floor
The whole room was swaying
And *The Sports* were playing
'*Strangers on a Train*'
I learnt to stand
In a place called Cloudland

They'd catch a tram from Adelaide Street
And with their brothel creepers on the seat
They'd head for the blue-lit arch
And try to sneak their gin past

And they were always letting
'*Golden Wedding*'
Carry them away
Billo Smith led the band
Every night at Cloudland

We Rise, We fall
We used to have a ball
She was too pretty
For such an ugly city
Unsound, unseen
Thanks to the brothers Deen
I lost my thrill
Up on Cintra Hill

Well they came at four a.m.
So nobody could bother them
Not even City Hall
Could stop that wrecking Ball
And all they left behind
Was an empty skyline
Oh and the memories
Town houses now stand
In this place called Cloudland.

THE CLOUDLAND MEMORIAL ARCH

memorial. It commemorates Cloudland Brisbane's skyline—and is called the *Cloudland Memorial Arch*. This 2004 design takes its lead from the former structure's inspiring and famous neon-lit arch:

> Panels feature historical images from the Cloudland site and ceramic ground tiles in the form of dance steps created by Sarah Greenwood relate stories of people with memories of the ballroom.

Artist Jamie Maclean was the creator of this celebratory arch which once stood atop the summit of Bowen Hills as a dominating

The arch is situated at Cowlishaw Street, Bowen Hills. *Below* are two views of the Cloudland Memorial Arch.

THE BALLET, CLOUDLAND

During 2004, a ballet, *Cloudland,* was choreographed by Francois Klaus. It had premiered at the *Brisbane Festival.* It has since been presented in a number of Australian and European cities. Since 2004, the work has regularly charmed audiences on a highly acclaimed tour to six cities across Switzerland and Germany.

The Queensland Ballet Company had this juicy titbit of information about its *Cloudland* production:

The lights dim, the music swells, and wrapped in the magical embrace of Cloudland, the dance begins...

An iconic Brisbane building for [four] decades, the Cloudland ballroom was the chief focus of the city's social life. Countless romances blossomed under its spinning mirror balls. Romantic, nostalgic, and humorous, Cloudland is based on real-life stories of romance, friendship and [of] war-time relationships. With the music performed live on stage by Sean O'Boyle and his fabulous band, the production gives an energetic and dynamic portrayal of life, love and dance in Brisbane from the 1940s to the 1980s.

Let the spirited dancers of Queensland Ballet whisk you back in time to Cloudland...

Ironically, the Ballet Theatre Company's own premises had itself been scheduled for demolition, making a ballet about the 'cruel' demolition of Cloudland Ballroom an interesting topic to portray in classical dance.

In January of 2005, QPAC (the Queensland Performing Arts Complex) mounted a display featuring the *ca.* 1980s band of Cloudland, *Razar.* The Brisbane City Hall held a similar display in May of 2005.

Cloudland, the ballet.

Queensland Ballet.

DANCE FOR A CAUSE

Cloudland Ballroom as a theme had also returned with a vengeance and a cause when local dancers performed swing and jive moves for charity at Samford Village on March 24th, 2007. Four of the five original members of the 'seminal' rock and roll band, *Waterloo*, played at the 'Dance for a Cause' fundraising event. *The RK Quintet*, featuring the voice of *Waterloo* guitarist, Chris Carroll, had also performed at this function. Evidently, *Waterloo* gigged regularly at Cloudland in the 1970s and '80s. Chris remembered playing—

to huge crowds when we supported bands like *Sherbert*, *Zoot* and *Skyhooks*. Some of these nights were harder to remember...[There were also] songs by *The Beach Boys*, *The Beatles*, the *Rolling Stones*, the *Doobie Brothers* and

Bee Gees [which] were frequently requested at shows, as were the 1950-era rock and roll of the likes of Elvis Presley and Roy Orbison.

The lead guitarist of Sherbert, Clive Richard Shakespeare.

The rock'n'roll group, *Waterloo*, jamming in 1975.   *The Westerner.*

612 ABC RADIO'S BACK TO CLOUDLAND

There was a tremendous response to 612 ABC Radio's *Back to Cloudland* event, held on November 2nd, 2008, at Brisbane's City Hall. According to journalist, Rebecca Sparrow:

> This call-out for memories saw the switchboard light up like a New York skyline with hundreds of callers wanting to share their memories.
>
> As for the event itself, no fewer that 700 couples went along to dance to the *Allan Brown Big Band* and reminisce about what was once Brisbane's favourite venue. (*Sunday Mail.*)

Evidently, the local radio station of our national broadcaster ran a 'nostalgic' series which culminated in the *Back to Cloudland* event.

The *Allan Brown Big Band* — playing at the Cloudland reunion.

Normie Rowe, one of the big headliners to perform at Cloudland with *The Playboys*, reminisced on radio with Kelly Higgins-Devine, plus promoter Ivan Dayman's wife, Niah; former rock jock, Johnny James; Gary McDonald from the popular *Sounds of Seven*; Tony Worsley who was front-man for the *Blue Jays*; and the late Pat Aulton, Dayman's right hand man, emcee and crooner.

Tim West and Maggie Adeney-West perform as the The *Baby Boomer Party Band*. Their claim to fame was that, not only did they win a double pass to 612 ABC Brisbane's *Back to Cloudland* event at the City Hall on November 2nd, 2008, they worked together to pen and record an original piece of music, as a commemoration about the time they had at Cloudland. In truth, Maggie's husband performed 'gigs' there in the 1960s; and Maggie herself danced there in the following decade. The Wests' song goes something like this:

Cloudland

Saturday night and moon is bright,

I'm gonna head uptown to see the city lights

Twinkling and a shining from a hill on high

There's magic in the air and music in the sky

At Cloudland,

I'll be dancing to the band at Cloudland

I met my love at a Cloudland Ball,

We dreamed a dream on a starlit night

I kissed my girl on the grand dance floor

I swung her to the left; I swung her to the right

At Cloudland,

We were dancing to the band at Cloudland

In 1940 Brissy came of age

With a brand new venue and a world class stage

In the '50s we were swingin'

To the Big Band sound,

In the '60s Thorpy had to turn the volume down!

We rock'n'rolled those nights away,

To *The Sounds of Seven* and the old *Blue Jays*

To Tony Worsley and Normie Rowe

The floor started jumpin'

When the saxaphones'd blow

At Cloudland,

Dancing to the band at Cloudland.

Solo

The music changed but the beat went on,

With a new generation and a brand new song

The kids were burning up the *Midnight Oil*

1980 was a different world

At Cloudland,

Still dancing to the band at Cloudland

One thing I know is all things must pass

But it's sad to see what took its place

I'm glad I've known an old world's grace

I'm glad I've known an old world's grace

At Cloudland

Dancing to the band at Cloudland

Catching the tram to Cloudland

Rolling down the hill from Cloudland

I remember it still, Cloudland,

And I always will

Cloudland.

As for the star-studded *Back to Cloudland* event itself, Normie Rowe sang his classic *Shakin' All Over*; couples danced the *foxtrot* and *gypsy tap*; and Kelly and Quentin Hull did the solo numbers *Fever* and *Have you met Miss Jones.*

As the *Courier-Mail* reported:

Back to Cloudland

There were no hard feeling when [the] demolition driver **George Deen** took to the stage at Sunday night's *Back to Cloudland* celebrations held at *The City Hall*. Deen, who had cemented his company's notoriety by taking down Cloudland inside a 20-minute excavation with his brothers way back in 1982, was met with apprehension from the crowd following his introduction by host Spencer Howson. But Deen remembered the job as good fun, adding: "I had the last dance".

As gasps turned to claps, the crowd was in a healing mood, not to let any bad memories linger among the wonderful celebratory atmosphere.

'George' Deen is the only brother left in the demolition business. Ray buys and sells trailers and trucks (as does Happy); Louie operates a heavy haulage business; and Funny also has trucks.

As Paul Henderson of Wynnum attests: '[The] infamy of the Joh Bjelke-Petersen era lingers over the Cloudland site 30 years later. The ballroom may be gone, 'but certainly not forgotten'.

'George' Deen.

CLOUDLAND COMES TO CLEVELAND

Cloudland arrived back in Cleveland, Brisbane, too, on Saturday, August 15th, 2009, when the Redlands Committee on Ageing (RDCOTA) brought back "nostalgic memories of a bygone era", as part of its celebrations for Senior Citizens Week in the Redlands.

The Master of Ceremonies was Terry Annesley alongside of Tony Worsley, *The Countdowns*, Dennis Knight, Julie Paris and locals *The Cat's Whiskers*. The music line-up had performed with many international and 'Aussie' artists from the 1950s, including Johnny O'Keefe, Johnny Farnham, Billy Thorpe, the *Dave Clark Five*, *The Delltones*, *The Easybeats*, *Manfred Mann*, Lonnie Lee and Gina Jeffreys.

Participants for the night were urged to put on their dancing shoes "for an evening of non-stop dance music, including ballroom, rock'n'roll, jive, swing and pop".

Tony Worsley and Julie Paris, lining up here for 'Cloudland comes to Cleveland'.

Bayside Bulletin.

THE NEW CLOUDLAND
IN FORTITUDE VALLEY

Cloudland Ballroom as an entertainment venue was to be 'immortalised' and reborn in 2009. It was used as the namesake of a brand new Brisbane 'Mega-Club' in Fortitude Valley, and is located approximately 1½ kilometres away from the former Cloudland Ballroom site. This 1500-capacity venue of *Cloudland*, costing almost $10 million, opened up to a great deal of fanfare and gaiety. The modern décor of this nightclub has been described as an 'urbane oasis', remarkably like its former original.

According to a recent *Courier-Mail* report, the new *Cloudland* will be well managed:

The biggest of the entire Valley's players remains Lou Bickle and his family with their venues the *Empire*, *Family*, *Birdee Num Num* and their newest addition, *Cloudland*.

Such was their faith in the Valley that the family pumped millions into creating the sprawling four-level *Cloudland*, the [most] ritziest nightclub Queensland has ever seen, with a design straight from a Tim Burton film set.

Bickle, 68, who got his foothold in the Valley in the aftermath of the Fitzgerald inquiry, says the standard of operators and venues is the best it's ever been. He doesn't feel the same about many of the patrons who attempt to get into his bars, saying patron standards are "terrible".

Two years ago Bickle told *The Sunday Mail* the Valley was now on the cusp of an unprecedented boom.

One 'first-nighter', who attended *Cloudland's* opening in 2009, had this to share:

I'd attended the opening of the new *Cloudland* venue in Fortitude Valley in Brisbane last Thursday night.

Wow—what an amazing place.

I can't remember ever walking out of any venue being so impressed. Then again, it is unlike any other venue I have ever been in (anywhere). The superlatives being bandied about in the early reports rolling out, are appropriate. This is a venue that is well and truly worthy of its history heavy name—and would seem to do justice to the gorgeous art deco ballroom that carried it, for many years.

I was there in a professional capacity, for the early part of the night, with a colleague of mine (and his camera) to film footage for a documentary film project. The party itself was exciting and interesting. An eclectic pastiche resplendent with plenty of posturing and posing—as you would expect at such a function—with plenty of well- known faces flown in from around the country; which all made for good film. I did a lot of crowd watching—the demographic was varied and intriguing and there were plenty of characters in the room. But invariably the lens (both the camera's and my own) turned to the walls, the floors, the lights, the plants, the water features, the bars…

An extremely striking sculpture for *Cloudland's Carnevale di Venezia*.

Cloudland's Wedding Showcase.

'Pure ritz', the four-level *Cloudland* in Fortitude Valley.

3D CLOUDLAND 'BUST' DESIGNS

Kyle Fysh, a 3D designer, using Cloudland as a theme, embarked on a "painstaking process" of gathering details about the ballroom's images and information to enable him to apply "meticulous detail" to his models about the iconic structure.

Kyle's angel model, copied from the wreckage of Cloudland Ballroom.

JOHN WATERS' CLOUDLAND ALBUM

Actor John Waters' debut album of originals, *Cloudland*, has also had a compelling "association with the defunct and the much lamented dance venue". It seems that, after John had finished work on a sheep station, he worked as a friend's offsider, delivering fruit and vegetables in a small truck. One of the places they delivered to was Cloudland.

Waters' album is "a blend of blues, roots, folk, country and rock". It also "covers the spectrum of love, loss, regret, retrospective hindsight; and inspirational salvation, as he takes you on a personal emotional journey". [*Waterfront Records*]. The album was released in July, 2011.

John Waters.

A BOOK, DOLLIES IN CLOUDLAND

In 2011, Clara Lieu, an author, was working on a children's book series, *Dollies*. She wrote the text and then created the illustrations. One of her titles for the works was: *Dollies in Cloudland*.

MIDNIGHT OIL'S SONG, 'DREAMWORLD'

Finally, *Midnight Oil*, who had headlined at Cloudland countless times, immortalised the destruction of the iconic ballroom in their song, *Dreamworld*. It was from their *Dust and Diesel* LP. In *Dreamworld*, Peter Garrett and the *Oil's* band attacked the Queensland Government's greedy pro-development forces.

Peter Garrett recalled on ABC radio that he was literally sick right to his stomach when he had found out about Cloudland's fate in November of 1982. He accused Joh Bjelke-Petersen's regime of not realising the true importance of Cloudland to Brisbane, Queensland, and Australia's live music scene; or connecting the historic structure to the satisfaction and happiness people had been bequeathed by its presence and smooth operation. Peter also lamented the lost opportunity for bands like *Midnight Oil* to ever perform again at this very magical venue.

BOUNDARY STREET

The musical, *Boundary Street,* examines racism, discrimination, fear, brutality (and additionally prejudice) in jazz-besotted Brisbane in 1942. There, 'respectable' Australian women are allured by African-American servicemen and their love of music and dancing, such as 'eye-popping' swing, jitterbug and jive (reminiscent of post-war Cloudland).

A dance sequence from *Boundary Street*.

Bee Gees Way & Statue unveiled on the 14th February, 2013.

ABOUT THE AUTHOR

Dr James G. Lergessner is one of Queensland's distinguished historians, biographers and memoir writers. He commenced his writing career in 1993 as a professional, contracted author with Boolarong Press, Brisbane. His books sell presently Australia-wide with library suppliers; and, in addition, to Dymocks, Angus & Robertson and Mary Ryan Bookstores where he has been on hand for book signings. Formerly a university professor of education and an academic consultant in Australia and Canada, James is a passionate observer and recorder of life and events in Brisbane, the State of Queensland and Australia. He has published twenty-three books (19 non-fiction and four fiction works) related to early Queensland; namely Brisbane, the Caboolture Shire and Moreton Bay Regional Council areas including Bribie Island, and Australia generally. James is also noted for the excellence of his research which underpins all of his published works, as well as the high standard of production and the friendliness of his writing style.

Since all his early years, James has taken an active interest in conservation, Aboriginal issues, the early Queensland pioneers, family dynasties and cultural heritage. During 2004 to 2009 Caboolture Shire Council, Moreton Bay Regional Council RADF and Jupiter's Gaming Community Benefits grants have most effectively endorsed James's entire body of work. From 2004 to the present time, James has spoken at well over 700 functions within the south-east Queensland area. He is particularly in demand as an invited guest and after-dinner speaker to special breakfast, lunch and evening events around Brisbane and the Moreton Bay Regional Council area. From 2009 to 2010, James was invited to be a special guest of the Brisbane Libraries to tour their Wynnum, Fairfield and Annerley facilities with his hilarious book, *Snippets from a Baby Boomer's Diary*. Moreover, he was also invited to tour the Moreton Bay Regional Council Libraries in Strathpine, Bribie, Caboolture and Woodford, with his evocative book, *Death Pudding: The Kilcoy Massacre*. As well, James has been a guest at various Queensland EXPOS; and the Redfest, Wynnum Spring and Central Park Wynnum Festivals; both reading from his work; and often being accompanied by Peter Meij from Jim's music duo, 'One-two', as they both perform the songs from the 'baby boom' era of 1946-1964.

An entry under James's name was significantly published in Crown Content's Inaugural Edition of *Who's Who in Queensland for 2007/2008*. As he is a confirmed sports 'nut', James felt most honoured for his entry to be placed between the legendary rugby league player, Wally Lewis, and Libby Lenton (now Trickett).

OTHER WORKS BY THE AUTHOR

White Specks on a Dark Shore: The Pumicestone Passage Castaways, Bowen Hills, Brisbane; Boolarong Press, 1993.

Bribie the Convict Weaver, Bongaree, Bribie Island: Victory Press, 2005.

A Shrine to the Artist Ian Fairweather, Bongaree, Bribie Island: Victory Press, 2005.

'Seaward', South Esplanade, Bribie Island, Bongaree, Bribie Island: Victory Press, 2006.

Oysterers of Moreton Bay, Narangba: Print Approach, 2007.

Embattled Seacows: Dugongers in Early Queensland, Narangba: Print Approach, 2007.

I, Thomas Welsby, Narangba: Print Approach, 2007.

Chief Bungaree: King of the Broken Bay Tribe, Kippa-Ring: John Schuurs Publishers, 2008.

Death Pudding: The Kilcoy Massacre, Kippa-Ring: John Schuurs Publishers, 2008.

Reborn, Kippa-Ring: John Schuurs Publishers, 2008.

Great Southern Land: Origins of the early New South Wales colony, Kippa-Ring: John Schuurs Publishers, 2009.

Snippets from a Baby Boomer's Diary, Kippa-Ring: John Schuurs Publishers, 2009.

Bribie Island: A Pictorial History (with Gladys [Blundell] Fedrick), Caboolture: Communicaé, 2009.

A Window into Caboolture Shire, Salisbury, Queensland: 3E Innovative, 2009.

The Sacred Ibis: Protector of Aborigines Archibald Meston and Queensland's Race relations, Kippa-Ring: John Schuurs Publishers, 2010.

serendipity: the road least travelled, Kippa-Ring: John Schuurs Publishers, 2010.

The Republic of Ausmania, Kippa-Ring: John Schuurs Publishers, 2010.

Body Harvest, Kippa-Ring: John Schuurs Publishers, 2010.

From olive grove to eucalyptus tree: An immigrant family in baby boomer

Australia, Kippa-Ring: John Schuurs Publishers, 2010.

Bribie Island's Seaside Culture: a potted History and Heritage, Kippa-Ring: John Schuurs Publishers, 2010.

Iconic Seaside Cottages of Bribie Island (with artist, Tony Ryan), Kippa-Ring: John Schuurs Publishers, 2011.

The Coburns of Pumicestone Passage, Kippa-Ring: John Schuurs Publishers, 2011.

SNIPPETS ... FROM A BABY BOOMER'S DIARY

Between 1946 and 1964, nearly four million babies—'baby boomers'—were born in Australia. As people had breathed huge sighs of relief at their new-found freedom after the war years, they had wanted to give to their children everything they'd perhaps missed out on—a far better life for their offspring: home, school, a secure family and a car for outings. The greatest wealth was no longer contentment with just a little.

Snippets embarked as an attempt to try and recall the majority of people's deep connection with Brisbane—a carefree place where numerous Australian baby boomers were born and became domiciled. It trawls through the conservative decades of the 1950s and the action-packed swinging 1960s; political upheavals in the 1970s; and the 'greed is good' agendas of the 1980s and beyond.

Within this racy narrative, I have attempted to embrace my love affair with the city's people, suburbs and local communities. As you'll undoubtedly read, all of this happened with a bit of 'cross-fertilisation' from within my own family, the Lergessners.

Images of Cloudland, by the author's late cousin, Claude Wagner of Toowoomba and Sydney.